The Secrets of True Happiness

If you know someone who wants a fabulous book that sets them on the path to happiness and resilience, despite the challenging times in which we live, *The Secrets of True Happiness* is the best gift possible. Farnaz, Bijan and Adib Masumian have written the single most comprehensible and comprehensive book on the secrets of true happiness yet. There is absolutely nothing that comes close in the existing literature. This book is euphoric and inspirational as it is informed by the latest and the greatest in science! The Masumians bring together in a wonderful symphony of integration all the key elements of spirituality, positive psychology and practice that contribute to 'true' happiness. They offer a fabulous, user-friendly and immediately accessible presentation of the very best knowledge to date on how spirituality, love, faith, service, prayer, meditation, marriage and family, mirth, gratitude, and positive thinking all make unique and highly important contributions to the happiness that we all seek. Other authors have written on how any single one of these connects with happiness, but no one to date has pulled all of these strengths together, and certainly not in a manner that respects all spiritual traditions so deeply, as is a special feature of the Bahá'í tradition out of which these authors write. This book is a vitamin pill for the soul and a ticket to a flourishing and meaningful life. As first a scientist, then a graduate of the University of Chicago Divinity School, as well as a professor in several of the nation's leading medical schools over three decades, I can easily state that this is the finest book on happiness that I have ever read with regard to both content, style, and potential to transform lives. I plan to give a copy ASAP to all of my family members, friends, and colleagues. Bravo!

Stephen G. Post, PhD
Founding Director, the Center for Medical Humanities, Compassionate Care and Bioethics of Stony Brook University School of Medicine
President, Institute for Research on Unlimited Love
www.unlimitedloveinstitute.org
Past Trustee, John Templeton Foundation
Best-selling author of *Why Good Things Happen to Good People*

The Secrets of True Happiness

Second edition

Farnaz, Bijan & Adib Masumian

GEORGE RONALD
OXFORD

George Ronald Publisher
Oxford
www.grbooks.com

© Farnaz, Bijan and Adib Masumian 2019
All rights reserved

This revised edition © Farnaz, Bijan and Adib Masumian 2023

A catalogue record for this book in available from the British Library

ISBN 978–0–85398–663–8

Cover Design: Steiner Graphics

CONTENTS

Foreword by Khalil A. Khavari	vii
Acknowledgements	x
1 The Purpose of Life	1
2 The Practice of the Presence of God	29
3 Love	41
4 Faith	61
5 Service	72
6 Prayer	88
7 Meditation	104
8 Marriage and Family Life	132
9 Positivity	153
10 Happiness Techniques	167
11 Gratitude	202
12 Daily Practices for Cultivating a Spiritual Attitude	224
Bibliography	233
Notes and References	243
About the authors	255

To Robert Emmons, Barbara Fredrickson, Khalil Khavari, Allan Luks, Sonja Lyubomirsky, Stephen Post, MJ Ryan, and Roger Walsh, whose research and great contributions have been major sources of inspiration for this book; and to the memory of Brother Lawrence and Norman Vincent Peale, whose heartwarming words continue to guide our souls in our spiritual journey.

FOREWORD

What exactly do we mean by happiness? Is it attainable or only a wish? Aiming to nail down what is meant by happiness, psychologists have concluded that happiness is a subjective state of wellbeing. According to this definition, happiness is not a universal human condition, such as feeling cold or having a fever. It is a private, personal state of feeling that may have many features in common with others, yet is experienced differently with each individual. It ranges from a mild feeling of contentment to an extraordinary condition of euphoria. The panorama of a magnificent sun, the laughter of children at play, the unexpected joy of good news – all boost the mind into a happier state. It can be felt as a briefly passing moment, or as a long-lasting state of mind which brings joy and contentment to an individual for decades.

This book is a comprehensive and scholarly compendium which draws from many sources, from ancient religions and philosophers to current scientists. The authors make a convincing case that happiness is both real and attainable. In the same way that psychologists defined, as best they could, what happiness is, the authors have decided to define what we happiness-seeking humans really are. They explain that, in essence, we are spiritual beings. The surest way to create happiness for ourselves is by leading a spiritual life; that is, a virtuous life lived by spiritual principles. Going far beyond simple exhortations, the authors provide us with insights from both science and religion, both sides of the same coin of truth.

Eminent brain scientists have concluded that the human brain/mind is arguably the most complex entity on the planet. One example of this complexity is the fact that the brain can be both inflexible as well as pliable. The rigidity feature of our minds makes for an orderly continuity of past experiences while its flexibility allows for the adjustment and accommodation to new conditions. The mind is a potent source of power that needs to be harnessed and trained to make good decisions and to do good work. This can happen at any age, even when the resiliency of youth has passed. Science now tells us that growing older does not mean the lessening of the mind's power to learn and to adapt.

When we are faced with some bad news or an adverse event, we can significantly diminish its emotional impact by thinking rationally about the situation, by turning to prayers and meditation for comfort and insight. With a mind thus focused, we can deal with what is necessary. We need to use the mind to outsmart the mind.

Feeling good can be had by means of the senses. The fragrance of a rose, a hug from a loved one, chocolate, and soothing music are uplifting examples of pleasure from the external, material world. There is a distinction between pleasure and happiness: it's not a pleasure to wake up at 2 a.m. to the sound of a crying baby, but there can be floods of happiness that comes when holding that same child.

Feeling good by spiritual means is also possible from deep within the individual through connecting with the Infinite with prayers and meditation. These are spiritual activities that are qualitatively different from sensual pleasures. They are available to any human being at any time. Those who make the effort to transcend the material world and to feed our souls by tapping into our spiritual nature can find our much longed-for serenity, contentment and joy. I know this well from personal experience.

This book contains a wealth of specific practices that enable us to live a spiritual life of inner contentment within the outer realm of the material world. For many people, this challenge is overwhelming; they seek relief through the use of alcohol and other mood and mind-altering chemicals. The 'happy hour' at the corner bar purports to offer happiness by numbing our brains at a discount, chemically regressing the brain and subverting its vital functions. In contrast to this, the practices and information in this book offer not only healthy but realistic ways of empowering the mind and heart that enable us to discharge our vital tasks under the optimal condition of greater serenity.

FOREWORD

This is not a book to be read quickly, but one to read with studied enjoyment: to savor, to reflect upon, to plumb the depths of the direct quotations provided from the treasuries of past and present wisdom, both spiritual and scientific. The authors give us a path to retune our minds and hearts, they lead us to a greater understanding of our true natures – which is the foundation of life-long happiness.

Khalil A. Khavari
Emeritus Professor of Psychology
July 2018

ACKNOWLEDGEMENTS

The authors gratefully acknowledge Dr Sonja Lyubomirsky, who allowed us to use the results of her invaluable research on happiness in the form of a redesigned pie chart, included in our chapter on happiness. We would also like to thank the HeartMath® Institute for sending us a copy of their Heart Rhythms graph, used in our gratitude chapter.

Additionally, we want to offer deep appreciation to our editor at George Ronald, Yas Taherzadeh, whose great insights significantly improved the quality of this work.

Finally, we would like to offer our heartfelt thanks to Jay Braden, a talented artist and friend of many years, who not only provided us with an original painting (the Virtues Tree) found in our chapter on the purpose of life, but also helped us improve the quality of several other graphics in this book.

1

THE PURPOSE OF LIFE

Have you ever met someone who didn't want to be happy? Probably not. Seeking happiness as a goal is one of the few things in life that everyone seems to agree on. However, most of us think happiness is about having *more* of the things we find desirable. We think that *if only* we had more popularity, more money, more love, more power, a better job, then we would be happy. Yet, if our happiness is dependent upon having *more* of these things, we will probably never find contentment because we may never know when *more* is enough. Paradoxically, the more we have of these things, the more of them we will probably want. Or worse, a new *if only* would arise:

> Somehow we've gotten the message that happiness is out there, something to be sought after – in the right job, the mate who never annoys you, the $50,000 BMW – rather than inside ourselves. We've trained ourselves to think in 'if onlys' – if only our spouse would come home from work earlier we'd be happy; if only we'd make $20,000 more a year we'd be happy; if only we could be a stay-at-home mom we'd be happy. We spend our time trying to make our 'if onlys' come true only to discover that even if we do achieve them, a new 'if only' arises.[1]

To reach a state of happiness in life, there are certainly skills and aptitudes that can help. For instance, having a high intelligence quotient (IQ) may be a good thing because it could help us make better decisions. However, is having a high IQ a requirement for achieving happiness? Probably not. Today, there are plenty of happy people in the world who don't have particularly high IQs. Also, recent studies[2,3] have shown that we might actually have multiple intelligences, not just IQ. Howard Gardner, Professor of Education and Cognition at Harvard University, first proposed and popularized the theory of multiple intelligences in 1983, with the publication of his classic work, *Frames of Mind: The Theory of Multiple Intelligences*.[4] This book revolutionized thinking in the worlds of education and psychology by postulating that, rather than having just one type of intelligence (IQ), humans may have multiple intelligences. Perhaps, thus, what is needed to achieve enduring happiness is aptitude in several or all of these intelligences. Gardner initially suggested eight different intelligences: musical-rhythmic, visual-spatial, verbal-linguistic, logical-mathematical, bodily-kinesthetic, interpersonal, intrapersonal, and naturalistic. He later added existential, or moral intelligence, to his list.[5]

Emotional intelligence

In the 1990s, Daniel Goleman – author, psychologist and science journalist – built on Gardner's work and popularized the theory of emotional intelligence (EI), also known as emotional quotient (EQ), when he published his internationally best-selling book, *Emotional Intelligence*. Goleman's book remained on the New York Times bestseller list for more than a year and a half. He has since published numerous other books on EQ, but the revised edition of his original work still remains highly popular.[6]

In simple terms, IE or EQ can be defined as the ability to monitor our own emotions and those of others, and use that information to properly guide our thinking and behaviour in relation to others. Therefore, individuals with high EQs can interact with other people (for example, within the context of their families, work or faith community) more appropriately and create more positive experiences for everyone involved. Even though, to date, tests measuring EQ have not yet replaced or supplemented IQ tests as a standard measure of intelligence, EQ continues to gain momentum as an important dimension of human intelligence.

Spiritual intelligence

Spiritual intelligence (SI), or spiritual quotient (SQ), was first introduced by Danah Zohar in her book, *ReWiring the Corporate Brain*. Zohar defined 12 principles that comprise SQ, including self-awareness, having vision and values in life, showing compassion and empathy towards others, and demonstrating humility in our relationships. Thus, if IQ helps us use numbers and formulas effectively, and EQ aids us to interact with others more successfully, then SQ can help us achieve inner peace and balance – which would contribute to feelings of happiness and satisfaction in life.

Unlike Zohar, Gardner prefers the use of the term existential intelligence to spiritual intelligence.[7] Gardner defines existential intelligence as the 'sensitivity and capacity to tackle deep questions about human existence, such as the meaning of life, why do we die, and how did we get here'.[8] Regardless of our preferred nomenclature, the theory that humans also have a set of spiritual skills that can be measured and developed is gaining momentum. Tools for measuring SQ are already being developed. For instance, author and leadership coach, Cindy Wigglesworth, has proposed 21 skills that define SQ, and provided insights into how to develop these skills.[9] Writer, lecturer and existential coach, David King, has proposed 24 such skills[10] and has built an SQ Self-Report Inventory that is freely available to the public.[11]

In 2000, Robert Emmons, professor of psychology at the University of California, Davis, defined spiritual intelligence as 'the adaptive use of spiritual information to facilitate everyday problem solving and goal attainment'.[12] He believes SQ consists of five components:

- The capacity to transcend the physical and material
- The ability to experience heightened states of consciousness
- The ability to sanctify everyday experience

- The ability to utilize spiritual resources to solve problems
- The capacity to be virtuous.

In his book, *Spiritual Intelligence*, professor emeritus of psychology at the University of Wisconsin-Milwaukee, Khalil Khavari, notes the importance of the spiritual dimension of human beings:

> We are indeed spiritual beings, presently going through a material experience that is both a challenge and an opportunity. It is here, in this life, that each one of us can make choices that have great implications for how we enjoy the experience, as well as how successfully we prepare ourselves for the spiritual journeys ahead . . . When life is used in the acquisition and practice of virtues, we enter the world of spirit educated and trained for the unending journey ahead; but when life is used to cater to our lower nature, then we are severely handicapped and hobbled on arrival.[13]

Stephen Covey – educator, organizational consultant and the renowned author of international bestseller, *The Seven Habits of Highly Effective People* – also believed in the social modeling power of spiritual intelligence: 'Spiritual intelligence is the central and most fundamental of all the intelligences, because it becomes the source of guidance for the others.'[14] So, if Covey is right, spiritually intelligent people can potentially create a great deal of goodwill in the world by simply modeling moral and ethical behaviour.

Of the three types of intelligence discussed above (IQ, EQ and SQ), spiritual intelligence is the only one that considers existential questions – the answers to which will probably have the deepest and longest lasting impact on human happiness. If we cannot provide satisfying answers to the profound questions in life, we may never experience lasting happiness, regardless of gains in wealth, power or popularity. Even corporations are noticing the importance of the spiritual side of their employees' lives and its role in overall employee satisfaction and happiness.[15,16]

The purpose of life

Do any of these questions sound familiar: Who am I? Why am I here? What is the purpose or meaning of life? Am I simply an accident that happened because it was statistically possible, or am I the deliberate creation of a loving God? These are examples of existential questions to which people with a high SQ have provided satisfying answers in their personal lives. For centuries, however, these and similar questions on the meaning of life have perplexed the minds of philosophers and thinkers. A question that is often reflected upon is: 'Is my life only the sum total of my education, my family, my job, my possessions, the bills I pay, and the vacations I take? Or is there more to life?' This search for meaning, and finding the answers that are right for us, is fundamental to feeling happy. Austrian neurologist and psychiatrist, Viktor Frankl, who was also a holocaust survivor, once said: 'Life is not primarily a quest for pleasure, as Freud believed, or a quest for power, as Alfred Adler taught, but a quest for meaning. The greatest task for any person is to find meaning in his or her own life.'[17]

It seems impossible to answer these tough questions without first providing a satisfying answer to a more fundamental existential question: 'What is the *purpose* of my existence?' The question about purpose is more central because the answer to this question makes responding to the other questions easier. Our answer to the question of purpose will give a sense of direction to our life, to our goals, and to all our activities, hopes and dreams. If we can't provide a satisfying, crystal-clear response to the question of purpose, things will start getting fuzzy and, in the confusion that ensues, our life may begin to lose its meaning. We may begin to feel empty and unfulfilled. We may find ourselves lacking the drive, initiative and the motivation to accomplish things. Eventually, we might become apathetic and lethargic, conditions that are dangerous to our psychological and spiritual health. We would continue to breathe and go through life, but we may not feel vital – and without vitality, we will have no hope for the future and little energy to accomplish much in life. At best, we will go through life

Fig. 1
The spirituality-materiality continuum

with a passive orientation towards everything and everyone – a far cry from a fulfilling life.

Of course, some of us feel empty or unhappy simply because we get so entangled in the mesh of life and its ups and downs that we rarely spend time even thinking about those profound questions of purpose and meaning, let alone asking them or seeking their answers. Yet, for those of us who do take the time, the answer to the *purpose* question usually falls along a continuum, at one end of which is the fulfilment of spiritual goals and desires and at the other end are physical or material desires. Whether we are willing to publicly acknowledge it or not, every one of us falls somewhere along this spirituality-materiality continuum (see Fig. 1).

The closer we are to the spiritual end of the continuum, the more likely it is that our life revolves around spiritual matters, and these may well include concentration on God and His[18] purpose for us. The closer we get to the material end of the continuum, the higher the probability that our life is focused on physical and material goals and desires, and that God and spiritual goals are secondary, or even entirely absent. The danger of living on the extreme material side of the continuum is that it usually brings out our worst traits, such as selfishness, greed, jealousy, cruelty, and even violence:

> Indeed the chief reason for the evils now rampant in society is the lack of spirituality. The materialistic civilization of our age has so much absorbed the energy and interest of mankind that people in general do no longer feel the necessity of raising themselves above the forces and conditions of their daily material existence. There is not sufficient demand for things that we call spiritual to differentiate them from the needs and requirements of our physical existence.

> The universal crisis affecting mankind is, therefore, essentially spiritual in its causes. The spirit of the age, taken on the whole, is irreligious. Man's outlook on life is too crude and materialistic to enable him to elevate himself into the higher realms of the spirit.[19]

If we allow our lives to revolve solely around fulfilling material or physical desires, we could lose our moral compass. Without that important guide, we may find justification for anything that will satisfy those desires. We will have only one goal in mind: 'Get what you want, at any cost.' On the contrary, when the purpose of life is defined in spiritual terms, the centre of one's attention will move away from what benefits oneself and toward the general welfare of society. The development and sanctification of one's character becomes a primary goal in life. As a result, we will find meaning in our lives – not in personal gain or comfort, but in things that benefit society as a whole. Of course, providing stability and essential means of comfort for oneself and one's family is still important, but it will not remain the sole focus of one's life. Rather, the welfare of others – and the establishment of a society that operates on such noble and lofty principles as justice, equity, honour, and compassion – will gain importance, too, as we realize that the surest way to achieving lasting prosperity and security for our loved ones is the founding of a spiritual civilization, where humans everywhere can live in relative comfort and with dignity and respect. In this kind of global society, people everywhere will also have the opportunity to develop their innate spiritual potential, which will enable them to establish a civilization that is not marked by violence, greed, corruption, and the extremes of wealth and poverty, but one that will be peaceful, prosperous, egalitarian, compassionate, and essentially divine in nature.

'Abdu'l-Bahá, the son and successor of the founder of the Bahá'í Faith, Bahá'u'lláh, explains that our primary motivation in life should be to help establish such a civilization:

> Some men's lives are solely occupied with the things of this world; their minds are so circumscribed by exterior manners and traditional interests that they are blind to any other realm of existence, to the spiritual significance of all things! They think and dream of earthly fame, of material progress. Sensuous delights and comfortable surroundings bound their horizon, their highest ambitions center in successes of worldly conditions and circumstances! They curb not their lower propensities; they eat, drink, and sleep! Like the animal, they have no thought beyond their own physical well-being. It is true that these necessities must be dispatched. Life is a load which must be carried on while we are on earth, but the cares of the lower things of life should not be allowed to monopolize all the thoughts and aspirations of a human being. The heart's ambitions should ascend to a more glorious goal, mental activity should rise to higher levels! Men should hold in their souls the vision of celestial perfection, and there prepare a dwelling-place for the inexhaustible bounty of the Divine Spirit.
>
> Let your ambition be the achievement on earth of a Heavenly civilization![20]

Self-absorbed individuals often live relatively lonely lives because they are used to having their needs, wants, ideas, and opinions taking priority over everyone else's. Thus, when they don't get their way, they frequently enter into conflicts with others. As a result, over time they begin to lose friends, one by one, until they wake up one day and realize that hardly anyone is left in their circle. The conflicts that lead to this eventual loneliness can also take an enormous psychological and emotional toll on such individuals. If continued, these pressures can lead to physical or mental issues, including hopelessness, fear and anxiety. Many take refuge in drugs. Yet, pills only alleviate the symptoms. They don't provide a cure for hopelessness, fear or anxiety. A more secure way, and a longer-lasting solution, is to gradually shift our sense of purpose and direction in life away from the material side of the continuum and move towards the spiritual side.

Spiritual design of creation?

> Man[21] is a child of God, most noble, lofty and beloved by God, his Creator. Therefore, he must ever strive that the divine bounties and virtues bestowed upon him may prevail and control him. Just now the soil of human hearts seems like black earth, but in the innermost substance of this dark soil there are thousands of fragrant flowers latent. We must endeavor to cultivate and awaken these potentialities, discover the secret treasure in this very mine and depository of God, bring forth these resplendent powers long hidden in human hearts. Then will the glories of both worlds be blended and increased and the quintessence of human existence be made manifest.[22]

But how appealing or practical does a God-centred, spiritually-oriented life sound? After all, we all have families, jobs and careers to worry about. We have bills to pay, kids to get to school, college or soccer games to attend, movies to see, musical performances to watch, novels to read, and so on. There doesn't seem to be any need for God or time for spiritual matters. And how can I *know* God, anyway, when most religions claim God is 'unknowable'?

While many scientists no longer believe in a purely naturalistic worldview, others are convinced that the universe and all forms of life on earth are mere accidents. There is no place for God or other spiritual matters in a purely naturalistic interpretation of the world. According to such a perspective, there is no pre-defined plan or purpose for our existence, and the primary focus of our life is the pursuit and fulfilment of our material needs. This is certainly a viable path in life. Many have, in fact, come to accept this as the only rational way to live; but, is it really the only way to experience life on earth? Or are there other paths to life that could open up whole new vistas to our understanding of the cosmos and our place in it? For instance, could there be a spiritual design and purpose behind the creation of the universe and our existence? If so, what kind of effect would this new understanding have on our outlook on life and the goals we pursue?

Let's take a minute to entertain the possibility that there is actually intelligence behind the design of the universe and our place in it. An analogy might be our computers and mobile phones; all their programmes or 'apps' didn't just pop up on our screens out of nowhere. Every one of them had a programmer behind it. How, then, could this vast, incredibly more complex universe have just popped into existence, with no 'programmer' behind it?

So, for now, let's at least entertain the idea that there may be more to this physical universe than meets the eye. Let's imagine that – in addition to atoms, molecules and physical laws – spiritual laws and principles might also be at work here. If so, then this vast machinery must have a 'programmer' behind it and, just as designers of computer programmes or mobile apps have a purpose for writing their programmes or apps, the Creator of this infinitely more complex 'programme' (the physical universe) must also have reasons and plans for designing the cosmos and for setting its elements in motion.

Simply more intelligent animals?

> Man's supreme honor and real happiness lie in self-respect, in high resolve, and noble purposes, in integrity and moral quality, in immaculacy of mind.[23]

We often hear that humans are merely animals, and that the main distinction between us and the rest of the animal kingdom is that we just happen to be more intelligent. On the surface, this certainly sounds plausible. After all, like other animals, we have a body, physical senses, a limited lifespan, and the same basic needs for eating, sleeping, waking up, and so on. We seek pleasure and comfort, avoid pain and suffering, get sick like other animals, and eventually die and disappear from the face of the earth. Nonetheless, we also appear to have significant differences with other life forms on earth:

> Consider how all other phenomenal existence and beings are captives of nature. The sun, that colossal center of our solar

system, the giant stars and planets, the towering mountains, the earth itself and its kingdoms of life lower than the human – all are captives of nature except man. No other created thing can deviate in the slightest degree from obedience to natural law. The sun in its glory and greatness millions of miles away is held prisoner in its orbit of universal revolution, captive of universal natural control. Man is the ruler of nature. According to natural law and limitation he should remain upon the earth, but behold how he violates this command and soars above the mountains in airplanes. He sails in ships upon the surface of the ocean and dives into its depths in submarines. Man makes nature his servant; harnesses the mighty energy of electricity, for instance, and imprisons it in a small lamp for his uses and convenience. He speaks from the East to the West through a wire. He is able to store and preserve his voice in a phonograph. Though he is a dweller upon earth, he penetrates the mysteries of starry worlds inconceivably distant. He discovers latent realities within the bosom of the earth, uncovers treasures, penetrates secrets and mysteries of the phenomenal world and brings to light that which according to nature's jealous laws should remain hidden, unknown and unfathomable. Through an ideal inner power man brings these realities forth from the invisible plane to the visible. This is contrary to nature's law.

It is evident, therefore, that man is ruler over nature's sphere and province. Nature is inert; man is progressive. Nature has no consciousness; man is endowed with it. Nature is without volition and acts perforce, whereas man possesses a mighty will. Nature is incapable of discovering mysteries or realities, whereas man is especially fitted to do so. Nature is not in touch with the realm of God; man is attuned to its evidences. Nature is uninformed of God; man is conscious of Him. Man acquires divine virtues; nature is denied them. Man can voluntarily discontinue vices; nature has no power to modify the influence of its instincts. Altogether it is evident that man is more noble and superior, that in him there is an ideal power surpassing nature. He has consciousness, volition, memory, intelligent power, divine attributes and virtues of which nature is completely deprived and bereft; therefore, man is higher and nobler by reason of the ideal and heavenly force latent and manifest in him.[24]

The dual nature of man

In the above passage, 'Abdu'l-Bahá offers compelling evidence that humans have powers which we simply don't see in nature or other animals. So, what if these powers come from a side of man that is absent in nature and in other animals? What if humans have two sides: a material side (or lower nature), and a spiritual side (or higher nature)? When it comes to our lower natures, we are just like other animals on earth. This is the side that uses our physical senses to operate in the natural world. However, in doing so, we sometimes have the tendency to get wrapped up in our material needs, to the point of having a hard time getting past the comforts of the body:

> Ye are even as the bird which soareth, with the full force of its mighty wings and with complete and joyous confidence, through the immensity of the heavens, until, impelled to satisfy its hunger, it turneth longingly to the water and clay of the earth below it, and, having been entrapped in the mesh of its desire, findeth itself impotent to resume its flight to the realms whence it came. Powerless to shake off the burden weighing on its sullied wings, that bird, hitherto an inmate of the heavens, is now forced to seek a dwelling-place upon the dust.[25]

It is this animal side that – if allowed to predominate – can make us selfish, greedy and violent to the extreme, beyond all other animals. Yet, we also seem to have a higher nature, a spiritual side capable of seeking knowledge of the Divine and considering and reflecting on complex metaphysical questions. It is this spiritual side of us that can choose to seek the 'Programmer' (God) and explore the possibility that this Creator may have a higher purpose in creating us and putting us on this earth. It is also this spiritual side that is capable of focusing on nobler goals in life, on the sanctification of character, and on developing and displaying virtues like love, compassion, justice, selflessness, and service to others:

> In man there are two natures; his spiritual or higher nature and his material or lower nature. In one he approaches God, in the other he lives for the world alone. Signs of both these natures are to be found in men. In his material aspect he expresses untruth, cruelty and injustice; all these are the outcome of his lower nature. The attributes of his Divine nature are shown forth in love, mercy, kindness, truth and justice, one and all being expressions of his higher nature. Every good habit, every noble quality belongs to man's spiritual nature, whereas all his imperfections and sinful actions are born of his material nature. If a man's Divine nature dominates his human nature, we have a saint.
>
> Man has the power both to do good and to do evil; if his power for good predominates and his inclinations to do wrong are conquered, then man in truth may be called a saint. But if, on the contrary, he rejects the things of God and allows his evil passions to conquer him, then he is no better than a mere animal.[26]

Perhaps that's why, throughout the centuries, our species has been able to produce spiritual giants such as Gandhi, Mother Teresa and Albert Schweitzer, and – at the same time – evil individuals such as Genghis Khan, Adolf Hitler and Pol Pot.

'Abdu'l-Bahá explains that 'Every child is potentially the light of the world – and at the same time its darkness.'[27] The following Cherokee folktale reaffirms this same truth:

> One evening an old Cherokee told his grandson about a battle that goes on inside people. He said, 'My son, the battle is between two "wolves" inside us all. One is Evil. It is anger,

envy, jealousy, sorrow, regret, greed, arrogance, self-pity, guilt, resentment, inferiority, lies, false pride, superiority, and ego. The other is Good. It is joy, peace, love, hope, serenity, humility, kindness, benevolence, empathy, generosity, truth, compassion, and faith.'

The grandson thought about it for a minute and then asked his grandfather: 'Which wolf wins?'

The old Cherokee simply replied, 'The one you feed.'

If we do indeed have two natures, then it is possible that our spiritual or higher side could be our true nature. In other words, we could potentially be spiritual beings whose first and last habitation is the realm of the spirit. If so, then our lives on earth could simply be a temporary physical experience and, when compared to the eternal life of the spirit, would last less than the twinkling of an eye!

> Our true identity is our rational soul, whose free will and powers of understanding enable us to continually better ourselves and our society. Walking a path of service to God and to humanity gives life meaning and prepares us for the moment the soul separates from the body and continues on its eternal journey towards its Maker.[28]

Hafez, the great 14th century poet of Shiraz notes:

> With candor do I speak, and in my speech I take delight
> A slave to love am I; from both the worlds I take my flight
> A bird I am of holy gard'ns; parting tales I can't convey
> Alas, I could not tell you how to fateful snares I fell so prey
> I was an angel, lofty paradise my former place
> 'twas Adam brought me low from high retreats to such disgrace.[29]

In an untranslated Persian Tablet, Bahá'u'lláh confirms Hafez's viewpoint on the true nature of humans as essentially spiritual beings, but adds that if we comprehended, even to the extent of a needle's eye, where our true nature came from and for what purpose we had been put on this earth, we would dedicate our entire lives to serving God and trying to achieve His good pleasure.[30]

'Abdu'l-Bahá reinforces the same notion with the words, 'Man is, in reality, a spiritual being, and only when he lives in the spirit is he truly happy.'[31]

Thanks to our scientific achievements, we are now experiencing longer and healthier lives, and physical comforts and safety like never before. However, as important as these attainments are, if there is a spiritual dimension to our being, shouldn't we also spend time on that aspect of our lives? Nonetheless, without a high SQ, experiencing lasting happiness may prove a tall order. Gaining knowledge of the Sacred is an indispensable element of spiritual intelligence.

The Bahá'í writings emphasise that gaining knowledge of God should actually be foremost in our minds, a knowledge that will eventually lead to genuine love for our Creator. We are also told that humans are the only species on earth that have been endowed with the unique capacity to know and love God:

> Having created the world and all that liveth and moveth therein, He [God], through the direct operation of His unconstrained and sovereign Will, chose to confer upon man the unique distinction and capacity to know Him and to love Him – a capacity that must needs be regarded as the generating impulse and the primary purpose underlying the whole of creation . . . Upon the inmost reality of each and every created thing He hath shed the light of one of His names, and made it a recipient of the glory of one of His attributes. Upon the reality of man, however, He hath focused the radiance of all of His names and attributes, and made it a mirror of His own Self. Alone of all created things man hath been singled out for so great a favor, so enduring a bounty.[32]

So, if the Creator has conferred upon humankind the unique capacity to know and love Him, shouldn't acquiring knowledge of God and demonstrating love for Him become the primary purpose of our lives? If this is so, then why so many of us are completely oblivious of it?

> Is it not astonishing that although man has been created for the knowledge and love of God, for the virtues of the human world, for spirituality, heavenly illumination and eternal life, nevertheless, he continues ignorant and negligent of all this? Consider how he seeks knowledge of everything except knowledge of God. For instance, his utmost desire is to penetrate the mysteries of the lowest strata of the earth. Day by day he strives to know what can be found ten meters below the surface, what he can discover within the stone, what he can learn by archaeological research in the dust. He puts forth arduous labors to fathom terrestrial mysteries but is not at all concerned about knowing the mysteries of the Kingdom, traversing the illimitable fields of the eternal world, becoming informed of the divine realities, discovering the secrets of God, attaining the knowledge of God, witnessing the splendors of the Sun of Truth and realizing the glories of everlasting life. He is unmindful and thoughtless of these. How much he is attracted to the mysteries of matter, and how completely unaware he is of the mysteries of Divinity! Nay, he is utterly negligent and oblivious of the secrets of Divinity . . . It is as if a kind and loving father had provided a library of wonderful books for his son in order that he might be informed of the mysteries of creation, at the same time surrounding him with every means of comfort and enjoyment, but the son amuses himself with pebbles and playthings, neglectful of all his father's gifts and provision.[33]

So far, we have proposed that humans may have two sides to their existence: a material side that constitutes our lower or animal nature, and a spiritual side that reflects our higher or noble side. We have also suggested that while it is legitimate to pay attention to the needs and comforts of the body, such attention should not come

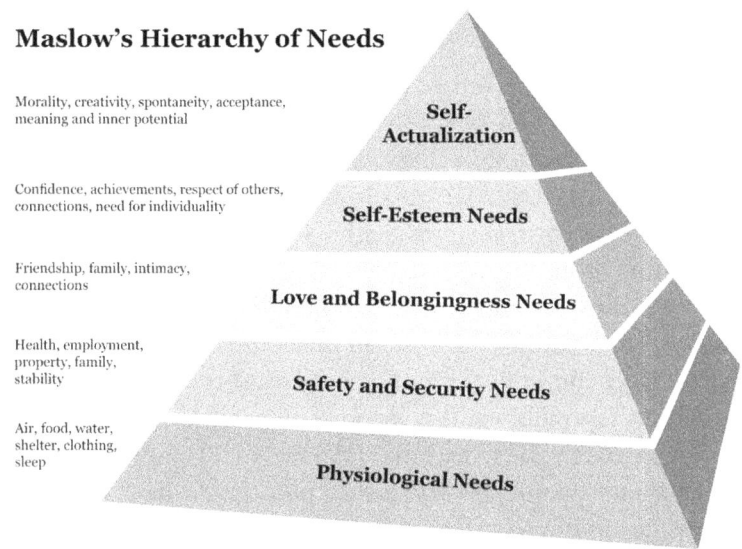

Fig. 2 Abraham Maslow's Hierarchy of Needs

at the expense of the needs of our soul. In fact, if the primary goal of our existence is to acquire knowledge and love of God, then this spiritual quest should take precedence over material pursuits.

Psychologist Abraham Maslow's hierarchy of human needs is widely recognized as a helpful guide for the elements that drive human motivation throughout life (see Fig. 2).

Naturally, we cannot pay serious attention to matters of the spirit before tending to our most fundamental physiological needs, such as air, food, water, or shelter. However, this doesn't mean we have to compete with others to ensure that the level of comfort or luxury we achieve in life is greater than theirs, and feel miserable if it is not. For example, we don't have to feel compelled to take out loans in order to buy the latest technological gadgets, expensive jewellery, a new car every three or four years, or take that exotic vacation – especially if we can't afford it. Many of us spend too much time and money on material comforts and pleasures, even if we have to spend beyond our means to do so. This often comes at the expense of the needs of the spirit. By spending beyond our means, we put extra pressure on ourselves and our families in the process. We then feel sad, depressed or edgy, and we, and everyone around us, suffers the consequences.

Yet, as we said earlier, this body may well be like a temporary temple for our souls. Eventually, we will have to leave this temple behind here on Earth. We also won't be able to take any of the luxuries we spend on creature comforts with us to the life beyond. In addition, even the wealthiest among us frequently get bored with our mansions and our most unique luxuries, because those luxuries cannot satisfy the needs of our souls. So, perhaps we will do well if we continue to remind ourselves of the self-evident fact that we come to this world stripped of all possessions, and we will leave it in exactly the same way.

So, again, one of the keys to happiness is to have very clear answers in our minds to the deep, existential questions we encounter in life, and then to keep reminding ourselves of those answers as we go through life. Is the journey solely – or even primarily – about the life of the body, which we will eventually leave behind, or also about the life of the soul, which we will take with us to the afterlife? Assuming it is the latter, what exactly are we supposed to do?

The life of the soul

If we come to the knowledge and conclusion that the life of the soul is also very important – pivotal, in fact – to our existence, then we should also acknowledge the fact that it takes personal initiative and volition to do something about it. In other words, we need to agree to spend time on the spiritual side of our existence. Nurturing the life of the soul is not something that we can delegate to others. Unlike managers in a corporate setting who can delegate certain tasks and responsibilities to others, nurturing our souls – an integral part of working towards achieving God's purpose for ourselves while on earth – takes personal initiative and precious time. Thus, our own volition plays a key role in our spiritual growth:

Fig. 3
The Virtues Tree
(original painting, by Jay Braden)
(see p. 21)

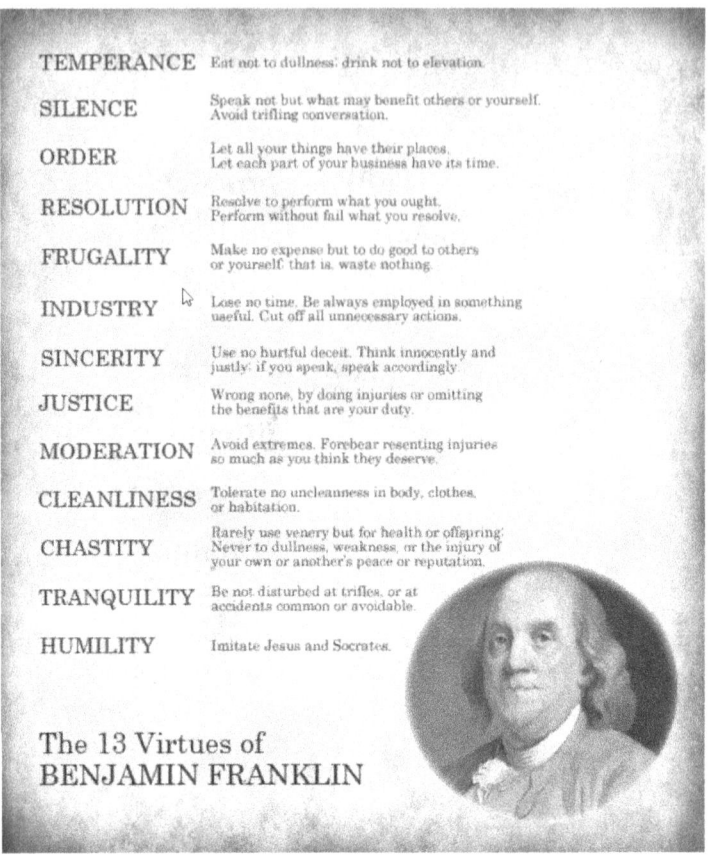

Fig. 4 The 13 Virtues of Benjamin Franklin
(see p. 22)

Form of the pages.
TEMPERANCE.
Eat not to dullness ; drink not to elevation.

	Sun.	M.	T.	W.	Th.	F.	S.
Tem.							
Sil.	*	*		*		*	
Ord.	*	*			*	*	*
Res.			*			*	
Fru.		*			*		
Ind.				*			
Sinc.							
Jus.							
Mod.							
Clea.							
Tran.							
Chas.							
Hum.							

Fig. 5
Benjamin Franklin's
Weekly Virtues Chart
(see p. 22)

All that which ye potentially possess can, however, be manifested only as a result of your own volition. Your own acts testify to this truth.[34]

Taking personal responsibility for our own spiritual transformation also means we should stop finding excuses for inaction, or blaming people or events in our past or present for dissatisfaction with our current spiritual condition, even if in some cases other people played pivotal roles that have led to our current conditions. Ultimately, we are each responsible and accountable for the life of our own soul:

> Mere knowledge of principles is not sufficient. We all know and admit that justice is good but there is need of volition and action to carry out and manifest it.[35]

Consistent nurturing of our soul will eventually lead to spiritual transformation. The fruit of such transformation is the development of divine qualities or virtues such as love, kindness, truthfulness, trustworthiness, compassion, forgiveness, justice, and the like. However, these are essentially good habits that we have to develop over time. Of course, habits can't be formed without practise, and practise takes patience and perseverance. Our spiritual transformation also involves abandoning undesired traits, such as jealousy, prejudice, dishonesty, and similar qualities. The same process works for establishing good habits and eliminating undesirable ones. Whether we are developing desirable habits and virtues or eliminating unwanted ones, if we show patience and perseverance, we can not only personally transform our own lives but also be examples for others (see Fig. 3).

> Man is like unto a tree. If he be adorned with fruit, he hath been and will ever be worthy of praise and commendation . . . The fruits of the human tree are exquisite, highly desired and dearly cherished. Among them are upright character, virtuous deeds and a goodly utterance . . . The Water for these trees is

the living water of the sacred Words uttered by the Beloved of the world.[36]

The most important goal that Benjamin Franklin, one of the Founding Fathers of the United States, set for himself in his life was to achieve what he called 'moral perfection'.[37] To attain this high ideal, Franklin came up with an elaborate plan that included identifying 13 different virtues (see Fig. 4), a weekly programme for developing each virtue and a visual chart to help him track his progress along the way (see Fig. 5).[38]

A key ingredient to lasting happiness: serving others

> Is there any deed in the world that would be nobler than service to the common good? Is there any greater blessing conceivable for a man, than that he should become the cause of the education, the development, the prosperity and honor of his fellow-creatures? No, by the Lord God! The highest righteousness of all is for blessed souls to take hold of the hands of the helpless and deliver them out of their ignorance and abasement and poverty, and with pure motives, and only for the sake of God, to arise and energetically devote themselves to the service of the masses, forgetting their own worldly advantage and working only to serve the general good.[39]

Benjamin Franklin also believed that God had given all humans natural talents to use in service to others. Many of us remember how the late actor, Christopher Reeve, famous for his portrayal of Superman, was paralyzed after a fall from his horse. For a while, he actually contemplated suicide. What saved him, however, was his decision to transcend his trauma and feelings of self-pity and focus his life on helping others who were also suffering from neurological damage. Examples of people like him abound today.

Thanks to the incredible advances that have been made in technology, mass communication, transportation, and other fields of human endeavour, we practically live in a global village. Now, more than ever before, our peace and tranquillity, our security and feelings of happiness or misery, are increasingly intertwined with the fortunes and deeds of people we have never heard of, and who may be living thousands of miles away from us. Thus, if we want to experience lasting happiness, more than ever before we should try to build a world around us in which the majority of people can enjoy an acceptable standard of living – a world that is free of hatred, violence, greed, prejudice, and other negative qualities. Such a herculean task can only be accomplished through collaboration with all those around us. We should invite others to join us in building this world – and the most effective way of getting others to join is by letting them see the beauty of this future world in our daily lives. How can we manifest that beauty? By focusing on the greater good of the society. In other words, by concentrating on service to others:

> Do not busy yourselves in your own concerns; let your thoughts be fixed upon that which will rehabilitate the fortunes of mankind and sanctify the hearts and souls of men. This can best be achieved through pure and holy deeds, through a virtuous life and a goodly behaviour.[40]

When others see positive changes in our behaviour at home, at work and at school, in our speech or dress, in our artistic pursuits, in the recreations we choose, and in the ways in which we interact with those around us, they are bound to be attracted to that positive change.

The benefits of living a spiritual life

Dr Roger Walsh, the author of *Essential Spirituality*, is a psychiatrist, philosopher, award-wining scientist, and spiritual practitioner. Walsh believes that if we choose to centre our efforts on the life of the soul by regularly engaging in spiritual practices, we will begin to realize many benefits:

Our heart begins to open, fear and anger melt, greed and jealousy dwindle, happiness and joy grow, love flowers, peace replaces agitation, concern for others blossoms, wisdom matures, and both psychological and physical health improve. Virtually all aspects of our lives are touched and transformed in some way.[41]

Living a spiritual life that includes practices such as regular prayer and meditation can offer a wide range of physiological, psychological and emotional benefits. Physiological benefits of meditation occur because 'meditation brings the brainwave pattern into an alpha state, which is a level of consciousness that promotes the healing state' (see Fig. 6).[42] Studies have shown that among the physiological benefits of meditation are lower levels of cholesterol and blood pressure, reduced frequency in headaches and colds, and lessening of hypertension and intensity of psoriasis in patients.[43] Other studies have demonstrated faster recovery from stomach problems, allergies, muscle tension, arthritis episodes, asthma, cancer, heart disease, skin problems, palpitations, and temporomandibular join syndrome.[44] Asthma patients have experienced improved airflow to their lungs, which enables them to breathe easier.[45] Harvard researchers also used functional magnetic resonance imaging (fMRI) to show the significant role of meditation in treating stress-related physical conditions such as digestive problems, heart disease and infertility.[46] Individuals who meditate regularly typically have lower levels of cortisol and lactate – two chemicals that are associated with stress.

There are also many psychological and emotional benefits associated with living a spiritual life. For instance, those who engage in spiritual practices generally tend to show greater self-control and sensitivity towards the feelings and needs of others. They use less alcohol and drugs, and rarely show signs of aggression and selfishness. Their marital lives are also typically more stable.[47] They are capable of showing more compassion and forgiveness towards others. They are generally more detached from the mundane and show deeper appreciation for the simpler things in life. These

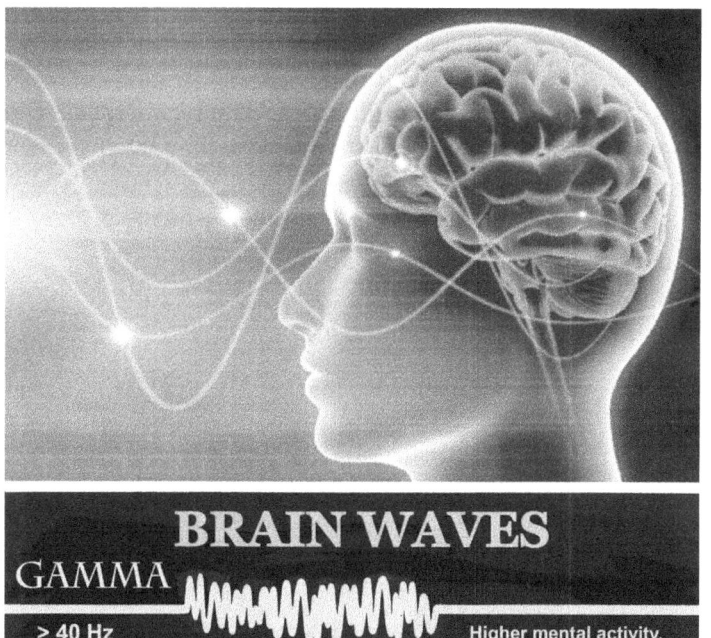
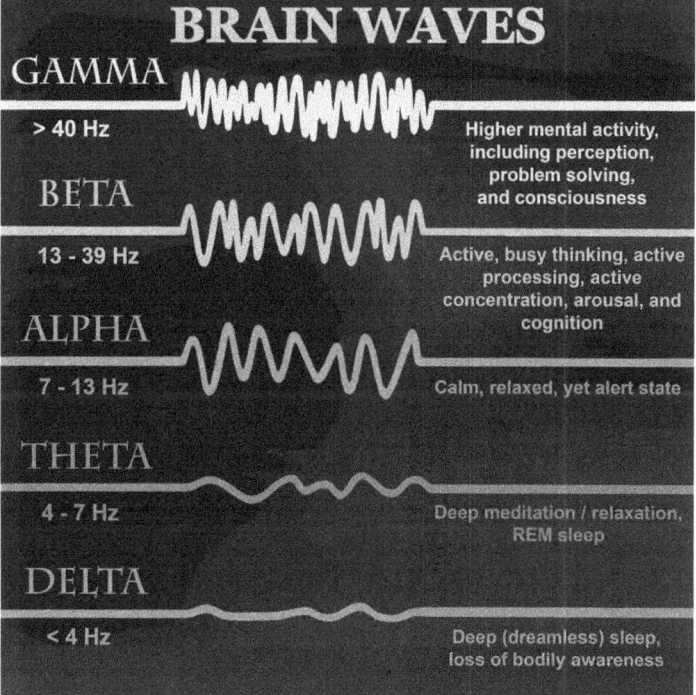

Fig. 6
Brain Waves
(see pp. 24, 50 & 115)

qualities enable them to face life and its problems with more serenity and a calmer attitude. Spiritually-centred individuals can also weather a range of storms, regardless of their severity, from terminal disease, to loss of a loved one, to dealing with the consequences of a natural disaster or a destructive war. Many people who initially turn to meditation for its self-regulatory benefits eventually discover that they are also becoming more spiritual:

> In her work with many cancer and AIDS patients, Dr Borysenko has observed that many [patients] are most interested in meditation as a way of becoming more attuned to the spiritual dimension of life. She reports that many die 'healed', in a state of compassionate self-awareness and self-acceptance.[48]

The station of human beings

After twenty years of spiritual practice and research into different world religions and philosophies, Roger Walsh, professor of psychiatry, philosophy and anthropology at the University of California, Irvine, discovered seven practices that he believes are central to human happiness:

1. **Transform your motivation**: Reduce craving and find your soul's desire.
2. **Cultivate emotional wisdom**: Heal your heart and learn to love.
3. **Live ethically**: Feel good by doing good.
4. **Concentrate and calm your mind**.
5. **Awaken your spiritual vision**: See clearly and recognize the sacred in all things.
6. **Cultivate spiritual intelligence**: Develop wisdom and understand life.
7. **Express spirit in action**: Embrace generosity and the joy of service.

In defining the above principles, Walsh integrates some of the most fundamental principles of religion and philosophy into a rewarding approach to life, in which love, kindness, joy, peace, vision, wisdom, generosity, and service become integral parts of everything we do on a daily basis. Walsh believes individuals who engage in these practices regularly will eventually come to the greatest discovery of their lives:

> Within ourselves we find our deepest self, our true Self, and recognize that we are not only more than we imagined but more than we can imagine. We see that we are a creation of the sacred, intimately and eternally linked to the sacred, and forever graced and embraced by the sacred.
>
> This is the greatest of all discoveries, the secret of all secrets, the priceless gift that is both the source and goal of the great religions. This is the aim of all our seeking, the answer to a lifetime of longing, the cause of the mystic's bliss, the source of overwhelming and enduring joy. This is the central message at the heart of the great religions and the basis for their ecstatic cries, such as those in the Western traditions.[49]

Therefore, by following the insights from Walsh and others, we can effectively raise our SQ over time and increase the likelihood that we will experience lasting happiness. In the process, we will learn that enduring happiness will involve the demonstration of certain skills; for instance, the ability to go beyond personal desires and enlarge our circle of love and compassion to include others, or the ability to live an ethical life. We will learn that happiness may also necessitate showing good will towards others on a regular basis, awakening our souls to the sacred, performing random acts of kindness and generosity, sending good thoughts and good wishes to others (even those we don't like), and discovering the joy of service to our fellow humans. In the following chapters, we will explore these and similar themes in more detail.

I sensed God's love for me and for all

Veronica was not sure if it was wasps or black hornets that stung her multiple times, but she was sure that her allergic reaction to these stings resulted in anaphylactic shock. Here is her description of her near-death experience:

I could hear the paramedics discussing how bad things were, and the last words I remember were, 'We don't have a pulse; she's flatlining.' Then I was gone.

I went directly to a place of light – no tunnel or any sensation of travel. It was immediate and calm. I perceived the place to be the exterior to an entryway, but not fully in heaven. There wasn't much light, but I could see vague outlines – of one major being of love and many other beings of love with souls.

There was nothing but love, goodness and truth, with no room for fear or evil, just all things that had to do with love. It was beyond perfect, and loving as we know in our human state. No words can describe it. I was so happy to be there.

I understood the major superior being of love to be God, and I sensed God's love for me and for all. That was the most emotionally intense and beautiful moment. There were other loving beings with God – like his spiritually evolved helpers or companions. God is perfect, heartbreakingly complete, highly evolved love; yet He is a being with a soul and identity. I sensed that we all are on a path to that love and to God.

Our main purpose is love and realizing the source of that love, which is God. Our purpose and goal is God and His perfect love: to serve God, to love and serve each other, to love ourselves, to grow spiritually. We must understand God's love – and the opposite of it, and how destructive and wrong it is. Then we must reach toward God to a beautiful and loving existence.

No words can describe my time with God and His perfect love. The type of love God exudes and is all about is beyond human comprehension. God, love, growing spiritually, serving in love, uniting in love are our goals. Our love is immature and 'seen through a glass darkly'. The answer is in God's light and love. The total bliss.[50]

2

THE PRACTICE OF THE PRESENCE OF GOD

> There is no peace for thee save by renouncing thyself and turning unto Me.[1]

Hardly anyone goes through life without tests and difficulties. Adversities come in all sizes: some are small and pass quickly, others are major and their impact can last a lifetime. Think of losing a close friend or family member in an accident, or imagine financial ruin or a life-threatening disease that might take you away from your family. Understandably, we often respond to severe blows in life with feelings of sadness and sorrow – or worse, despair and depression. To battle these conditions we often turn to family and friends for support and comfort, as we should. Yet, we all live very busy lives. As much as they might want to, family and friends can't always be with us. So, how can we experience lasting inner peace? Can we find a constant companion to whom we can turn in our hour of need? Someone who is always there when we need them?

The sacred texts of the major religions of the world tell us that we indeed have such a Friend in God, our Creator. With Him, we are never alone:

> Fear thou not; for I am with thee . . . I will strengthen thee; yea, I will help thee. (Is. 41:10)

In an untranslated Persian Tablet, 'Abdu'l-Bahá also notes that God is our companion and comforter, and that those who believe in God are never alone, even if they are in the midst of a vast and arid desert with no one else in their company.[2] Thus, we have the assurance that we are not alone in this world, and that there is a loving Creator Who loves us more than we can imagine. He is always with us and will see us through the challenges of life, as long as we live according to His teachings to the best of our ability and put our trust and confidence in Him.

Once we become aware of the existence of this Friend and begin to become conscious of His presence in our lives, we can expect a gradual transformation in our thoughts, words and deeds. For instance, we cannot live close to an almighty, all-powerful, omniscient, omnipresent Being and still feel insecure:

> I keep the Lord always before me: because he is at my right hand, I shall not be moved. Therefore my heart is glad, and my soul rejoices: my body also dwells secure. (Ps. 16:8–9)

The practice of living in His presence will help us develop confidence. It will help us overcome fear and anxiety. When we come to believe for a fact that God is with us, our fears will disappear. It will give us perseverance and strength because we feel we have the most powerful Ally on our side:

> The sense of God's presence steadies us, it gives us an anchor in the storm, and provides a reservoir of personal power . . . if we live with God as a friend, God will become so real that He will be our sturdy companion day and night. Then, even when the going is hard, our hearts can be happy within us, for we have His assurance.[3]

We also begin to feel more joy and happiness:

> In Thy presence there is fullness of joy. (Ps. 16:1)

Living in His presence also makes us continuously conscious of God's plan for humanity and His desire for us to live a decent, moral and ethical life, all of which lead to human nobility:

> Verily, the noblest of you in the sight of God is the one who is most deeply conscious of Him. Behold, God is all-knowing, all-aware. (Qur'an 49:13)

How do we practise living in His presence?

American minister and author, Norman Vincent Peale, widely regarded as the progenitor of positive thinking, believes that human happiness rests on two pillars. One is moral decency, the other is consciousness of God and the act of living in His presence:

> There are two pillars upon which happiness rests. One is moral decency, mastery over self. The other is the knowledge of the love of God and of His presence at all times, come what may.[4]

One of the best methods for cultivating God-consciousness within ourselves is by engaging in the practice of daily contemplation and reflection on the Sacred Word, especially those verses that focus on developing faith.[5] Regular reflection and contemplation on such words or verses will gradually instil within us a sense of trust in God and the belief that He will guide and protect us in times of trouble. Thus, we can turn to Him in moments of weakness, restlessness, fear, anxiety, or whenever negative thoughts arise within our mind:

> Cast thy burden upon the Lord, and he shall sustain thee. (Ps. 55:22)

> Rely upon God. Trust in Him. Praise Him, and call Him continually to mind. He verily turneth trouble into ease, and sorrow into solace, and toil into utter peace. He verily hath dominion over all things.[6]

To accustom our souls to a peaceful life lived in God's presence, we can have what biochemist and author of *Let Go and Let God*,

Albert Cliffe, describes as, 'an hourly contact with God'. Cliffe describes this practice as follows:

> The most wonderful thing that ever happened to me was this; many years ago I let go my past and let God take over my life. When I completely surrendered my life to Him, I lost my temper, my fears, my years of deadly illness and sicknesses. It meant facing life every hour with the truth that was in me to replace the negative thinking of a lifetime. It meant an hourly contact with God, in the streetcar, the bus, my own car, my laboratory – no matter where I went I had an appointment with Him. What came of it? Peace of mind, health and spiritual prosperity.[7]

Another way to grow the seed of faith and trust in God within our souls is to concentrate on the meaning of the religious and faith verses that focus on the constant presence of God as a faithful Friend in our lives.

> And surely I am with you always, to the very end of the age. (Matt. 28:20)

The 'Four Gs' daily practice

This practice can be done before the start of any task during the course of the day until it becomes a habit.

1. **Gratitude:** Think of one thing you are grateful for at this moment and express it verbally or mentally to God.
2. **Guidance:** Seek God's assistance in any small or big task you are about to undertake. It could be as small as writing an answer to an e-mail.
3. **Gaze (loving gaze):** As you are engaged in the task at hand, remember God in your heart periodically, and turning to Him with an inner or outer smile, say or think of such words of love, as, 'O God my God, my Beloved, my heart's Desire',[8]

or 'Please help me live according to Your good-pleasure', or 'I love You, my Beloved, with all my heart and my soul'.
4. **Gratitude:** Thank God for His assistance.

Through this practice, our actions can become little acts of communion with our Creator.

Another practice can be a simple affirmation of God's constant presence in our life, especially when we feel weak or when we face problems. In such moments, we can repeat to ourselves such comforting thoughts, as, 'God loves me more than I can ever imagine. He is with me. He wants the best things for me. He guides and protects me'. We can repeat these affirmations several times a day.

Brother Lawrence's approach to practising the presence of God

An inspiring resource for living a God-centred life is a small book titled, *The Practice of the Presence of God*, which contains the words of Nicholas Herman of Lorraine, a 17th century Carmelite, now remembered as 'Brother Lawrence'. This book, compiled after Brother Lawrence's death, is a treasure-trove of practical advice for practising the presence of God in our daily lives. The language of the book is simple, engaging and inspiring. Its central theme is to encourage the reader to live a life of 'continual conversation' with God:

> That we might accustom ourselves to a continual conversation with Him, with freedom and in simplicity. That we need only to recognize God intimately present with us, to address ourselves to Him every moment, that we may beg His assistance for knowing His will in things doubtful, and for rightly performing those which we plainly see He requires of us, offering them to Him before we do them, and giving Him thanks when we have done. That in this conversation with God we are also employed in praising, adoring and loving Him incessantly, for His infinite goodness and perfection.[9]

Brother Lawrence states that our main objective in life should be to become 'the most perfect worshipers of God we can possibly be'.[10] To do so, 'we must watch continually over ourselves that we may not do nor say nor think anything that may displease Him'.[11] We should make the love of God the end of all our actions. To Brother Lawrence, perfect resignation to God is 'a sure way to heaven',[12] and 'God always gave us light in our doubts when we had no other design but to please Him'.[13] For Brother Lawrence, God was the end of all of his thoughts and desires, and everything he did was for His love[14]:

> When he [Brother Lawrence] began his business, he said to God, with a filial trust in Him: O my God, since Thou art with me, and I must now, in obedience to Thy commands, apply my mind to these outward things, I beseech Thee to grant me the grace to continue in Thy presence; and to this end do Thou prosper me with Thy assistance, receive all my works, and possess all my affections. As he proceeded in his work he continued his familiar conversation with his Maker, imploring His grace, and offering to Him all his actions.[15]

In his letters, Brother Lawrence recommended the following approach for practising the presence of God in order for it to become habitual:

> I should communicate to you the method by which I arrived at that habitual sense of God's presence . . . I renounced, for the love of Him, everything that was not He, and I began to live as if there was none but He and I in the world . . . I beheld Him in my heart as my Father, as my God. I worshiped Him the oftenest that I could, keeping my mind in His holy presence, and recalling it as often as I found it wandered from Him . . . I made this my business as much all the day long as at the appointed times of prayer; for at all times, every hour, every minute, even in the height of my business, I drove away

from my mind everything that was capable of interrupting my thought of God . . . I have found great advantages by it . . . by often repeating these acts, they become habitual, and the presence of God rendered it as it were natural to us.[16]

To Brother Lawrence, living in God's presence could be practised even during our meals and in the company of others:

> Lift up your heart to Him, sometimes even at your meals, and when you are in company; the least little remembrance will always be acceptable to Him. You need not cry very loud; He is nearer to us than we are aware of.[17]

Such conversation with God provided him with great joy and spiritual elation:

> And I make it my business only to persevere in His holy presence, wherein I keep myself by a simple attention and a general fond regard to God, which I may call an actual presence of God; or, to speak better, an habitual, silent and secret conversation of the soul with God, which often causes me joys and raptures inwardly, and sometimes also outwardly, so great that I am forced to use means to moderate them and prevent their appearance to others . . . There is not in the world a kind of life more sweet and delightful than that of continual conversation with God. Those only can comprehend it who practice and experience it . . . while I am so with Him I fear nothing, but the least turning from Him is insupportable.[18]

Brother Lawrence explains that his most useful method is the simple attention or awareness of God's presence. He advises us that, in our practice of the presence of God, we should be gentle with our mind, 'that we must do our business faithfully, without trouble or disquiet, recalling our mind to God mildly, and with tranquillity, as often as we find it wandering from Him'.[19]

He also encourages us to:

Think often on God, by day, by night, in your business, and even in your diversions. He is always near you and with you; leave Him not alone. You would think it rude to leave a friend alone who came to visit you; why, then, must God be neglected? Do not, then, forget Him, but think on Him often, adore Him continually. We must make our heart a spiritual temple, wherein to adore Him incessantly . . . If we knew how much He loves us, we should always be ready to receive equally and with indifference from His hand the sweet and the bitter.[20]

Brother Lawrence sums up his approach to attaining unto the presence of God in the following steps:

1. We must first purify ourselves and guard against thoughts, words or deeds that might be displeasing to God and, if we did engage in such practices, to ask for His forgiveness.
2. We must faithfully practise His presence and keep our soul's gaze fixed on God in faith, calmly, humbly, and lovingly.
3. Before taking up any task, we should look to God, even if it is for a moment, and do the same during and after the task. We should not be discouraged if we don't succeed at first, as developing this habit is not easy and will take time. However, when we have developed the habit, we will gain great joy in performing it.
4. We should keep our thoughts fixed on Him by mentally uttering such phrases as these in our mind: 'My God, I am wholly Thine. O God of Love, I love Thee with all my heart.'
5. Practising the presence of God is hard at first, yet, when pursued faithfully, it will gradually and imperceptibly work within the soul and will have marvellous effects. It will draw down God's grace, and lead our soul insensibly to the ever-present vision of God.[21]

According to Brother Lawrence, among the greatest benefits of practising God's presence is growing one's faith in God's grace and protection, becoming more hopeful, and learning to live by His Will. By practising a 'steadfast gaze on Him', our lives can consist of 'unceasing acts of love and worship . . . of praise and prayer, and service; at times indeed life seems to be but one long unbroken practice of His Divine Presence'.[22]

Other inspiring sources for the practice of God's presence

Another inspirational source for the practice of the presence of God is the Muslim mystic and poet, Rabi'a al-Basri (717–801 CE). Rabi'a was a female mystic saint who many consider to be the first true saint in the Muslim Sufi tradition. Rabi'a's fame excelled that of many men in early Muslim Sufism. She owes at least some of her renown to the Persian mystic, Farid ad-Din Attar (c. 1145–1221), who included many of the stories of Rabi'a's life in his classic work, *Memorial of the Saints*. Rabi'a lost her parents as a child and was sold as a slave in her youth. Her master, who witnessed Rabi'a's exemplary devotion and love for God, eventually decided to set her free so she could dedicate more of her time to living in the presence of God. Rabi'a's impact on the Muslim world was so great that many believed some of the stories of her piety, her unparalleled love for God and for other people, as well as her ascetic lifestyle, played a major role in the development of Islamic mysticism.

She is also credited as a pioneering mystic who preached and practised a brand of Sufism in which love, rather than the fear of God, was placed at the centre of devotional life. Rabi'a later became a teacher of both women and men and referred only to God as her Master. Her complete trust in and submission to God eventually became the stuff of legend.

Rabi'a's profound sense of love and adoration for God can be seen in this beautiful poem:

> O God . . . Give the goods of this world to Your enemies – Give the treasures of Paradise to Your friends – But as for me – You are all I need.

O God! If I adore You out of fear of Hell, burn me in Hell! If I adore You out of desire for Paradise, lock me out of Paradise. But if I adore You for Yourself alone, Do not deny to me Your eternal beauty.[23]

Your hope in my heart is the rarest treasure
Your Name on my tongue is the sweetest word
My choicest hours
Are the hours I spend with You –
O God, I can't live in this world
Without remembering You –
How can I endure the next world
Without seeing Your face?[24]

Rabi'a – Rabi'a – how did you climb so high
I did it by saying: 'Let me hide in You
From everything that distracts me from You,
From everything that comes in my way
When I want to run to You.'[25]

Let go and let God

Thou wilt keep him in perfect peace whose mind is stayed on Thee; because he trusteth in Thee. (Is. 26:3–4)

A single constant affirmation that the everlasting arms of God are holding you up, repeated hour by hour until you become convinced that God is now your guide and stay, will often bring you out of worries and fears . . . Suppose that you have a broken watch and you take it to a watchmaker, asking him if he can repair it. He takes out his glass and looks at the works and says that he most assuredly can repair it. Suppose then that you say to him, 'Thank you', place it back in your purse or pocket and leave the store. Will you get that watch repaired? Most certainly not, for you have to leave the watch with the watchmaker.

It is just the same with your religious life. You have to get into the habit of leaving your troubles with God. The only complete and sure cure for your bad nerves, as you call them, is to relax in the hands of God and know that He is now looking after your troubles, that He is now guiding you into the quiet waters of inner peace . . . The most wonderful thing that ever happened to me was this: many years ago I let go my past and let God take over my life. When I completely surrendered my life to Him, I lost my temper, my fears, my years of deadly illness and sicknesses. It meant facing life every hour with the truth that was in me to replace the negative thinking of a lifetime. It meant an hourly contact with God, in the street car, the bus, my own car, my laboratory – no matter where I went I had an appointment with Him. What came of it? Peace of mind, health and spiritual prosperity . . .

Friend, you are not alone. You are not facing life alone, you are facing a future, an eternity with God. I do not know nor do I ask what the future holds for me, but I do know who holds my future. I know with an absolute faith that God will never let anything come my way that He and I cannot handle together. You first have to surrender, then you have to supply the willingness and the tools, and God supplies the power. When God actually becomes a reality in your life, anxiety goes, but when anxiety dominates your mind, then God goes.[26]

God's Sunshine

John Oxenhamb[27]

God's Love is Always Shining
Never once since the world began
Has the sun ever stopped his shining.
His face very often we could not see,
And we grumbled at his inconstancy;
But the clouds were really to blame, not he,
For, behind them, he was shining.
And so – behind life's darkest clouds
God's love is always shining.
We veil it at times with our faithless fears,
And darken our sight with our foolish tears,
But in time the atmosphere always clears,
For his love is always shining.[28]

3

LOVE

The love of God

> The essence of love is for man to turn his heart to the Beloved One, and sever himself from all else but Him, and desire naught save that which is the desire of his Lord.[1]

In the previous chapter, we noted the importance of faith and trust in God, and said that among the many benefits of having faith and trust in God were developing a sense of security, hope and inner peace, and finding meaning and purpose for our existence. However, showing faith and trust in God is not possible without first developing a love relationship with Him. Fortunately, we know that the seed of that love has already been planted within us:

> My love is in thee, know it, that thou mayest find Me near unto thee.[2]

In fact, the sacred literature of the Bahá'í Faith tells us that the purpose underlying our creation is the love that our Creator has for us:

> Veiled in My immemorial being and in the ancient eternity of My essence, I knew My love for thee; therefore, I created thee, have engraved on thee Mine image and revealed to thee My beauty.[3]

Therefore, if the purpose of creation was God's love for humanity – and He also planted the seed of His love in our inner essence – then the more we nurture this mutual love relationship, and the deeper our love for God becomes, the more in tune we will become with the purpose of our existence, which will then lead to a sense of self-fulfilment and enduring happiness:

> Thy Paradise is My love; thy heavenly home reunion with Me. Enter therein and tarry not.[4]

The Book of Psalms also confirms the relationship between humankind reaching out to God in love and the Creator returning that love:

> Because he cleaves to me in love, I will deliver him; I will protect him, because he knows my name. When he calls to me, I will answer him; I will be with him in trouble, I will rescue him and honour him. (Ps. 91:14–15)

Thus, human prosperity and lasting peace and joy can be achieved more easily if we develop a relationship of love with God – a relationship in which He is the Beloved and we are the lover seeking after Him. A true lover strives, with heart and soul, to do whatever he can to please his Beloved and draw closer to Him. This search after the Beloved becomes easier when we realize that He has created us as inherently spiritual beings, who have been invested with a spark of God's own reality and immortality within our souls.

If the human heart remains devoid of the love of God, this vacuum will, more than likely, be filled with other things. These other things could range from a love for material things – which usually doesn't last long without constantly seeking 'bigger and better' replacements – to filling our hearts with negative feelings, such as anxiety, apathy, jealously, hatred, depression, and boredom.[5] None of these will bring us peace of mind or lasting joy. To flee from these negative forces, some of us may even resort to addictive substances, such as alcohol or drugs, which can not only ruin us physically, psychologically and emotionally, but also spiritually, as they will move us further and further away from our true destiny. On the contrary, when our hearts are filled with the love of God, the result can be peace of mind, hope and happiness.

How to nurture the love of God in our hearts

There are a number of methods we can use to strengthen God's love in us. Among these are:
- Persistent prayers to be guided to the path of His love and His good pleasure.
- Living a God-centred life.
- Praying for steadfastness, resignation to God's will, and perseverance.
- Contemplating His Word.
- Associating with spiritual people who can be a source of inspiration to us.
- Engaging in charitable deeds and service to humanity.

Prayers like the one below from Bahá'u'lláh can nurture the love for God within us and help strengthen our relationship with the Creator:

> O Thou Whose face is the object of my adoration, Whose beauty is my sanctuary, Whose habitation is my goal, Whose praise is my hope, Whose providence is my companion, Whose love is the cause of my being, Whose mention is my solace, Whose nearness is my desire, Whose presence is my dearest wish and highest aspiration, I entreat Thee not to withhold from me the things Thou didst ordain for the chosen ones among Thy servants. Supply me, then, with the good of this world and of the next. Thou, truly, art the King of all men. There is no God but Thee, the Ever-Forgiving, the Most Generous.[6]

Another way to strengthen our love for God is to demonstrate that love to His creatures. We can choose to show divine qualities

– such as generosity, mercy and compassion – towards our fellow human beings:

> To grow in the love of God, we must always remember Him and pray to Him. To grow in our love for His loved ones, we must share the blessings we receive with others, and seize every opportunity to engage in acts of kindness and service.[7]

Contemplating on scriptural passages that emphasise the cultivation and nurturing of love in our hearts, such as the one below, can also be of great help:

> O FRIEND! In the garden of thy heart plant naught but the rose of love.[8]

Serving others is also a great avenue for increasing our love for them – so much so, in fact, that Bahá'u'lláh regards service to others as inseparable from our humanness. In other words, human beings cannot claim 'humanness' if they do not have the willingness to serve others:

> That one indeed is a man who, today, dedicateth himself to the service of the entire human race. The Great Being saith: Blessed and happy is he that ariseth to promote the best interests of the peoples and kindreds of the earth. In another passage He hath proclaimed: It is not for him to pride himself who loveth his own country, but rather for him who loveth the whole world. The earth is but one country, and mankind its citizens.[9]

By engaging in consistent service to others, we will come to the realization that, as Saint Francis of Assisi stated, 'It is in giving that we receive.' Before long, we will begin to observe the positive effects of our actions on the recipients and on ourselves. We will witness how serving our fellow human beings becomes an outward manifestation of demonstrating love towards God. This love and its outward manifestation – serving others – will help us to develop and mature spiritually. Over time, this maturity will give us the mental resilience to withstand the toughest tests in life, including witnessing the suffering of our loved ones.

The author, Dr Stephen Post, has done extensive studies of Alzheimer sufferers, including his own grandmother. By observing Alzheimer patients, he came to realize 'the simple truth that love is our core'.[10] Despite his grandmother's terribly difficult situation, Post noticed he could still communicate with her through the language of love: 'I knew that even in the haze of dementia, she could still give and receive love – in fact, it was the only language left to her.'[11] His recommendation to others is to 'give love, and you'll discover life in all its force, vitality, joy, and buoyancy. In generosity lies healing and health.'[12]

Norman Vincent Peale also strongly believed that our own happiness was closely tied to learning to love and respect others, and to seeing the best in people. He was convinced that what we thought about people, and how we treated them and reacted to them, was critical to our own happiness: 'Treat each man as a child of God is the secret . . . Hold him in esteem and it will make both him and you happy.'[13]

Cultivating love for others begins with self-love

We cannot engage in service to others unless we first feel genuine love towards them. In a world scarred by national, religious, racial, and ethnic hatred, it may at first be difficult for some of us to cultivate or demonstrate love towards our fellow human beings. However, we can change that. The first step in this transformation is to develop self-love. This may sound contradictory or counterintuitive, but, in reality, most of us cannot manifest love towards others if we do not love ourselves. It is only when we approve of ourselves as individuals worthy of respect, and thus develop an abundance of love in our lives, that we can draw from that reservoir and consistently demonstrate that love towards others. Yet, many of us struggle with low self-esteem.

So, how do we combat the thoughts that negate our self-worth? One way is to study and contemplate scriptural passages that give us insights on our inherent value as God's noblest creation, and which make the special relationship we have with Him clear to us. Consider the following three passages from Bahá'u'lláh's *Hidden Words*:

> O SON OF SPIRIT! I created thee rich, why dost thou bring thyself down to poverty? Noble I made thee, wherewith dost thou abase thyself? Out of the essence of knowledge I gave thee being, why seekest thou enlightenment from anyone beside Me? Out of the clay of love I molded thee, how dost thou busy thyself with another? Turn thy sight unto thyself, that thou mayest find Me standing within thee, mighty, powerful and self-subsisting.[14]

> O SON OF BEING! Thou art My lamp and My light is in thee. Get thou from it thy radiance and seek none other than Me. For I have created thee rich and have bountifully shed My favor upon thee.[15]

> O SON OF BEING! With the hands of power, I made thee and with the fingers of strength I created thee; and within thee have I placed the essence of My light. Be thou content with it and seek naught else, for My work is perfect and My command is binding. Question it not, nor have a doubt thereof.[16]

Feeling valuable as human beings should not be mistaken with feeding selfishness in ourselves. The former is a positive attribute because it is an acknowledgement of our self-worth as God's noblest creation on earth, while the latter is a negative feeling that can lead to narcissism and self-infatuation.

In addition, we all have unique talents and qualities. Focusing on our God-given gifts and talents can be a helpful way to learn to develop self-respect and love for ourselves. Sometimes it takes another person to bring our good qualities and gifts to our attention. If such compliments are expressed, accept and acknowledge them by expressing your gratitude. Don't rebuff them out of excessive humility. If numerous people keep telling you that you are a gifted writer, speaker or teacher, or how loving, nurturing, patient, and generous you are, make a mental note of it. Better yet, write it down in a notepad or a computer file. Build this list over time and, if need be, go back and review these qualities. It will gradually help you to develop a positive mental image of yourself as you continue to work on improving yourself as an individual. By becoming conscious of our God-given qualities and talents, and leveraging them to the fullest possible extent in the path of service to humanity, we can also begin to experience lasting joy.

Metta meditation

Another complementary approach for cultivating self-love, as well as instilling love for others in ourselves, is the Buddhist practice of Metta meditation. 'Metta' is a Pali[17] word that literally means 'loving kindness'. The concept entails a display of benevolence, friendliness and goodwill towards all, and taking an active interest in the comfort of everyone. Metta is considered a compassionate form of meditation that teaches us how to tap into our innate reservoir of love and helps us to become a friend to ourselves and to the rest of the world. Among the other benefits of Metta meditation is an increase in self-respect, developing an attitude of care and consideration for others, and acknowledging the importance of living a harmonious existence with all forms of life on the planet.[18]

Buddhists believe if we adopt an attitude of loving kindness towards everyone, and manifest this love through our thoughts, words and deeds, we will find peace both within ourselves and with the outside world. Advocates of Metta meditation believe that love is the only force that has the power to unite all humans and bring true and lasting happiness. They are also convinced that practising loving kindness towards others can nurture other desirable qualities in us, including compassion, self-control and sympathetic joy – feeling truly happy for others, without having any self-interest in mind. Another benefit of Metta meditation is that it can help us overcome the false sense of separateness from others, which usually leads to feelings of sadness, fear, loneliness, and alienation. Scientific research has shown that consistent engagement in Metta meditation can actually help us replace feelings of separateness with a genuine sense of interconnectedness, which can, in turn, generate confidence, security, unity, and ultimately happiness for ourselves and for society at large.[19]

Metta meditation helps keep our minds pure and radiant. If we don't practise Metta meditation, certain negative states – such as anger, hatred, fear, guilt, and greed – can arise within us over time and lead to the defilement of our mind. Subsequently, as our mind loses its natural state of radiance, we begin to experience suffering and unhappiness. Fortunately, we have control over these states of being and can combat them. Anger can be confronted with calmness, hatred with love, fear with courage, guilt with forgiveness, greed with contentment, and so on.[20]

The Buddha taught that the negative forces in the mind that bring suffering are able to temporarily hold down the positive forces, such as love or wisdom, but they can never destroy them. The negative forces can never uproot the positive, whereas the positive forces can actually uproot the negative forces. Love can uproot fear or anger or guilt, because it is a greater power.

The practice of Metta meditation begins with positive affirmations for ourselves. This is not out of selfishness, but rather an explicit recognition that until and unless we value and respect ourselves and acknowledge our self-worth, we will not be able to fully unleash our potential for having positive feelings and aspirations for others. With the Metta practice, we uncover the possibility of truly respecting ourselves.

In Metta meditation, we gently repeat phrases that express a worthwhile and enduring wish – first for ourselves and then for others. The words we choose should focus on things that are truly significant to us. For instance, we can say phrases such as: 'May I be happy', 'May I be peaceful', 'May I be healthy', 'May I be healed', 'May I live with ease', or 'May I live in peace'.

Practising Metta meditation

A typical Metta meditation session takes between 20 to 30 minutes.[21] To start a Metta meditation session, sit comfortably with your eyes closed while you focus on your breathing for a few minutes. Then, visualize yourself at any age and in any surroundings with which you feel comfortable. Choose three or four phrases that convey your deepest wish for yourself, and gently repeat them over and over again. For instance, picture yourself as a child held by your mother and, with love and gentleness,[22] repeat the following silently to yourself for about ten minutes: 'May I be well, may I be happy, may all things go well for me.'[23] If your mind begins to wander, lovingly bring it back to the Metta phrases. If you feel any discomfort arising, just let the feeling pass by like clouds in the sky and take a few breaths.

Again, sending ourselves care may sound selfish and egotistical, but, in reality, it is not. We can only love others if we first manifest love and respect towards ourselves. Imagine the opposite: if you hate yourself and have little or no self-respect or confidence, would you be able to manifest *genuine* love and respect towards others?

Next, visualize a person who is important to you. This could be a family member, a friend or a colleague. Think of their inner goodness, their kindness to you and their contributions to the world. Then, silently and slowly, send them the same Metta phrases you have sent yourself. For instance, you can say: 'May you be well, may you be happy, may all things go well for you.'[24]

Now picture someone you may or may not know quite as well – perhaps someone you saw in a store or on the street – and send them the same Metta you sent to your family member, friend or colleague. It would be helpful to choose someone you see occasionally. This way, the Metta meditation will help you experience a sense of interconnectedness with them. Over time, you may develop warmth and care toward this other person, even if you have never said a word to them. This is a good way of breaking down the barriers between us and others.

Finally, if there are people towards whom you have negative

feelings, bring them to mind and send them the same Metta you sent to the other two groups. This last step is a very powerful stage in your Metta meditation practice, because it will help you transform your conditional love for others into an unconditional one. Here, you learn an incredibly powerful lesson: like the sun, true love can and should shine on everyone and everything.

When you are done with your Metta for this last group, sit quietly for a few minutes and enjoy the positive feelings you have experienced by being loving and compassionate toward all things. Leave your meditation with a smile on your face and with a firm resolve to carry those positive feelings with you in all that you do and say in the course of the day.[25]

There is now scientific evidence that we can use this practice to train our brains to overcome feelings of fear and anxiety. Metta meditation can achieve this by affecting the hippocampus, a major component of the brain in humans and other mammals. The hippocampus plays a significant role in consolidating information from short-term to long-term memory. Unfortunately, it is also the first part of the brain that can be damaged by tension, anxiety and anger. Individuals with a damaged hippocampus are unable to form or retain new memories, which makes them susceptible to ailments like Alzheimer's disease and amnesia (see Fig. 7). Studies by neuroscientists, Andrew Newberg and Mark Waldman, have shown that Metta meditation can help us suppress negative feelings that can damage our hippocampus, and even help us grow new nerve cells in that region of the brain.[26]

In addition to Metta meditation, other meditation practices can also be of great benefit in cultivating self-love.

'Remembering the good within ourselves' meditation practice

Another method of strengthening self-love is the practice of 'remembering the good within ourselves'. In her book, *Loving Kindness: The Revolutionary Art of Happiness*, Sharon Salzberg explains the technique of this practice:

Sit comfortably, in a relaxed way, and close your eyes. As much as possible, let go of analysis and expectation. For ten to fifteen minutes, call to mind something you have done or said that you feel was a kind or good deed – a time you were generous, or caring, or when you contributed to someone's wellbeing. If something comes to mind, allow the happiness that may come with the remembrance. If nothing comes to mind, gently turn your attention to a quality you like about yourself. Is there an ability or strength within yourself you can recognize? If still nothing comes to mind, reflect on the primal urge toward happiness within you, and the tightness and beauty of that.

In any of the above reflections, even if impatience or annoyance or fear should arise, don't be disheartened or anxious – see if you can return to the contemplation without guilt or judgment. The heart of skilful meditation is the ability to let go and begin again, over and over again. Even if you have to do that thousands of times during a session, it does not matter. There is no distance to traverse in recollecting our attention; as soon as we realize we have been lost in discursive thought, or have lost touch with our chosen contemplation, right in that very moment we can begin again. Nothing has been ruined, and there is no such thing as failing. There is nowhere the attention can wander to, and no duration of distraction, from which we cannot completely let go, in a moment, and begin again.[27]

It is only when we feel secure about ourselves and God's love for us that we can begin to manifest consistent love and acts of love towards others. If we succeed in extending our love towards others and rendering service to our fellow human beings, we can gradually begin to achieve humanity's greater goals, such as unity and brotherhood:

Strive to attain a station of absolute love one toward another. By the absence of love, enmity increases. By the exercise of love, love strengthens and enmities dwindle away.[28]

The 'celebratory love' meditation

Another love-based meditation practice that can also help cultivate love in our hearts towards others is the 'celebratory love' meditation:

> Find a location where you can sit undisturbed. Place your feet flat on the floor and adjust your position and posture until your body feels both alert and open. Lengthen your spine as if it were an antenna. Lift your heart as if you were offering it up as a gift.
>
> Take a few slow and deep breaths, bringing your awareness to each as it rises and falls. Then bring your awareness to your intention for this practice session. Perhaps it's to learn to be an even better friend, or to reduce pernicious envy and instead learn to celebrate others' successes . . .
>
> Now, gently call forth the visual image of someone for whom you know something good has happened. This good event may be big or small. Perhaps this person's family has been expanded to include a healthy newborn child. Or maybe he or she got a raise or had an important project at work meet with success. Or maybe this person is simply feeling healthy and strong, and enjoying a sense of ease in daily life. No matter the circumstances, let your mind slowly absorb the scope of this person's good fortune, knowing that, like all events – good and bad – this, too, shall fade with time. Then, lightly remind yourself of how people worldwide yearn to be happy, and that – at this particular moment, for this particular person – this universal wish is coming true. Into this context, say the following classic phrase, or your own version of it, speaking from your heart: 'May your happiness and good fortune continue.'
>
> Repeat this ancient wish over and again, with each new breath you take. Let the phrase infuse and soften your heart and your face. Visualize yourself supporting this person, celebrating his or her unexpected good fortune, coaxing whatever goodness he or she experiences to linger just a bit longer.

As your practice deepens, try out new ways to soften and expand your heart's capacity. Take in new people, ranging from those you know well to those you don't know at all. Remember that your aim is not to make this or any other person's good fortune last forever. That's hardly possible.[29]

If we learn to rejoice in the good fortune of others, our own happiness multiplies and that is the best cure for negative feelings such as envy.[30]

Science and love

It may be hard to believe that physical manifestations of love and affection can actually have health benefits too. Yet, scientific studies are proving just that. For instance, Dr Kathleen C. Light, of the University of North Carolina at Chapel Hill, has done groundbreaking research on the effects of physical affection – especially hugs – on our health. According to her findings, people who get hugs daily have higher levels of oxytocin and lower blood pressure.[31] Oxytocin, widely referred to as the 'love hormone', is a hormone that is made in a region of the forebrain called the hypothalamus. Oxytocin not only makes us feel good, but also lowers the levels of stress hormones in the body, improves our mood, increases our tolerance for pain, and lowers our blood pressure.

In a study at Pennsylvania State University,[32] students were divided into two groups. One group was given the assignment of either giving or receiving a minimum of five hugs daily for a month, and were asked to record the details. These nonsexual hugs had to be front-to-front and using both arms of the participants, but the length and the strength of the hugs were left to the participants' discretion. Additionally, the students had to try to hug as many different people as they possibly could. The second group was only given the assignment of recording the number of hours they spent reading daily for a month. By the end of the one-month study, the students in the first group, who had an average of 49 hugs over the course of the study, described themselves as happier. There was no change, however, in the second group.

Harvard Behavioural Psychologist, David McClelland, also conducted a study with students in the 1980s, which showed that spending time watching a film about Mother Teresa taking care of orphans in Calcutta significantly increased students' protective antibody salivary immunoglobulin A (S-IgA), compared to students who watched a neutral film. While watching the film, the students in the first group were also asked to focus their minds on times when they had loved or been loved. Results showed that the S-IgA levels of the students watching the film with Mother Teresa were significantly higher in the first group and that those levels remained high even an hour after watching the film. McClelland referred to this as the 'Mother Teresa Effect'. While there may be alternative explanations to this, the idea that such care-related emotions have an impact on biology is the most plausible and well established.[33]

Different kinds of love

There are, of course, different kinds of love: love for oneself; love for other people, including family and friends; love for animals; love for things and objects, such as our home or our cars; love for creation, like when we fall in love with the awesome majesty of the Grand Canyon or with the beauty of a sunset; and love for the Creator. We have already explained that by love for oneself we do not mean the kind of love that promotes selfishness or self-centredness. Rather, we are referring to the kind of love that helps nurture a sense of self-confidence within us – as noble creatures worthy of respect from ourselves and others. This is a kind of love that will help us to grow spiritually and make us better, happier individuals. Without this foundational love, it becomes very difficult for us to demonstrate love towards other people. However, if we conflate love for oneself with selfishness or self-centredness, we will severely hinder our spiritual progress. In fact, from an early age, children should be encouraged to widen the circle of their love. The wider we make that circle, the greater the benefits, both for ourselves and the rest of humanity:

> Every imperfect soul is self-centered and thinketh only of his own good. But as his thoughts expand a little he will begin to think of the welfare and comfort of his family. If his ideas still more widen, his concern will be the felicity of his fellow citizens; and if still they widen, he will be thinking of the glory of his land and of his race. But when ideas and views reach the utmost degree of expansion and attain the stage of perfection, then will he be interested in the exaltation of humankind. He will then be the well-wisher of all men and the seeker of the weal and prosperity of all lands. This is indicative of perfection.[34]

Barbara Fredrickson's scientific experiments

Dr Barbara Fredrickson, a Stanford University graduate, is the Kenan Distinguished Professor of Psychology at the University of North Carolina. As a social psychologist, she has been conducting research on human emotions and positive psychology for many years. She is also the recipient of sixteen consecutive years of research funding from the National Institutes of Health, one of the world's foremost research centres.

While love as a positive human emotion remains at the centre of her investigations, Fredrickson believes there are ten major emotions that contribute to lasting health and happiness: love, joy, gratitude, serenity, interest, hope, pride, amusement, inspiration, and awe.[35] Fredrickson conducts her experiments with her colleagues at the Positive Emotions and Psychophysiology (PEP) Laboratory. Their experiments show that while love is not a 'magic bullet', the steady and wide range of a loving moment, even when short-lived, can lead to physical and mental health and happiness.

In her book, Love 2.0,[36] Fredrickson describes one of her PEP lab experiments that provides some of the most direct causal evidence that love improves our bodily systems in lasting ways. Participants in a study were randomly selected to either learn how to self-generate love more frequently, or how not to do that. Their daily reports of love and social connection diverged across the two groups, and these differences accounted for significant improvements in people's resting levels of vagal tone, which is a key indicator of the health of our parasympathetic nervous system. Vagal tone can slow a racing heart and help us regain calm after an episode that generates fear or anxiety.

Since heart disease has been the leading cause of death in the United States, physicians can use knowledge of the individual's vagal tone to predict, with some accuracy, the likelihood of patient heart failure, as well as a person's odds of surviving heart attacks. People's vagal tone also reflects the strength of their immune system, especially as it relates to chronic inflammation – a well-known risk factor for heart failure, as well as stroke, arthritis, diabetes, and some cancers. What Fredrickson's experiment showed was that, by learning to love more frequently, we can actually reduce our risks for some of the worst health conditions many of us frequently worry about.

The PEP lab is now focusing on experiments that investigate how love might change humans at the cellular level. Fredrickson and her colleagues are now testing the hypothesis that learning to increase the frequency of loving connections could potentially alter human gene expression in ways that strengthen our immune system and increase our body's resistance against various forms of disease.[37]

Insight into how everyday moments of love register and resonate within the human body helps make sense of the groundswell of evidence that links experiences of positive social connections to health and longevity. A plethora of research has documented that people who have diverse and rewarding relationships with others are healthier and live longer. A more recent wave of longitudinal studies specifically ties positive emotions to healthy longevity. These studies suggest that a lack of positivity resonance is in fact more damaging to your health than smoking cigarettes, drinking alcohol excessively or being obese. Specifically, these studies show us that people who experience more warm and caring connections with others have fewer colds, lower blood pressure, and less often succumb to heart disease and stroke, diabetes, Alzheimer's disease, and some cancers.[38]

Sir John Templeton and the Institute for Research on Unlimited Love

A fitting end to this chapter is to mention Sir John Templeton, his dedication to the scientific study of love, and the outward manifestation of that dedication – the Institute for Research on Unlimited Love. Sir John, as he was called by many, was a business icon and the founder of the well-known Templeton Mutual Fund, as well as a philanthropist. The John Templeton Foundation currently gives away about US$70 million annually to research grants and programmes that engage in spiritual or scientific projects. One of his foundation's annual prizes, amounting to US$1.5 million, is the Templeton Prize for Progress Toward Research or Discoveries About Spiritual Realities. Among the recipients of this prize have been personalities such as Mother Teresa, Russian novelist and historian, Aleksandr Solzhenitsyn, and English physicist, Paul Davis.[39]

Sir John's lifelong passion and hope was that, someday in the future, science and religion (or spirituality) might fully converge on the same view of God, or the 'Ultimate Reality'. Sir John believed that love was the greatest force in the universe and worthy of world-class research. So, in 2000, he invited Stephen Post, author and professor of bioethics and family medicine at the School of Medicine at Case Western Reserve University, to start an institute solely dedicated to the scientific study of love. Post accepted the proposal and Sir John became the initial benefactor of the Institute for Research on Unlimited Love, which became a public charity just a few months later. Today, the Institute's website identifies its mission as the following:

> We seek to increase public awareness of the growing dialogue on Unlimited Love that is taking place at the interface of (1) new scientific investigations (e.g. in the health sciences, psychology, sociology, neuroscience, physics, and mathematics);

(2) insights of the world's great philosophical, spiritual and theological traditions; and (3) inspiring works of love by exemplars across the world.[40]

The proposal to conduct scientific studies of love goes back to at least 1951. During that year, psychologist, Harry Harlow, gave a powerful presidential address to the American Psychological Association, in which he challenged the participants to begin investigating positive human emotions such as love, instead of continuing their focus on negative human traits such as hatred, violence and fear. Harlow himself was a pioneer in such studies, which included controversial research on baby monkeys who clung to their cloth-and-wire 'mothers'.[41]

When people ask Post what exactly the Institute for Research on Unlimited Love does, he provides three answers:

1. It funds pioneering empirical research on selfless love in different areas, from human development and genetics to positive psychology and sociology.

2. It keeps an eye on those who act as helpers in situations that involve human suffering or disasters. When Mr Rogers[42] was asked what parents should tell their children after the September 1 terrorist attacks, he said: 'Keep your eye on the helpers.' The institute tries to study good hearts, good works and good lives, and come up with simple lessons we all can live by.

3. It tries to live by the motto: 'In the giving of self lies the unsought discovery of self.' In other words, when we give, we find our true selves. At the institute, we aid that discovery as we can.[43]

Best breakfast ever

My dad worked in construction. His day started early and ended late. All he wanted to do was crash on the couch and relax when he got home. For the most part that was what he did. No one complained; we were just happy when he was home.

But one hot and muggy summer, when my parents' 19th anniversary was coming up, they made plans to go out, just the two of them. The big day finally arrived and Dad got home at seven. Mom had fed all five of us early. She was dressed in her finest and wearing his favourite pair of high heels when he came in. They kissed, as they always did, when he came through the kitchen and headed for the family room. It was obvious he was hot and tired.

'Honey, I just need a thirty-minute nap and then I'll get ready and we will go out to eat,' he said, as he sat down on the couch.

Mom was already on her way over to the couch to give him a fresh cup of hot coffee. She bent over and kissed him on the head and said, 'I'll be ready whenever you are.'

I knew how important this evening was to my mother, but before long Dad was fast asleep. Then I watched my mother do the strangest thing. She reached into the refrigerator and took out eggs and bacon. Soon she had a batch of biscuits baking in the oven. I never said a word. I just watched her.

Breakfast was my dad's favourite meal. Before my eyes she piled a plate full of his favourite foods. As she set another fresh cup of coffee on the end table she bent down and kissed him while whispering in his ear, 'It's time to wake up, honey'.

He ran his fingers through his head of natural curly snow-white hair and sat up on the edge of the couch. As he looked up he found my mom standing in front of him with his dinner. I will never forget the look of love that passed between them as they made eye contact.

'Honey, I promised you I would take you out to dinner and I meant it,' he said sincerely.

Mom sat down beside him on the couch as he took the plate of food. She kissed him on the cheek. 'I know you would, but I also know you've had a hard day and you're tired. What's important is that we are together. We can go out any time for dinner.'

I was seventeen then, and that lesson in love is still with me today, five decades later.[44]

Count that Day Lost

George Eliot

If you sit down at set of sun
And count the acts that you have done,
And counting find
One self-denying deed, one word
That eased the heart of him who heard;
One glance most kind,
That fell like sunshine where it went –
Then you may count that day well spent.

But if, through all the livelong day,
You've cheered no heart, by yea or nay –
If, through it all
You've nothing done that you can trace
That brought the sunshine to one face –
No act most small
That helped some soul and nothing cost –
Then count that day as worse than lost.[45]

4

FAITH

> As a bee needs a hive, a bird needs its nest and a ship a harbour in time of storm, so do we every day of our lives need a refuge in time of stress and trouble. That refuge is faith.[1]

In the previous chapter, we identified some of the physiological, psychological and emotional benefits of living a spiritual life. We observed that, for many, this means putting a benevolent God at the centre of our lives. However, living a God-centred life requires that we first establish a personal relationship with Him as our spiritual Parent or our close Friend, a Being who is there for us when times get tough – much like a biological parent or a friend who is there for us whenever we need help. The difference here is that, unlike a parent or a friend who can be seen and touched, God is invisible to our outward-looking eyes. He can be felt by many, but cannot be physically observed. Thus, believing in Him and trusting that we can enter into a personal relationship with Him requires faith.

In their book, *Spiritual RX: Prescriptions for living a meaningful life*, Frederick and Mary Ann Brussat offer a succinct definition of faith and its implications:

> In the broad scope of the spiritual life, we see faith not as something you have but as something you are in – a relationship. It involves an awareness of and an attunement to God's presence in our everyday experiences. Practising faith, then, is like developing any relationship. You have to give it time and attention. It requires you to see, hear, feel, and constantly remember your partner – God. Have confidence in the

relationship's viability, even when you are facing mysteries, doubts and paradoxes. Trust in this faith, even to the point of staking your life on it. [2]

What is faith?

In the context of living a God-centred life, faith can be defined as having complete trust and absolute confidence and assurance in the grace and bounty of God as a benevolent Friend and a loving Protector who is always with us, sees us through hardships in life and, as His wisdom sees fit, protects us from the changes and chances of this world:

> For the Lord thy God will hold thy right hand, saying unto thee; Fear not; I will help thee. (Is. 41:13)

However, life's challenges can sometimes weaken our sense of faith and trust in God. Some of us tend to expect positive outcomes from all the difficulties we face in life. So, when we don't get what we want – or worse, what we thought we were entitled to in the first place – we start to question our entire relationship with God, and doubt begins to creep in. In such situations, the tests we are facing can eventually drive a wedge between us and God – and may last a lifetime. For others, tests and trials can have the opposite effect. They can galvanize us and act as magnets that will actually draw us closer to God.

Difficulties can act as catalysts to faith. During a dark night of the soul, sometimes all we can do is trust that this, too, will pass. Facing illness, death or the myriad other challenges in our lives, we are strengthened by the knowledge that a Greater Power watches and waits with us.

Thus, living a God-centred life requires that we use our God-given gifts and talents to solve tough challenges when we are faced with them, and, at the same time, also confidently put our trust in God, His grace and His bounty, believing that He is there to help us if and when we need it:

He that giveth up himself wholly to God, God shall, assuredly, be with him; and he that placeth his complete trust in God, God shall, verily, protect him from whatsoever may harm him.³

The Buddha promises that those who show faith will 'overcome the sorrows of life'.⁴ When we show faith, we are essentially accepting the notion that the purpose of tests in life is not to defeat or humiliate us, but to make us stronger individuals. If we are able to respond to tests positively, we will gradually transform into a loving, caring person who can become a source of grace and bounty to our own family and to countless others around us. We will learn to ignore our own weaknesses and frailties, and fix our gaze 'upon the invincible power of the Lord'.⁵ After all, 'things which are impossible with men are possible with God' (Luke 18:27).

Beyond this, when we realize that God is on our side, and become convinced that 'God hath never burdened any soul beyond its power',⁶ then we recognize that what we have perceived to be calamities, are, in fact, bestowals and blessings. In other words, the challenges we face become gifts and opportunities that can help us grow spiritually and mould us into stronger individuals who can withstand the toughest tests in life and come out of them unscathed. We can also take comfort in the fact that 'adversity is followed by success and rejoicings follow woe',⁷ and that God will eventually 'turn trouble into ease and sorrow into solace, and toil into utter peace'.⁸ Thus, as we deal with the tough challenges that life throws at us, we need to keep reminding ourselves that this, too, shall pass, but 'in God's time' (Ps. 27:14), not necessarily in our time frame, or in some other way that meets our expectations.

When we have a positive attitude towards life, we can also gradually overcome fear and anxiety because we will have accepted the notion that 'he who trusts in the Lord is safe' (Prov. 29:25). This acceptance will, in turn, lead to a greater sense of peace and joy within us, which will produce inner calm and serenity and leave no room for sorrow and sadness.

In an untranslated Tablet, Bahá'u'lláh states that the hearts of those who come to the true recognition of God will be so filled with the remembrance, the praise, the love, and the fellowship of God, that they will have no room for the sorrows of this world and calamities will not affect them.[9]

Faith can be cultivated through these practices:

1. **Living with God as our constant Companion:** This practice can help us develop a strong faith, which will, in turn, lead to a profound sense of security, peace and comfort. The practice will help us realize that, regardless of our conditions in life, we are never alone, and that there is a loving God Who is always with us and Who will guide, protect and help us in everything to the end. This practice requires us to begin our day with thoughts of God. If we learn to fill our minds with God, we will leave little room for worry, fear or anxiety. We will replace such negative thoughts with thoughts of faith, steadfastness, hope, and courage.

2. **Engaging in daily prayer:** We should think of prayer as communion with our spiritual Beloved. We should engage in prayer regularly, humbly and persistently. If our faith is not strong at first, we can always pray for assistance to develop that strength.

3. **Showing pure trust in God**: When it comes to trusting God, sometimes what is required of us is to show an attitude of child-like trust in Him. This means that we need to do our best in every situation and, as we seek guidance and assistance from God through prayer and supplication, leave the rest in His hands.

In his book *The New Art of Living,* Norman Vincent Peale explains this relationship beautifully:

One reason we find perfect peace by keeping our mind on God is that, in a remarkable way, faith in Him, in His goodness and His constant care, removes fear from us. I have a distinct memory out of the past. It was when I was a very little boy. Walking through crowded city streets with confusion and clamorous noise all about, with hundreds of people passing whom I did not know, I became frightened. Then I recall putting my hand in my father's hand and looking up into his face. He smiled down at me reassuringly and I was no longer afraid. I knew everything would be all right, for my father was big and strong and he loved me, and that was enough. The situation fundamentally is no different when we become adults and find ourselves in the midst of a dark and confused world. Put your hand in the hand of the Father. Look up and by the long vision of faith see His smile. He is big and strong and He loves you and will take care of you.[10]

4. **Deep contemplation on Scriptures:** We have a treasure trove of wisdom and guidance in the scriptures of different religions. These sacred texts are mankind's spiritual heritage that should not only be cherished, but studied and deeply contemplated time and again. Over time, the valuable insights contained in these books can positively reshape our mental attitude towards events, people and life in general.

    We can begin and end each day by reading and reflecting on the meaning of a single passage from the sacred literature of different religions on the subject of faith.[11] As we take short breaks over the course of the day, we can also review the gist of the message in the passage we have read, contemplate on its meaning and think about how it applies to our life and our relationship with others.

5. **Keeping a faith journal:** Another effective way to cultivate faith is to keep a record of the times we feel our prayers are answered. To do this, we can buy a notebook and, for added inspiration, write a few scriptural verses that deal with the

subject of faith on the first couple of pages. Then, each time we think our prayers for a particular occasion are answered, we can put the date on top of a new page and write the details of the event in our faith journal. This type of journal can prove to be an invaluable resource in life. As we encounter tests and trials in life, and despair overcomes us to the point that we feel our prayers are no longer heard, we can pick up that faith journal and refer back to numerous examples of how our prayers were heard in the past. That will give us the patience and faith to go on and wait for 'God's time'.

Keeping a faith journal can be a good approach for both strengthening our faith and for cultivating faith. If we struggle with the belief in God, next time a test comes our way and we are desperate and don't know where to go, we can try to believe that there is a Power in the world that can help us overcome our test. Then with all our heart and soul, we can turn to that Power for assistance. Then if our prayer is answered, we can write about it in our faith journal. The more prayers are answered, the stronger our faith will become. With a strong faith, comes peace of mind, tranquillity and happiness.

6. **Holding a weekly 'faith night'**: Holding a faith night as a weekly event can be a joyous and inspiring way for us to nurture the seeds of faith in the hearts of our family members. Simply pick a certain day and time when everyone in the family is available, and start the weekly meetings with some prayers. Follow this by reading a passage or two on the subject of faith, then contemplate on the inner meaning of the faith passage that has been read and how it applies to the life of each member of the family. End the session with reading inspirational faith stories from various sources. For the past few years, our own family of three has found a great deal of joy, solace and inspiration in this weekly practice.

7. **Repeating a faith verse before we sleep:** What we think about the last five minutes before sleep has a strong influence

on our consciousness. One way to cultivate faith is to repeat a faith verse a few times before we fall asleep. We can also repeat the same verse silently in our minds as we wake up in the morning the following day. This way, we will begin and end our days with God and His Word.

Levels of faith and trust in God

In his book, *The Spiritual Design of Creation*, Hushidar Motlagh notes that there is a direct relationship between the degree of our awareness and knowledge of God and how much faith and trust we will place in Him. The more we get to know Him, the more we will show faith and trust in Him. Motlagh identifies four levels in the journey to becoming fully conscious and aware of God in our lives:

1. **The level of absolute unawareness**: This is the state of total unawareness, ignorance, denial, or avoidance of God as a being or subject of discussion. At this level, consciousness of God has no influence or role in the conscious life of the individual.

2. **The level of mental awareness**: At this stage, God is in the back of the mind of the individual, but has only marginal influence on one's feelings or daily living.

3. **The level of perceptual awareness**: At this stage, God has moderate influence on one's feelings and daily living.

4. **The level of absolute inner awareness**: At this level, God has a profound influence on one's feelings and daily living. He is at the very core of one's life.[12]

True joy and inner peace come when we attain the fourth level: the stage of absolute inner awareness of God. This should be the ultimate goal of every human being. Mutlagh believes that humans should develop a love relationship with God. Among the fruits of such a relationship for humans are:

- A sense of security, inner peace, meaning and purpose
- A healthy and humble self-esteem
- Basic values to live by
- A diminished fear of death
- A sense of accountability and a desire to pursue a noble life
- A healthy attitude toward adversity
- A sense of fellowship with people and with the entire universe
- A lingering sense of gratitude
- An undying hope for the future.[13]

But how do we go about establishing a loving relationship with God? The first step is to show willingness. The next is to develop a strong desire for beginning such a relationship. Fortunately, as noted in Chapter 3, the seed for developing this relationship seems to have already been planted within us:

> My love is in thee, know it, that thou mayest find Me near unto thee.[14]

Motlagh explains:

> We can take ourselves out of God, but we can not take God out of ourselves . . . People look everywhere in their search for meaning and purpose except in their own souls. They think contentment is locked up in tomorrow and happiness is to be found in the next home. They think like a little girl who entered her parents' bedroom and said, 'In my room there aren't any good dreams. Let me try your room.'[15]

The 'Faith Factor' and scientific evidence

Dr Herbert Benson is a prominent cardiologist and a professor of mind/body medicine at Harvard Medical School. He is the author of 12 books and close to 200 scientific publications. His contributions to the field of mind-body research are well known. In his book, *Beyond the Relaxation Response*, he reflects on the subject of faith and science:

> I'm not at all interested in promoting one religious or philosophical system over another . . . I'm most concerned with the scientifically observable phenomena and forces that accompany faith . . . My research and that of others has disclosed that those who develop and use the Faith Factor effectively can:
>
> - Relieve headaches.
> - Reduce angina pectoris pains and perhaps even eliminate the need for bypass surgery (an estimated 80 per cent of angina pain can be relieved by positive belief!).
> - Reduce blood pressure and help control hypertension problems.
> - Enhance creativity, especially when experiencing some sort of 'mental block'.
> - Overcome insomnia.
> - Help alleviate backaches.
> - Prevent hyperventilation attacks.
> - Enhance the therapy of cancer.
> - Control panic attacks.
> - Lowers cholesterol levels.
> - Alleviate the symptoms of anxiety that include nausea, vomiting, diarrhoea, constipation, short temper, and inability to get along with others.
> - Reduce overall stress and achieve great inner peace and emotional balance.
>
> The Faith Factor should be used in conjunction with modern medicine. It should be an addition to the awesome cures that the medical profession can now perform. The two approaches – the Faith Factor and modern medicine – can enhance each other's impact and, together, bring about optimal results.[16]

The Runaways

One winter morning the year before I started school, my dad came in and asked if I would like to go with him to feed the cows. That sounded like fun, so I dressed in my warmest clothes, including the mittens connected by a string through the sleeves of my jacket, and went out with my dad to take my place in the world of work.

It was a pleasant morning. The sun shone brightly, but it was cold and the ground was covered with a blanket of new snow. We harnessed the team, Babe and Blue, and went over the hill with a wagon full of hay. After we found the cows and unloaded the hay for them, we started home. Then my dad came up with a good idea. 'Would you like to drive?' he asked. And I responded in typical manly fashion. I like to drive anything: cars, trucks, golf carts or donkey carts. I think the attraction must be the power. There is such a sense of power to be in control of something larger than I am, and it's good for my male ego.

I took the lines from my dad and held them looped over my hands as he had shown me, and we plodded back home. I was thrilled. I was in control. I was driving. But the plodding bothered me. I decided that while I was in control, we should speed up. So I clucked the horses along, and they began to hurry. First they began to trot, and I decided that was a much better pace. We were moving along, and we would get home much faster. But Babe and Blue came up with a better idea. They decided if they would run, we would get home even sooner.

The horses went to work on their plan and began to run. As I remember it, they were running as fast as I have ever seen horses run, but that observation might have a slight exaggeration factor built in. But they did run. The wagon bounced from mound to mound. As the prairie dog holes whizzed by, I concluded that we were in a dangerous situation, and I started to try my best to slow down this runaway team. I pulled and tugged on the lines until my hands cramped. I cried and pleaded, but nothing worked. Old Babe and Blue just kept running.

I glanced over at my dad. He was just sitting there, looking out across the pasture and watching the world go by. By now, I was frantic. My hands were cut from the lines, the tears streaming down my face

> were almost frozen from the winter cold, stuff was running out of my nose and my dad was just sitting there watching the world go by.
>
> Finally, in utter desperation, I turned to him and said as calmly as I could, 'Here, Daddy. I don't want to drive anymore.'
>
> Now that I am older and people call me Grandpa, I re-enact that scene at least once a day. Regardless of who we are, how old we are, how wise or how powerful we are, there is always that moment when our only response is to turn to our Father and say, 'Here. I don't want to drive anymore.'[17]

5

SERVICE

> That one indeed is a man who, today, dedicateth himself to the service of the entire human race.[1]

The world's great religions teach us that one of the most potent approaches to lasting joy is service to humanity. The Bible teaches us to use our 'gifts' (1 Pet. 4:10). We are told that these gifts are God's grace to us so that we can serve others, and we should do so with love. Hindu scriptures tell us that 'God is present in every act of service',[2] while the Bahá'í teachings note that, 'service to humanity is service to God',[3] and that our glory and majesty is in our servitude to fellow humans. Beyond that, we are also told that our 'eternal happiness is contingent upon giving'.[4]

The great philosopher, theologian and physician, Dr Albert Schweitzer, believed that the Gospel needed to be spread through the Christian labour of healing, rather than the verbal process of preaching. Thus, he spent more than half a century in remote locations in Africa, where few other western doctors dared even visit, let alone live. In the process, he provided care for thousands of patients and saved countless lives from a variety of horrific and deadly diseases, including leprosy, dysentery, malaria, and yellow fever. Later, his wife also joined him and, by the 1950s, his small hospital had three other unpaid physicians, seven nurses and thirteen volunteer aides. When he died in 1965, at the age of 90, Schweitzer's little hospital had grown into a compound of 70 buildings, 350 beds, and a leper colony for 20.[5]

A truly exemplary life of service had taught Schweitzer an important lesson regarding the connection between service and happiness:

I don't know what your destiny will be, but one thing I do know: the only ones among you who will be really happy are those who have sought and found how to serve.[6]

While few of us may have the potential to become the next Schweitzer, all of us have the capacity to render some service to others. And the sooner we learn to live a life of service, the better, because life-transforming acts of service often begin with small things in childhood.

In addition to being the president of The Institute for Research on Unlimited Love, Dr Stephen Post is the author of over 300 articles in peer-reviewed journals, as well as several books on the importance of service, including, *Why Good Things Happen to Good People*. As a child, Post once complained of boredom to his Irish mother. Her response was, 'Stevie, why don't you just go out and do something for someone?'[7] So, he went across the street and gave elderly Mr Muller a hand in raking leaves – an act of service that made the young Stevie feel really good. Post explains that his mother's advice, which he continued to share with other people, turned out to be more fundamental in the course of his life than his mother could have ever imagined.[8]

The good news is that, today, beyond scriptural admonitions and suggestions by the wise and educated, we now have plenty of scientific evidence that serving others is actually good for our own physical and mental health, and that the more we do for others, the better we feel and the happier we become.

In his best-selling book, *The Healing Power of Doing Good*, Allan Luks, an expert in volunteerism and non-profit leadership, who coined the now internationally recognized expression, 'helper's high',[9] explained the relationship between good health and volunteering. Following the analysis of an open-ended survey, to which more than 250 people across the country responded in just the initial wave, Luks came to the conclusion that helper's high is 'a rush of physical pleasure and wellbeing, increased energy, warmth, and actual relief from aches and pains'[10] that occur when people are directly helping others. Luks' research has now shown that:

Helper's high involves physical sensations that strongly indicate a sharp reduction in stress and the release of the body's natural painkiller, the endorphins . . . Endorphins are naturally occurring opiates in our bodies that seem both to relieve pain and to promote a sense of well-being, even euphoria . . . This initial rush is then followed by a longer-lasting period of improved emotional wellbeing.[11]

Here is how Tammy, a volunteer in Luks' research, describes her helper's high:

'It was a tremendous rush, like I could run for a hundred miles,' said Tammy Foley, a twenty-four-year-old kindergarten teacher in Othello, Washington, of her own experiences with helper's high. 'I felt like I had been zapped by an energy bolt. It was very euphoric. My whole body, especially my hands, really tingled. I felt very light and happy and content. My stomach tingled like "butterflies" and I felt like I bounced while I walked.'

Tammy taught at a school with many students from low-income families, and she 'sort of adopted them'. Some days she would take students home with her and make cookies.

'I have known for a long time', Tammy said, 'that, for me at least, when I'm helping someone, I feel the best. As soon as I finish up one project, I want to start right away on another. When I was in college, I would get really stressed out and get bad headaches. As soon as I would volunteer somewhere, my headaches would stop, my energy would improve. I would do fantastically on my tests, and I enjoyed even dreary tasks more. Sometimes I was elated and had such a rush, I couldn't settle down for hours. I kept charging all over the house, smiling and hugging everyone, singing. It was wonderful. And then, when I calmed down, I was so relaxed.'[12]

Luks' research concluded that regular helpers are ten times more likely to be healthy than those who don't do volunteer work. The biochemical explanation is that regular volunteer work not only helps our brains release its own morphine-like substances, such as endorphins, but it also produces powerful good feelings – even euphoria.

Self-centredness, as well as inordinate preoccupation with ourselves and our own needs, is not healthy. When we are fixated solely on our own needs and wants, we tend to lose a joyous and excited attitude towards life. On the contrary, when we lose ourselves in service, we will often be filled with vigour, enthusiasm and joy. Refocusing on others by performing acts of service could help us overcome difficulties in life.

> When your interest and appreciation are widened to include the whole great world, life becomes even more fascinating. Interest, projected outside yourself, has the power to force even hardship, suffering and pain into the background. The more vital your interest, in others and in the world, the more certainly you can live triumphantly over your own difficulties.[13]

Nurturing others also makes our lives more wholesome. In their book, *Altruism in Later Life*, authors Eva Midlarsky and Eva Kahana state five reasons why we should be generous with our time and energy and serve others:

- We gain a greater sense of the meaning of our life.
- We can cope with our own stress by shifting our focus to others.
- We feel socially integrated and connected.
- We feel more competent and effective.
- Nurturing others may lead to a more active lifestyle.[14]

Volunteering as a form of meditation

It is more blessed to give than to receive. (Acts 20:35)

In the field of medicine, Dr Herbert Benson, of Harvard University, is known for his pioneering contributions to the field of mind-body research. He is the author of 12 books and author or co-author of more than 180 scientific publications. His now classic 1975 book, *The Relaxation Response*, was the work that gave the major boost to today's alternative medicine movement. No publication has played as significant a role as this book in popularizing mind-body medicine. *The Relaxation Response* was the outcome of the studies Benson conducted at Boston's Beth Israel Hospital and at Harvard Medical School.

Through these studies, Benson showed that relaxation techniques, such as meditation, had tremendous physical benefits, including lowered blood pressure and reduction in heart disease. Benson considered volunteering as a form of meditation and actually prescribed it to his patients as an important step in achieving good health.[15] Benson is not alone. Physicians who are part of a large California health maintenance organization have also been prescribing volunteerism as a step towards restoring health to patients through a program they call *Rx: Volunteer*[16]:

> The key, both in helping and in meditation, whether you're repeating a mantra or teaching an illiterate adult to read, is that you're concentrating on a point outside of yourself. What happens physically is that the out-of-self focus breaks into the person's usual tension-producing thought patterns, decreasing the activity of the sympathetic nervous system and thereby countermanding the body's stress reactions . . . For many people, helping produces more powerful experiences than meditation, since it can often be easier to 'get outside yourself' and so break the usual chain of the stress reaction by coming to another person's aid than by sitting motionless in a quiet, darkened room silently repeating a phrase to yourself. Yet helping does duplicate meditation's complete shift of attention outside of one's daily focus. Helping is both a form of single-focus meditation, in which you concentrate on others instead of a sound or phrase, and a variation on what is known as 'mindfulness', a state of heightened awareness of all the emotions, thoughts, and sensations that come to you.[17]

On a spiritual level, service can help us connect to other people and can awaken within us a sense of compassion, care, and even love. It can give us a sense of peace, true joy, enthusiasm, optimism, and fulfilment. It can also be a boost to our self-esteem, which is the result of feeling needed and valued by those we help. Lowell Levin, professor of public health at Yale University, says that 'when you're a helper, your self-concept improves. You are somebody. You are worthwhile. And there's nothing more exhilarating than that.'[18]

On a physical and psychological level, volunteering can also enhance our immune system and help alleviate such conditions as headaches, backaches, insomnia, acid stomach, arthritis, Lupus, asthma, heart disease, depression, and alcoholism.[19] In *The Giving Heart,* author, MJ Ryan, gives the example of her friend who has been suffering from a terrible case of lupus for twenty years. This friend, however, has learned through experience that when she does volunteer work – in her case, volunteering at a soup kitchen – she feels better. Her pain is not as severe and she has more energy.[20]

Regular volunteer work can be a great tool in the treatment of depression in a lasting way. Barbara Bush, the former First Lady of the United States, is a great example. Bush said that when she and her husband returned to the US in 1976, after a two-year stay in China, she began to suffer from severe depression. However, she managed to defeat her depression through her volunteer work. She told reporters: 'I would feel like crying a lot and I really painfully hurt.'[21] However, she explained, after working at Washington Home – a health-care facility for people with serious illnesses – for six months, her depression permanently left her.[22]

In his work, *Adaptation to Life,* which we will discuss in Chapter 10 as the outcome of the longest running longitudinal study of adults in history, author George Vaillant concluded that adopting an altruistic lifestyle was a critical component of mental health.[23] In a 2005 study that was published in the *Journal of Molecular Psychiatry,* researchers looked at 354 families who had more than one child, and learned that 'our most common genetic subtype of dopamine – known as the D4.4 – is significantly linked to generous, giving behaviour.'[24] For instance, when a small child tries to comfort his baby sibling, 'innumerable dopamine-loving neurons are lighting up his brain with bliss. So, we can say that by nature we are hardwired to feel good when we do good.'[25]

As the following quote, attributed to the great American philosopher, poet and essayist, Ralph Waldo Emerson, says:

> It is one of the most beautiful compensations of this life that no man can sincerely try to help another without helping himself.[26]

When it comes to volunteering, however, there are certain critical steps that will lead to acquiring the best results. For example: personal contact with those we assist, frequency of help, assisting strangers as well as family members, having a supportive organization, a connection with one's fellow helpers, the use of one's gifts and talents, and letting go of results.[27] Another benefit of service is that we will gradually enlarge our inner circle by letting the people we help enter it. As members of society, this can also help us come together and feel more united. In addition, giving will help us find our true self, inasmuch as 'in the giving of self lies the unsought discovery of self.'[28]

In his book, *Man's Search for Meaning*, holocaust survivor, Viktor Frankl, says:

> Being human always points, and is directed, to something, or someone, other than oneself – be it meaning to fulfil or another human being to encounter. The more one forgets himself – by giving himself to a cause to serve or another person to love – the more human he is and the more he actualizes himself . . . self-actualization is possible only as a side-effect of self-transcendence.[29]

Think of Susie Valdez, who was nicknamed the 'Queen of the Dumps'. Her life is a great example of how self-sacrifice can change not only one's own life for the better, but countless other lives too. Susie was born in the slums of Mexico and, following a series of misfortunes, moved to El Paso with her children. She eventually founded a mission and raised money for the establishment of two medical centres, various subsidized schools, and began to feed 3,000 poor people daily. Many of those who met her were moved by her charisma. Now, Susie's motto is: 'Give love, and you'll discover life in all its force, vitality, joy, and buoyancy. In generosity lies healing and health.'[30]

Stephen Post notes that giving protects our overall health twice as much as aspirin protects against heart disease: 'If giving weren't free, pharmaceutical companies could herald the discovery of a stupendous new drug called "Give Back" – instead of "Prozac" – and run TV ads about love.'[31]

In his book, *Essential Spirituality*, Roger Walsh offers this inspiring story on Mother Teresa:

> Mother Teresa's nuns offer dramatic examples of royal giving and the joy it produces. Theirs is an austere lifestyle. They leave the comforts of home and live like the poorest of the poor people they serve. At their central house in Calcutta they are packed three or four to a room, and their only personal possessions are two dresses and a bucket for washing. They eat the same food as the poor, and despite the suffocating Indian heat they have no air conditioning. They rise before dawn and spend their days working in the slums. It is an existence that most of us would regard as difficult, if not downright depressing. Yet when a television interviewer visited Mother Teresa, he exclaimed: 'The thing I notice about you and the hundreds of sisters who now form your team is that you all look so happy. Is it a put-on?'
>
> 'Oh no,' she replied, 'not at all. Nothing makes you happier than when you really reach out in mercy to someone who is badly hurt.'
>
> 'I swear', wrote the interviewer afterward, 'that I have never experienced so sharp a sense of joy.'[32]

Walsh believes that serving others has many benefits for the individual rendering the service, as well to the one receiving the service. For instance, service strengthens positive forces like love, compassion and kindness, and weakens negative forces like greed, jealousy, envy, and resentment within our minds.

American psychologist and author, Abraham Maslow, once conducted a study of psychologically healthy people. At the end of the study, he came to the conclusion that 'the best way to become a better helper is to become a better person. But one necessary aspect of becoming a better person is via helping other people. So one must and can do both simultaneously.'[33]

How to cultivate an attitude of service

Some of us go through life hardly ever thinking about service and the value of serving others. After all, by definition, serving others usually means that you give and expect nothing in return. Yet, there are many among us who would like to get involved and to be of service, but don't know where to start. Alternatively, we may simply not be used to the whole idea of investing our time and energy in providing different kinds of service to other people. Such service could range from helping others to meet their basic necessities of life, to offering various opportunities for growth, such as in education and training.

A first step, if we have the desire to be of service to others, is to first find out where we are in terms of our own attitude towards service. If we first need to develop a positive outlook towards service and its value in general, a good source might be the sacred literature of the great religions of the world. We can begin by reading such passages, and then spending time contemplating on why these rich sources of spiritual guidance for humanity through the ages have emphasised service so much. We may ultimately come to the understanding that our comfort, safety, happiness, and spiritual joy are ultimately tied to the comfort, safety, happiness, and spiritual joy of our fellow humans.

Once we decide to get involved, we should seek out the areas of service in which we can offer the greatest benefit to others. Choosing the right kind of volunteer work can be tricky because we want to make sure to choose an area that leverages our talents, skills or interests. For instance, if we have good life skills, can communicate well and can easily connect with others, we may be a good candidate to mentor an underprivileged child. If our strong suit is teaching, perhaps we can teach immigrants to read, write and speak the language of the country they have immigrated to or tutor children in public schools on topics such as reading, writing and math. If we are not sure where to start, we can visit various online volunteer sites for guidance.[34]

Associating with people who do acts of service regularly can also be a great tool for learning from their experiences and for gaining inspiration. While some of us may begin serving others with the expectation to be acknowledged and appreciated, we will eventually learn that the reward is in the act itself. Thus, over time, our need for recognition or acknowledgment will diminish and may be completely eliminated. Doing good work quietly and without fanfare goes a long way in lowering such expectations.

Giving anonymously can also be a good approach. Roger Walsh offers a great example of this:

> A friend of mine had a delightful experience of 'helper's high' and a potent lesson in the power of anonymous giving when he was on a spiritual retreat. The food at the retreat was rather sparse and plain, so when he received a cake in the mail he was ecstatic. However, after eating a piece he began to think of the other people at the retreat, all of whom would enjoy a treat just as much as he would. After a moment's hesitation, he went into the kitchen and placed a piece of cake in each person's bowl. Then he hid and watched the expressions of astonishment and delight as each person filed into the kitchen and found not an empty bowl, but an unexpected delicacy. This happened twenty years ago and he says that he can't recall the taste of the cake he ate himself, but he still remembers with delight the look on people's faces that day. He has had twenty years of enjoyment from one cake.[35]

Service and science

For a long time, we had a very mechanical view of the human body. We viewed it as a machine that was simply controlled and run by an organ we called the brain, which acted as a computer with short-term and long-term memory. However, more recent research seems to indicate that the brain can also be considered a social organ that uses its cells and pathways to create feelings of empathy. As a result, a person could experience the joys and sufferings of others as if they were our own.

Stephen Post believes that 'our brain, our hormones and our immune system are an intimately related care-connection system'.[36] We all have this system. Unfortunately, however, many of us learn to turn this system off with negative feelings such as fear, vengefulness, anger, or other emotional states. If we could overcome these negative feelings, the care-connection system will reassert itself. We can use a variety of religious and spiritual practices – including meditation, contemplation, prayer, visualization, and positive affirmation – to gain self-control over these destructive emotions and replace them with feelings of genuine love for others.

As humans, we appear to be hardwired to show love and care towards others, because, when we do, our brains often reward us by releasing oxytocin – a hormone that generates feelings of joy and satisfaction. That's why when we ask volunteers why they help others, one of the most frequently given responses is that it makes them feel good, or they feel that they are getting as much out of it as those that are being served.[37]

Post also cites a collaborative effort called 'The Cognitive and Emotional Health Project: The Healthy Brain'. Researchers at three different national organizations – the National Institute of Neurological Disorders and Stroke, the National Institute of Mental Health, and the National Institute on Aging – collaborated on this project. The project's goal was to uncover the neurology of unselfish deeds that went beyond family members and reached out to strangers. Nineteen individuals were each given a sum of money and a list of causes to which they could contribute. Functional magnetic resonance imaging (fMRI) on the brains of the subjects showed that the mere act of donating the money activated the mesolimbic pathway – the brain's reward centre – which releases dopamine, a hormone that produces a sense of euphoria.[38]

Although America is known largely as a materialistic society, polls still show that most Americans see their happiness closely linked to building meaningful relationships and friendships, as well as in making positive contributions to the lives of others. A survey by *Time* magazine, conducted on 13-14 December 2004, asked Americans where their happiness came from. Three in four ranked 'contributing to the lives of others' among the top three things that made them happy. The two items that topped this were: 'friends and friendships' (76%) and 'relationship with children' (77%). Both of those also show the importance of social connectedness, generous behaviour and social support.[39]

A 2013 Gallup poll also showed that 46 per cent of Americans volunteered their time at a religious organization, and 49 per cent to another type of charitable group. Some 65 per cent donated their time to at least one of these types, and 30 per cent donated to both.[40]

In his books on the value of service, Post offers a number of different scientific studies that show the diverse benefits of service. Some studies showed that volunteering in adolescence:

> . . . enhances social competence and self-esteem, protects against antisocial behaviours and substance abuse, and protects against teen pregnancies and academic failure. Simple chores – helping with dishes, making one's bed, helping cook meals, doing laundry, and the like – are daily practices that make helping second nature. The kitchen table wisdom is the basis of scouting, Montessori schools, healthy families, and flourishing communities . . . Adolescents who are giving, particularly boys, have a reduced risk of depression and suicide. And giving during the high school years predicts good physical and mental health more than fifty years later, according to an ongoing study that began in the 1920s.[41]

In his book, *Why Good Things Happen to Good People*, Post offers a long list of studies involving thousands of subjects with different backgrounds to show the wide range of positive effects generosity and giving can have on our lives. Among the conclusions drawn from these studies are:

- Giving reduces mortality significantly in later life, even when you start late.
- Giving reduces adolescent depression and risk of suicide.
- Even the simple act of praying for others can reduce the impact of health difficulties in old age.
- Teens who are giving in high school live significantly longer, happier lives than their less giving counterparts. Nurturing others when you are young becomes a lifestyle.
- For other adults, studies show that giving protects and improves psychological wellbeing.
- Giving is linked to leadership, high self-esteem and attaining a feeling of control over our lives. It is also linked to enhanced spirituality and social competence.[42]

A 2007 publication by the Corporation for National and Community Service summarizes the results of over two decades of research on the potential benefits of service and volunteering activities. The publication draws on 32 different reports that looked at such studies and came up with the following conclusion:

> This research has established a strong relationship between volunteering and health: those who volunteer have lower mortality rates, greater functional ability, and lower rates of depression later in life than those who do not volunteer. Comparisons of the health benefits of volunteering for different age groups have also shown that older volunteers are the most likely to receive greater benefits from volunteering, whether because they are more likely to face higher incidence of illness or because volunteering provides them with physical and social activity and a sense of purpose at a time when their

social roles are changing. Some of these findings also indicate that volunteers who devote a 'considerable' amount of time to volunteer activities (about 100 hours per year) are most likely to exhibit positive health outcomes.[43]

The findings included the following:

- Those who engage in volunteer activities are less likely to suffer from ill health later in life, and may be introduced into a positive reinforcing cycle of good health and future volunteering.
- Even when controlling for other factors, such as age, health and gender, research has found that when individuals volunteer they are more likely to live longer.
- Individuals must meet a 'volunteering threshold' in order to receive the positive health outcomes from volunteering; that is, they need to commit a considerable amount of time – or at least one or two hours a week – to volunteering activities.
- States with higher volunteer rates are more likely to have lower mortality rates and less incidence of heart disease.

The following quotes from 'Abdu'l-Bahá are reflective of the attitude towards service that we can all strive towards:

> Is there any deed in the world that would be nobler than service to the common good? Is there any greater blessing conceivable for a man, than that he should become the cause of the education, the development, the prosperity and honor of his fellow-creatures? No, by the Lord God! The highest righteousness of all is for blessed souls to take hold of the hands of the helpless and deliver them out of their ignorance and abasement and poverty, and with pure motives, and only for the sake of God, to arise and energetically devote themselves to the service of the masses, forgetting their own worldly advantage and working only to serve the general good.[44]

This is worship: to serve mankind and to minister to the needs of the people. Service is prayer.[45]

The Surgeon and the Newsboy

In a mid-Western city, some years ago, was a great surgeon who was also a professor in the medical school. This surgeon was a true physician in that he not only had superlative skills but also loved people and went about doing good. He became deeply interested in the little [disabled] newsboy at the corner, where the doctor regularly bought his paper. He was a bright little fellow, this newsboy, and the famous surgeon said to him one day, 'Johnny, would you like to have me cure that leg of yours so that you could run and play like other boys?' 'Oh, Doctor,' said the little lad, 'that would make me so happy!'

Accordingly, the surgeon arranged to operate upon the boy and explained to him that he wanted to perform the operation in the presence of his class of medical students to teach the students how to help other little boys when they became doctors. Johnny agreed. He was placed before the surgeon and the students were arranged in tiers, as in an amphitheatre so that they could witness the operation. The doctor explained the disease and operative procedure he was to follow.

When all was ready, he said, 'Now, Johnny, we are going to fix that leg of yours', and attendants started to administer the anaesthetic. Johnny raised his head, and said in a voice that could be heard all over the room, 'God bless you, Dr Dawson, for you have been so good to me.' The surgeon looked down at him. Tears came into his eyes. He put his hand on the head of the little fellow and said, 'Thank you, Johnny.'

After the successful operation, the surgeon said to the students, 'I have operated on many great and prominent men, upon millionaires, senators, governors, and have received many large fees, but what that little boy said was the greatest fee I ever received in my life.'[46]

6

PRAYER

What is prayer?

Prayer is the act of communion with God. Those who engage in prayer believe that, just as we feed our bodies to physically survive and grow, we need to regularly feed our souls, too, for spiritual sustenance and growth.

> O SON OF LIGHT! Forget all save Me and commune with My spirit. This is of the essence of My command, therefore turn unto it.[1]

Since the object of our prayer is not outwardly visible, it takes faith to rely on prayer as a form of communication with God. However, to those who demonstrate faith in the power of prayer, this form of communication with God can prove to be a great source of solace in times of trouble, and a refuge for attaining calm, peace and inner tranquillity. Today, prayer continues to help millions of people who are faced with troubles, illnesses, grief, hopelessness, and loss. The American philosopher and psychologist, William James, considered prayer a great remedy for overcoming negative states of mind, saying, 'The sovereign cure for worry is prayer.'[2]

Why should we pray?

As we will see later in this chapter, science has shown that those who pray generally enjoy greater physical, emotional and psychological health. Prayer can contribute to one's overall happiness.

However, for religious and spiritual people, prayer can also be a means of communicating with the Supreme Being, drawing closer to Him and deepening one's love for Him as the Creator and Sustainer of the universe. Someone once asked 'Abdu'l-Bahá what the wisdom of prayer was. He responded:

> The wisdom of prayer is this: That it causeth a connection between the servant and the True One, because in that state man with all heart and soul turneth his face towards His Highness the Almighty, seeking His association and desiring His love and compassion. The greatest happiness for a lover is to converse with his beloved, and the greatest gift for a seeker is to become familiar with the object of his longing; that is why with every soul who is attracted to the Kingdom of God, his greatest hope is to find an opportunity to entreat and supplicate before his Beloved, appeal for His mercy and grace and be immersed in the ocean of His utterance, goodness and generosity.[3]

Thus, prayer gives us the option to turn to a Friend and communicate with Him at virtually any time, anywhere, to unburden ourselves. It can also be looked upon as our expression of love for the Beloved (God). The Qur'an speaks of God as being closer to us than our jugular vein:

> We are closer to him than [his] jugular vein.[4]

In the Bahá'í Writings, God is described as our true Friend:

> Worldly friends, seeking their own good, appear to love one another, whereas the true Friend both loved and doth love you for your own sakes; indeed He hath suffered for your guidance countless afflictions.[5]

Author and professor of psychology at the University of California, Davis, Robert Emmons, notes that:

Prayer is at the front and centre of the spiritual life. It has been referred to as 'the soul and essence of religion' and 'the most spontaneous and personal expression of intimacy with the divine'. Prayers of gratitude are among the most common form of prayer, and religious scriptures of various traditions are replete with prayers of this type.[6]

How to cultivate the habit of praying

As humans, we cannot pray by instinct. Praying is a habit, the formation of which takes time and effort. To form the habit of praying – as with any other habit – we need to exercise self-discipline, regularity and perseverance.[7] To practise these three elements, we need motivation – which comes from conviction or faith in God as the Creator who loves us and cares about our wellbeing. Such a view of God leads us to want to express our love for Him through prayer – by exercising the three elements of self-discipline, regularity and perseverance.

Self-discipline

The practice of self-discipline requires praying, regardless of our mood. When we first try to form the habit, there may be times when it takes special effort on our part to engage in prayer. Since we are aware of the importance of the role that prayer plays in our lives, even at such times we can gradually pray ourselves into the mood and focus our minds on the words we say.

If, during prayer, our mind begins to wander, we need to be patient with ourselves and gently bring our thoughts back to our communion with God.

Regularity

In some religions, including Islam and the Bahá'í Faith, adherents are asked to engage in a particular category of prayers known as 'obligatory prayers'. Additionally, Bahá'ís are also required to read excerpts from their holy writings once in the morning and once in the evening, and reflect on the content of those words and how they apply to their lives. Once prayer becomes a part of our daily routine, the practice will come to us more naturally, and its regularity will feel like having spiritual sustenance. Soon, much like we try not to skip physical meals during the day, skipping daily spiritual nourishment will also become more difficult.[8]

Perseverance

Finally, as with any other habit, if we want to form the habit of praying, we need perseverance. We have to discard the notion that unless we truly 'feel' the presence of God during our prayers, we are not really praying. Regardless of the outcome, we should persevere in the practice of praying and leave it to God to use our prayers as He sees appropriate, and not desire any superficial or temporary gain.[9]

How to pray

In his book, *the Power of Positive Thinking*, Norman Vincent Peale sums up what he calls rules for effective praying. Some of these rules are as follows:

- Pray as you go about the business of the day, on the subway or bus or at your desk. Utilize 'minute prayers' by closing your eyes to shut out the world and concentrating briefly on God's presence. The more you do this every day, the nearer you will feel to God's presence.
- Do not always ask when you pray, but instead affirm that God's blessings are being given and spend most of your prayers giving thanks.
- Always express willingness to accept God's will. Ask for what you want, but be willing to take what God gives you. It may be better than what you ask for.
- Practise the attitude of putting everything in God's hands.

Ask for the ability to do your best and to leave the results confidently to God.
- Pray for people you do not like or who have mistreated you. Resentment is blockade number one of spiritual power.
- Make a list of people for whom to pray.[10]

What should we pray for?

Gaining material means or possessions

Some among us may see prayer simply as a means to supplicate to a higher force to give us what we want or need. While we may seek assistance with anything, according to 'Abdu'l-Bahá, the ultimate goal of prayer is far from seeking personal gain of any sort:

> The true worshipper, while praying, should endeavour not so much to ask God to fulfil his wishes and desires, but rather to adjust these and make them conform to the Divine Will. Only through such an attitude can one derive that feeling of inner peace and contentment which the power of prayer alone can confer. Thou hast asked about material means and prayer. Prayer is like the spirit and material means are like the human hand. The spirit operateth through the instrumentality of the hand. Although the one true God is the All-Provider, it is the earth which is the means to supply sustenance. "The heaven hath sustenance for you" but when sustenance is decreed it becometh available, whatever the means may be. When man refuseth to use material means, he is like a thirsty one who seeketh to quench his thirst through means other than water or other liquids. The Almighty Lord is the provider of water, and its maker, and hath decreed that it be used to quench man's thirst, but its use is dependent upon His Will. If it should not be in conformity with His Will, man is afflicted with a thirst which the oceans cannot quench.[11]

Praying for the Will of God

In the above passage, 'Abdu'l-Bahá advises us that, instead of using prayer as simply a means for asking God to grant us wishes, we should use prayer as a tool for conforming our wishes to the Will of God. This makes sense. After all, if we reflect a bit on the notion of God as an All-Knowing, All-Loving Being, we would see Him as a spiritual Parent to us. Therefore, just as our biological parent always has our best interests in mind, so does He as our spiritual Parent. Yet, we humans see only part of the picture, whereas God, who is All-Perceiving, sees the full picture of what is best for us now, and in the future. Hence, if at times we feel that our prayers go unanswered, it is perhaps because the answer was, in fact, 'no':

> God is merciful. In His mercy He answers the prayers of all His servants when according to His supreme wisdom it is necessary.[12]

> I swear by My life, nothing save that which profiteth them can befall My love ones.[13]

Surrendering one's will to God's is not an easy exercise, especially if we strongly believe that we know what's best for us and we don't want to leave our destiny in anyone else's hands. Yet, for the exact reasons stated above, those who believe in an All-Knowing God should try to conform their will to the Will of God, and work towards developing the attitude of submitting to God's Will through prayers such as the one below:

> I implore Thee, O my Lord, by Thy name the splendors of which have encompassed the earth and the heavens, to enable me so to surrender my will to what Thou hast decreed in Thy Tablets, that I may cease to discover within me any desire except what Thou didst desire through the power of Thy sovereignty, and any will save what Thou didst destine for me by Thy will.[14]

One way we can accept the wisdom of praying for God's Will, instead of the realization of our own wishes, is to have trust in God and feel the assurance that, if we abide by His laws and make Him the centre of our daily lives, we will attain to the destiny He has ordained for us. However, as humans, we have been given free will. God does not want puppets, but thinking human beings. Therefore, He allows us to choose either His path or our own. Either way, we will be responsible for the choices we make in this life. So, for instance, we can choose to put the focus of our lives on acquiring wealth, becoming popular or living for the world alone. Or we can concentrate on understanding God's plan and purpose for our existence, which will lead to a focus on developing our spiritual side and attaining God's good pleasure.

According to Bahá'u'lláh, humanity's true heaven lies in nothing but the satisfaction of God's good pleasure:

> As to Paradise . . . in this world, it is realized through love of Me and My good-pleasure. Whosoever attaineth unto it, God will aid him in this world below, and after death He will enable him to gain admittance into Paradise whose vastness is as that of heaven and earth.[15]

In the process, we will experience difficulties in life. Let's not forget that the first of Buddha's Four Noble Truths – that suffering is universal.[16] In other words, all humans will go through some suffering. The belief in God's infinite knowledge – as well as a genuine and firm conviction in His love for humanity – are not only essential for effective praying, but will also prove beneficial in times of tests and trials. After all, as our Spiritual Father, He knows and wants what is best for us. Therefore, tests and trials in our lives could well be one of the methods He uses to draw us closer to Him.

Praying to express gratitude

We can also use prayer as a way to express gratitude for what we already have in life. In fact, Bahá'í scripture states that counting our blessings can result in an increase in the bounties we receive in life:

> Be thou happy and well pleased and arise to offer thanks to God, in order that thanksgiving may conduce to the increase of bounty.[17]

In his book, *Thanks! How the New Science of Gratitude Can Make You Happier,* author and psychologist, Robert Emmons, says:

> Praying for gratitude is strongly sanctioned in religious scriptures. The Hebrew Bible is replete with the motif that man owes God gratitude for life, health and sustenance. There are numerous 'thanksgiving' psalms and other prayers in which the person or the community that is praying pours forth expressions of gratitude. The message is clear: Be thankful. Accept the gifts you have been given. Don't forget God.
> If you find that because of circumstances you cannot pray from gratitude, then I would suggest praying for the ability to be grateful . . . that petitionary prayers 'work' better if people also practice gratitude.[18]

In fact, gratitude as a concept and expressing it as a practice are so critical to achieving long-lasting happiness that we have dedicated a chapter to it.

Praying for protection

Prayers can also be used to seek protection from the tests and trials of life. In his book, *Spiritual Intelligence,* psychologist, Dr Khalil Khavari, explains why we could also engage in this type of prayer:

> Praying for protection, above all, from the self – from the ever-active, ever-demanding impulses of the lower nature – is of high priority. Impulses are often the main source of our troubles and missteps in life. It is the submission to these potent impulses

that prevents and even reverses our spiritual progress. We also pray for protection from others. Others who may tempt us, others who may awaken and fuel our dormant evil inclinations, others who pose great tests to our standards of righteousness.[19]

Praying for others

The sacred literature of most religions also encourages us to pray for the wellbeing, happiness and forgiveness of all. These prayers can help sanctify our hearts and promote bonds of friendship and affection with others.

> Pray ye for all; ask ye that all be blessed, all be forgiven.[20]

Praying for the deceased

We can also pray for the forgiveness and progress of the souls of those who have departed from this world:

> O my God! O Thou forgiver of sins, bestower of gifts, dispeller of afflictions! Verily, I beseech Thee to forgive the sins of such as have abandoned the physical garment and have ascended to the spiritual world.
>
> O my Lord! Purify them from trespasses, dispel their sorrows, and change their darkness into light. Cause them to enter the garden of happiness, cleanse them with the most pure water, and grant them to behold Thy splendors on the loftiest mount.[21]

Praying for them will also help comfort our own hearts and leads to the progress of their souls in the afterlife.

Praying for guidance

We can also use prayers to seek guidance when making important decisions in life. For instance, in Psalms, we find this prayer:

Show me your ways, Lord, teach me your paths. Guide me in your truth and teach me, for . . . my hope is in you all day long. (Ps. 25:4–5)

Praying for strength

Prayer can be a great instrument for developing strength and mental toughness as well, especially when we face the tests and trials of life. Contemplation on verses like the one below helps us achieve that goal:

He gives strength to the weary, and increases the power of the weak. (Is. 40:29)

Seek the Lord and His strength; seek His presence continually. (Ps. 105:4)

Are our prayers answered?

This, of course, is the big question many of us ask, especially when we ask God for something and we don't receive it. The primary issue with such a perspective is that we reduce God to the level of a genie, whose main role is to grant our wishes. If we believe in the existence of God as a spiritual Parent, who genuinely loves us and wants what is best for us, then it is only natural to believe that He also hears and wants to answer our needs, wants and wishes, positively. However, in His inscrutable and all-encompassing wisdom, God may decide that what we want is not in our best interest.

Therefore, just as our biological parents may at times deny us what we think is in our best interest, our spiritual Parent – who has the full picture of the present and the future – may also deny what we perceive to be a critical need or want for us at that time. Hence, while it is safe to assume that God hears our prayers, we should not forget that He answers those prayers according to His all-encompassing knowledge and wisdom. Sometimes, that knowledge and wisdom requires the answer to be a resounding 'no'. It is in those situations that we tend to think that God has not answered our prayer at all, forgetting all along that 'no', too, is an answer. There could be a host of reasons for a 'no' in response to what we have prayed for:

1. The 'no' may actually be a blessing in disguise.

> My calamity is My providence, outwardly it is fire and vengeance but inwardly it is light and mercy.[22]

2. The answer may be 'no' now, but 'yes' later.

Sometimes, the answer to a prayer may appear as a 'no' because we are in a hurry to get a 'yes' now, forgetting that, unlike we humans who can see only part of the picture at a given time, God is All-Perceiving and sees the whole picture from the outset. Consequently, we may fervently pray to God to give us something that is just not timely for us. God's reply to such a prayer may essentially be 'wait for the right time'. In one of His writings, Bahá'u'lláh confirms that God has always answered human prayers and will continue to do so. If, at times, there are delays in His answers, it is for the benefit of the individual.[23]

3. What we want or think we need is not in our best interests.

We may think what we are praying for is the best thing for us, whereas, in reality, it may be harmful to us:

> O SON OF SPIRIT! Ask not of Me that which We desire not for thee, then be content with what we have ordained for thy sake, for this is that which profiteth thee, if therewith thou dost content thyself.[24]

Scientific studies of the positive effect of prayer

Many question the very notion of scientifically studying the power or efficacy of prayer. They argue that prayer is not an appropriate subject for scientific research. Others see prayer as an indispensable part of religion, and the same objection is raised to the scientific study of religion. Richard Sloan, professor of behavioral medicine at Columbia University, and the author of *Blind Faith: The Unholy Alliance of Religion and Medicine*, explains this succinctly:

> The problem with studying religion scientifically is that you do violence to the phenomenon by reducing it to basic elements that can be quantified, and that makes for bad science and bad religion.[25]

However, this hasn't stopped researchers from conducting numerous studies over decades on the effectiveness of prayer. Most of these studies can be classified into two broad categories: intercessory prayers and personal prayers. Results for both have been mixed, yet more positive effects have been observed for personal prayers.

Intercessory prayers

These are prayers that are said for the healing or general wellbeing of others. Intercessory prayers can be said in the presence of the subject or remotely. One of the original intercessory prayer studies was done by Dr Randolph Byrd, a cardiologist at San Francisco General Hospital. Byrd randomly divided a group of 393 heart patients into two groups. The first group consisted of 192 patients who received intercessory prayers from ministers and laypeople for a period of one month. The second group (the control group), which consisted of 201 patients, received no such prayers. Neither group had any knowledge of who was and who was not receiving prayers during the study. The results were quite provocative:

The heart patients who were prayed for suffered significantly fewer complications than those who received no prayer. Patients who were prayed for were five times less likely to require antibiotics for infections (a sign of good immune response), two and a half times less likely to suffer congestive heart failure, and had a significantly lower risk of sudden cardiac arrest.[26]

The largest and perhaps most well-known intercessory prayer study is 'The STEP Project' (Study of the Therapeutic Effects of Intercessory Prayer), also known as the 'Templeton Foundation Prayer Study' (named after its financial sponsor) or 'The Great Prayer Experiment'. Herbert Benson, a professor from Harvard, conducted this study together with his colleagues.[27] It was a decade-long, double-blind, randomized research that involved 1,802 coronary artery bypass surgery patients at 6 different hospitals in the United States. Results of the study showed no statistically significant differences between the post-surgery healing of those who received intercessory prayers versus those who did not.[28]

A meta-analytic study by John Astin, that summarized the outcomes of 23 intercessory prayer studies comprised of 2,774 patients, found that 13 studies showed statistically beneficial results for intercessory praying, 9 showed no results and 1 showed a negative result.[29] A 2003 study found 'some' evidence for the hypothesis that patients who suffered from acute illnesses experienced improved recovery if they were prayed for.[30] However, of the 23 studies included, only 3 had sufficient rigor.

Another 2007 meta-analytic study that examined the results of 17 studies on the efficacy of intercessory prayer found 'small, but significant, effect sizes for the use of intercessory prayer' in 7 studies, but 'prayer was unassociated with positive improvement in the condition of client' in the other 10 studies.[31]

Personal prayers

Personal prayers are those in which individuals engage for their own healing or general wellbeing. Some studies have shown positive effects for individuals who pray for themselves. For instance, Jankowski and Sandage found a positive relationship between the prayerfulness of the subject, and the amount of hope and the degree of forgiveness they expressed.[32] In a series of 4 studies involving a total of 2,390 subjects, Lambert and his associates looked at the strength and direction of the relationship between prayer and gratitude. Results of their research showed positive evidence that those who prayed regularly showed increased gratitude.[33] A study of 407 men in a rural Georgia county who had shown to be free of cardiovascular disease or hypertension showed that diastolic blood pressures of the men with high church attendance in that group who prayed regularly were significantly lower than those of the men in the group that found religion to be of low importance in their lives. The difference remained even after the researches adjusted for age, body-mass index, socioeconomic status, and smoking.[34]

In 1986, Dr Harold Koenig of Duke University, together with his colleagues, decided to examine the potential relationship between religious activities – such as attending worship and engaging in prayer – with blood pressure. For their research, they randomly chose 3,963 men and women, 65 years and older, who had previously participated in a large study by the National Institute of Health. They intentionally chose this age group because the negative effect of cardiovascular disease typically becomes more severe later in life. The participants were individually interviewed and asked a set of questions, including how often they attended religious meetings or service, and how frequently they prayed or studied the Bible. When Koenig and his colleagues compared actual blood pressure measurements of the participants with religious attendance, they found that both systolic and diastolic pressures of the subjects who attended religious services, regularly prayed or studied the Bible more frequently were significantly lower. These differences were maintained over a six-year period in which the study continued with all the surviving members of the population.[35]

Sending Prayers and Overcoming Frustration

Try the experiment of praying in an outgoing manner, affirming good will toward those who irritate or frustrate you, and discover for yourself that you have the amazing power of eliminating frustration.

I [Norman Vincent Peale] demonstrated this for myself while staying in a beautiful hotel at Stresa on Lake Maggiore in Northern Italy. This is one of the loveliest places in Europe. The lake and the great hotel resemble an old painting, serene and tranquil. The village is a colorful riot of flowers. The placid lake stretches away toward the hazy, towering hills in a charming vista. The fascinating little island villages, which seem to float in the lake, give the illusion of being out of a medieval picture book.

I went to bed that night expecting a restful night's sleep in that idyllic spot. But the hotel is on the main road which skirts the shore of the lake, and a constant and unending stream of noisy Vespas and lambrettas (motorcycles) turned the night into bedlam. I lay in bed listening hopefully for just one brief interlude of quietness between the racing motorcycles and strident horns, but none ever came. The noise was always either trailing off, or coming up, or bursting upon me in devastating power.

Soon I found myself getting into a state of agitation. Then I realized that I was actually getting mad at those motorcyclists. I arose and shut the windows, but the heat was more than I could bear. It was either heat, or noise, or both, for the sound was so penetrating that it came through the windows, even though they were double ones. I tried plugging my ears with cotton, but this was uncomfortable. I tossed restlessly on my bed and, with mounting asperity told my wife what I thought of people who would race with open cutouts through the still night with a total disregard for people who were trying to sleep.

I gradually worked myself into a state of frustration where sleep would be quite impossible. Then it occurred to me ... to send good will thoughts toward the motorcyclists. Why were they riding those motorcycles? Simply to get some joy and happiness out of life. Or perhaps they were on their way to some destination that was important to them... Therefore, every time I heard a motorcycle approach, which seemed about every half minute, I prayed specifically that the person riding it would have a wonderful life, that God would guide and bless him.

I became so positively engrossed in my spiritual contact with those nice Italian people speeding along on those ear-shattering motorcycles that I forgot my irritation, the frustration left me, and the next thing I knew it was seven-thirty in the morning. Those Vespa riders did not bother me from that time on throughout my entire stay in Stresa. It is a fact, that by prayer, if you really mean it and actually believe in it, you can block out frustration.[36]

7

MEDITATION

> Invisible and subtle is the mind, and it flies after fancies wherever it likes; but let the wise man guard well his mind, for a mind well-guarded is a source of great joy. (The Dhammapada 3:36)

The word meditation means contemplation or reflection. Meditation can also be defined as the skill of paying attention. The main goal of meditation is to free the mind from the grasp of automatic, random thoughts. When the mind learns, through meditation, to focus on our breath, or an object like a flower, it can slowly gain peacefulness. A quiet, centred mind can then lead to a calm and relaxed body.

As we grow up, many of us learn to become slaves, rather than masters, of our minds. Fortunately, regular meditation can reverse that trend. We can learn to master the mind by consciously slowing down our thinking processes, welcoming only positive thoughts we approve of and simply letting go of negative thoughts that are unproductive and harmful. When meditation becomes an indispensable part of our daily lives, we will learn to control our thoughts and, thus, our actions. This is a highly liberating, empowering and rewarding experience.

Regular practice of meditation can also help bring out some of our innate qualities such as creativity, patience, love, wisdom, faith, peacefulness, and so on. In some religious traditions, such as the Bahá'í Faith, the practice of meditation as contemplation is considered a valuable method for sanctifying the human heart, which is considered to be the seat of the Divine.

MEDITATION

The Baháʼí writings offer the analogy of the sun and the mirror to help explain how prayer and meditation can help remove the dust of worldliness from the mirror of the human heart, so the heart can faithfully reflect the divine light that is hidden in our innermost reality:

> Man possesses two kinds of susceptibilities: the natural emotions, which are like dust upon the mirror, and spiritual susceptibilities, which are merciful and heavenly characteristics.
> There is a power which purifies the mirror from dust and transforms its reflection into intense brilliancy and radiance so that spiritual susceptibilities may chasten the hearts and heavenly bestowals sanctify them. What is the dust which obscures the mirror? It is attachment to the world, avarice, envy, love of luxury and comfort, haughtiness and self-desire; this is the dust which prevents reflection of the rays of the Sun of Reality in the mirror. The natural emotions are blameworthy and are like rust which deprives the heart of the bounties of God. But sincerity, justice, humility, severance, and love for the believers of God will purify the mirror and make it radiant with reflected rays from the Sun of Truth.[1]
> Consider how a pure, well-polished mirror fully reflects the effulgence of the sun, no matter how distant the sun may be. As soon as the mirror is cleaned and purified, the sun will manifest itself. The more pure and sanctified the heart of man becomes, the nearer it draws to God, and the light of the Sun of Reality is revealed within it. This light sets hearts aglow with the fire of the love of God, opens in them the doors of knowledge and unseals the divine mysteries so that spiritual discoveries are made possible.[2]

> These energies with which the Day Star of Divine bounty . . . hath endowed the reality of man lie, however, latent within him. . . The radiance of these energies may be obscured by worldly desires even as the light of the sun can be concealed beneath the dust and dross which cover the mirror.[3]

Therefore, the dust and dross that cover the mirror of our heart – and prevent it from reflecting the divine light – originate in our lower nature. By concentrating on a life of virtues – characterized by prayer and meditation – we can gradually sanctify our heart so it can become worthy of manifesting divine light and guidance.

> O friend, the heart is the dwelling of eternal mysteries, make it not the home of fleeting fancies; waste not the treasure of thy precious life in employment with this swiftly passing world. Thou comest from the world of holiness – bind not thine heart to the earth; thou art a dweller in the court of nearness – choose not the homeland of the dust.[4]

Meditation and science

Scientific studies have shown that regular meditation can help quiet the internal chatter of the mind and contribute to achieving a tranquil state. As the mind becomes steady, our central nervous system finds balance. This, in turn, allows our physical systems to relax and our entire body to find the opportunity to steadily repair and renew itself. Hence, there seems to be a direct link between a relaxed state of mind and physical health. That is why meditation and relaxation practices are increasingly finding their way into mainstream medicine. Many physicians now regularly prescribe meditation as a beneficial practice for reducing patient stress and anxiety.

The gradual shift in attitude toward meditation within the scientific community and the medical profession goes back to the 1960s and the daring experiments in the labs of pioneers such as Dr Herbert Benson and Dr Gregg Jacobs, both of Harvard Medical School. Benson is a professor, author, cardiologist, and the founder of Harvard's Mind/Body Medical Institute. He coined the term 'Relaxation Response', which he defines as the personal ability to encourage our bodies to release chemicals and brain signals that make our muscles and organs slow down and increase blood flow to the brain. Benson also describes the scientific benefits of relaxation and explains how regular practise of the 'Relaxation Response' can be an effective means for treating a wide range of stress-related disorders.[5]

With the 'Relaxation Response', Benson essentially redefined meditation. This played a huge role in demystifying meditation and bringing the practice into the mainstream. His studies, spanning over two decades (the 1960s and 1970s), provided plenty of scientific evidence that meditation promoted better health, especially in individuals with hypertension. Benson showed that regular meditators enjoyed lower stress levels and blood sugar levels. Their resting heart rates were also lower, and their overall wellbeing also increased.

The 'Relaxation Response' essentially counteracts the physiological effects of stress and the 'fight or flight' response. When we perceive a physical or psychological threat, our sympathetic nervous system intervenes and immediately generates a number of physiological changes, such as increased metabolism, higher levels of blood pressure, heart and breathing rate, dilation of pupils, or constriction of blood vessels. All these conditions help us prepare to fight or flee from a stressful or dangerous situation:

> It is common for individuals experiencing the fight or flight response to describe uncomfortable physiological changes like muscle tension, headache, upset stomach, racing heartbeat, and shallow breathing. The fight or flight response can become harmful when elicited frequently. When high levels of stress hormones are secreted often, they can contribute to a number of stress-related medical conditions such as cardiovascular disease, GI diseases, adrenal fatigue, and more.[6]

Therefore, it is hardly surprising that findings from other studies show that regular use of the 'Relaxation Response' helps other health issues that are caused or exacerbated by chronic stress, including anxiety disorders, hypertension, fibromyalgia, gastrointestinal ailments, insomnia, hypertension, and anxiety disorders.[7]

Those interested in eliciting the 'Relaxation Response' in

themselves can choose from a wide range of methods, including prayer, different meditation or visualization techniques, yoga, progressive muscle relaxation, massage, or acupuncture. These, and other methods that help quiet the mind and generate inner peace and tranquillity, will elicit the 'Relaxation Response'. Perhaps the best time to practise the 'Relaxation Response' is early in the morning before the daily stresses of life begin to affect our mind and body. Studies by Benson and Jacobs led to a substantial body of positive evidence for meditation. Over subsequent decades, many others, including Daniel Goleman of Harvard, Jon Kabat-Zinn of the University of Massachusetts, neuroscientists Andrew Newberg of the University of Pennsylvania and Mark Waldman of Loyola Marymount, Zoran Josipovic of New York University, and Richard Davidson of the University of Wisconsin, provided a large body of evidence for physiological, psychological and spiritual benefits of meditation.

Physiological benefits of meditation

Perhaps the most frequently cited physiological benefit of meditation is the lowering of blood pressure. In fact, the National Institutes of Health (NIH) has identified meditation as the most effective means of treating mild hypertension.[8] The NIH closely examined results of 17 published studies from the medical literature, in which over 1,000 subjects with high blood pressure were treated with 5 different stress reduction techniques: simple biofeedback, relaxation-assisted biofeedback, progressive muscle relaxation, stress management training, and transcendental meditation (TM). Only one of these methods (TM) showed significant clinical and statistical reductions in blood pressure. The studies also showed that relaxation through meditation lowered blood cholesterol levels, reduced the impact of arrhythmia (irregular heart beat) and helped diabetic patients deal better with the emotional reactions that often occurred before the onset of heart attacks.

Other studies have shown meditation can actually lessen the frequency of headaches and colds, and can treat hypertension.[9]

Neuroscientists Andrew Newberg and Mark Waldman have reported cases of patients who, through meditation, overcame drug addictions and reduced the severity of psoriasis in their bodies.[10] Lorin Roche provides scientific evidence of patients who, after regular meditation, were able to reduce symptoms or accelerated the healing of stomach problems, allergies, muscle tension, arthritis, headaches, asthma, cancer, heart disease, skin problems, palpitations, and temporomandibular joint (TMJ) dysfunction.[11] Tension is a contributing factor to worsening the condition of all these diseases.

In a study of health insurance statistics, Dr David Orme-Johnson found that meditators had 87 per cent fewer episodes of hospitalization for heart disease, 55 per cent fewer for benign and malignant tumours, and 30 per cent fewer for infectious diseases. On average, they also had more than 50 per cent fewer doctor visits than did non-meditators.[12]

Meditation can also be an effective means for treating insomnia. In one study, by Dr Gregg Jacobs of Harvard Medical School, 75 per cent of long-term insomniacs who were trained in relaxation and meditation, and were taught simple lifestyle changes, were able to fall asleep faster than those taking sleeping pills.[13] Donald Miskiman, a researcher at the University of Alberta in Canada,[14] and Robert Woolfolk, at Rutgers University, replicated these results in their own respective studies with insomniac patients.[15]

Additional studies at Harvard Medical School showed that meditation can actually activate parts of the brain that control involuntary bodily functions such as digestion and blood pressure, which are functions that can generally be affected by stress. By using Functional Magnetic Resonance Imagery (fMRI), Harvard researchers monitored the subjects' brain activity during meditation and found that meditation played a significant role in treating stress-related physical conditions, such as digestive problems, heart disease and infertility.[16]

Psychological benefits of meditation

Another factor that directly affects our physical health is the psychological state of our mind. If we are constantly anxious or fearful, these emotions can raise our level of stress, which takes a toll on our bodies. However, anxiety or fear are not necessarily negative or useless feelings that should be entirely eliminated – even if we could eliminate them. We have those emotions for a reason. In fact, a part of our brain known – as the amygdala – is set aside to be responsible for emotions such as fear (see Fig. 7). When we encounter a scary or alarming situation, or when we have any reason to be afraid of someone or something that is outside of our control, the amygdala generates fear in us because it detects a situation that could potentially endanger our health or safety. Therefore, essentially, the amygdala's role is to keep us alive. It is a survival mechanism in the human body that is constantly scanning and monitoring our environment – even when we are sleeping – for things that it perceives as a threat to our life or our wellbeing. When we face threatening situations, such as an attack, the amygdala triggers other parts of the brain to generate a flow of adrenaline through our body, resulting in a fight or flight response. If we are convinced we can fight off the attack, we stay and face the threat. If not, we will flee from the scene as fast as we can to protect ourselves.

The challenge is that the amygdala does not differentiate between a physical threat and a psychological one. Physical threats, such as an oncoming car or a potential attack by a wild animal, are usually easier to detect. Hence, responses to these are typically quick: 'Uh oh – get out of the way as fast as you can!'

Psychological threats, however, are often not as clear-cut. For instance, if your employer says, 'Where have you been? I've been looking for you for an hour!', the amygdala may respond to this psychological threat the same way as a physical threat. It may force the body to release a hormone called adrenaline, which is also known as the 'fight-or-flight' hormone. The amygdala can't be calm because it feels your boss is unhappy with you, and that puts your comfort and emotional wellbeing in danger.

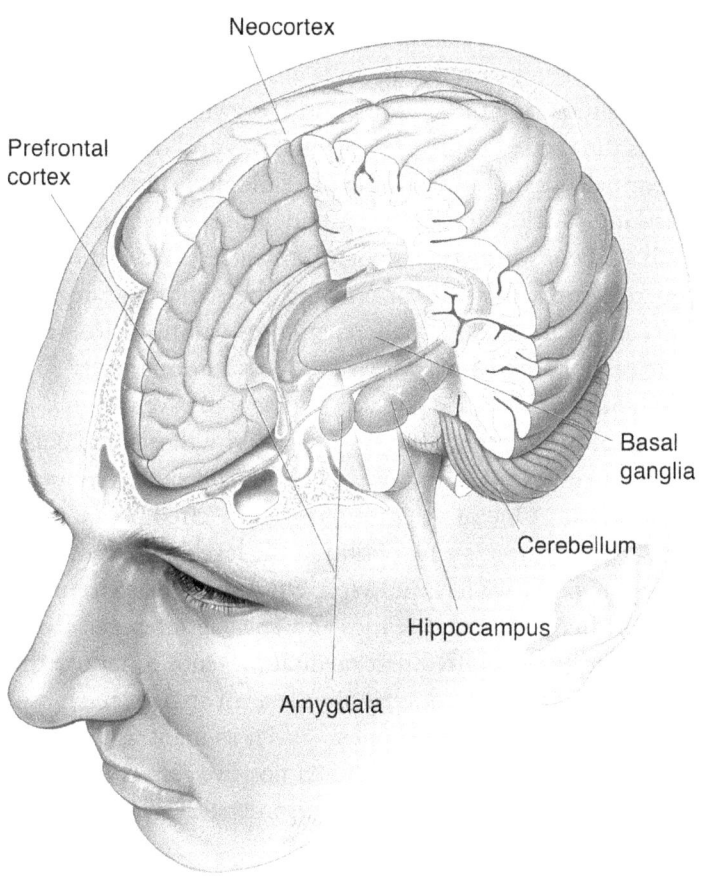

Fig. 7
Parts of the human brain that are involved in memory
(© Dr Levent Efe, CMI)

The same thing might happen if you receive a phone call from the dean's office in your daughter's school and are told that the dean wants to speak with you about your daughter in her office. That, too, could cause psychological stress, which could lead to the release of adrenaline by amygdala. Our brains like consistency and calm – at home, at work and everywhere else. Whatever interrupts those conditions – be they the physical danger of being robbed or held at gunpoint, or the psychological threat of a negative encounter with your boss, or reading unexpected bad news in an email – all constitute psychological threats. As far as the amygdala is concerned, they are all one and the same. The degree of intensity may vary, but all such experiences will ultimately result in the release of adrenaline, which produces fear or anxiety.

When our level of stress goes up, a variety of psychological and physiological problems can occur. That is why those who engage in regular meditation and prayer learn to gain better control of their emotions.[17] One of the more frequently cited psychological benefits of meditation is a reduction in the level of anxiety. When we are less anxious, we feel more relaxed. A more relaxed mindset leads to less frequent mood swings and episodes of anger. Even if such episodes do occur, frequent meditation tends to reduce their intensity. In addition to reducing one's level of anxiety, meditation practices that focus on mindfulness – such as mantra meditation and walking meditation – have shown positive results in treating hypertension, depression and eating disorders.[18]

Chemical warfare

Most of us don't realize that when we experience an emotion – such as happiness, sadness, stress, fear, or anxiety – it releases a variety of chemicals in our bodies. While some of these chemicals are good for our health, others are not so good. Hence, to borrow an expression from former Yahoo executive and current author and motivational speaker, Tim Sanders, a 'chemical warfare'[19] is taking place in our bodies every day and we don't even realize it. If we do not learn to deal with stress properly, our adrenal gland produces a steroid hormone called cortisol, which increases the level of sugar in our blood. Cortisol is not good for us because it essentially tells our immune cells to stop fighting. If we experience prolonged periods of stress, our immune cells become bathed in cortisol, and our immune system and inflammatory pathways will be suppressed. Therefore, if we are exposed to the flu or common cold virus, our body will be less able to react to the disease and is more susceptible to infection. In this area, studies by Dr Esther Sternberg, professor of medicine at the University of Arizona, are noteworthy.[20]

However, if we learn to respond to stressful situations in a more positive way, and actually engage in stress reduction or elimination practices – such as prayer and meditation – our body will start releasing serotonin, which is a neurotransmitter that is good for the body. Serotonin is known as 'the happiness hormone', but that is actually a misnomer because serotonin is a neurotransmitter, not a hormone. Neurotransmitters are brain chemicals that facilitate communication between our brain and our body. For example, the brain uses neurotransmitters to tell the heart to beat, the lungs to breathe and the stomach to digest. Neurotransmitters can also affect mood, sleep, concentration, and weight, and can cause adverse symptoms when they are out of balance.[21] Serotonin is a neurotransmitter that makes us feel happier, more confident and in control of our behaviours. That's why individuals with high levels of serotonin usually demonstrate more composure and are calmer in chaotic or stressful situations.

Another neurotransmitter that is good for our health is dopamine, which helps us focus better. If we keep forgetting where we left our keys or what a friend or family member told us just a few minutes ago, we are probably suffering from low levels of dopamine. Low levels of dopamine can also lower our drive or desire to get things done; in other words, it lowers motivation.

Positive practices like prayer and meditation release helpful neurotransmitters, including dopamine and serotonin, into our body and brain. These neurotransmitters will help us function properly. When the neurochemistry in our brain is in proper balance, we will feel a sense of joy, calm and safety, and thus eliminate symptoms of tension, sadness and anxiety.[22] Hence, meditation can have a significantly positive influence on our mental and emotional wellbeing. It is a powerful tool in treating depression, insofar as it increases the availability of positive chemicals like serotonin and tryptophan in our central nervous system – both of which play a critical role in our mood elevation. In addition, regular meditation can help us feel more confident and optimistic about life in general. People who show discipline in meditation also show fewer experiences of guilt, decreased levels of unreasonable internal expectations, improved self-esteem, and less intense reactions to grief. They also show a diminished level of separation anxiety.[23]

Spiritual benefits of meditation

Engaging in regular meditation also has many spiritual benefits. For example, those who engage in regular meditation often develop a deeper level of spiritual relaxation that goes beyond simple stress reduction and the calming of the mind. Individuals who regularly practice meditation tend to develop a greater appreciation for life in general. They begin to notice and appreciate the little things in life that others often miss entirely, take for granted or consider unimportant. They learn to 'stop and smell the roses'. They become aware of the countless blessings, big and small, that surround them every day. Consistent meditation helps them become more loving, more compassionate and more forgiving towards others – qualities that go a long way in establishing and solidifying long-lasting friendships with others. Such relationships bring joy and stability to our lives. In addition, regular meditation frequently leads practitioners to adopt a more spiritual orientation in life in general and develop a sense of detachment from the mundane. They start reflecting and contemplating on the bigger picture, which will lead them to ask the big questions in life, such as, 'What is the meaning of life?', 'Why are we here?' and 'Where are we going?' Asking these questions will, in turn, help such individuals gain deeper insight into what matters most in life. It is precisely these insights that will give such individuals the faith, patience, perseverance, and solace to face even the most complex and challenging problems in life, such as terminal disease, the loss of a loved one, or dealing with the consequences of a natural disaster or a ravaging war.

Jacobs and Benson were among the first scientists to study the positive spiritual effects of meditation. In one such study, Jacobs compared the electroencephalograms (EEGs) of a group of meditators to a group that was asked to simply listen to books on tape. Over the next few months, the brains of meditators produced far more theta waves than those of the book listeners. This meant that meditators were in a much more relaxed state of mind, because the more theta waves our brain produces the more relaxed we are (see Fig. 6):

> Jacobs's study demonstrated that meditators successfully deactivated the frontal areas of their brains that receive and process sensory information. They were also able to lower the activity in the parietal lobe – a section of the brain near the top of the head that orients us in space and time. By shutting down the parietal lobe, meditators lost their sense of boundaries and felt more 'at one' with the universe.[24]

The field of neuroscience has also provided plenty of scientific evidence for spiritual benefits of meditation. In this area, the works of Newberg and Waldman – the authors of *How God Changes Your Brain* and *Why God Won't Go Away* – are noteworthy. Their experiments provided solid evidence for the fact that regular meditation can actually lead to neurochemical changes in our brains. In some of their experiments, Newberg and Waldman observed brain functions of people of various faith traditions as they meditated, and concluded that such practices, even if practitioners were not focused on God or some other deity, increased the neural functioning of individuals' brains and improved their emotional and physical wellbeing. They also discovered that concentrated, long-term meditation and reflection on God permanently changes even the physical shape of those parts of the brain that control our moods:

> One of the most unusual findings in our brain-scan studies involves the thalamus . . . The thalamus is the Grand Central Station of sensory processing. Every sensation, mood and thought passes through it as the information is relayed to other parts of the brain . . . The Thalamus plays a crucial role in identifying what is and isn't real, and it gives a sense of emotional meaning to the thoughts that emerge in the frontal lobe . . . the more you meditate on a specific object, be it God, or peace, the more active your thalamus becomes . . . if you exercise an idea over and over, your brain will begin to respond as though the idea was a real object in the world . . . The more you focus on God, the more God will be sensed as real . . . For advanced meditators . . . God, tranquillity, and unity become an integral part of their lives, no longer a thought but a palpable experience.[25]

Newberg and Waldman also learned that meditation helped practitioners become more peaceful and compassionate towards others, while anger had negative consequences on brain activity.[26]

For the first time ever, neuroscientists have now also helped us document how mere thoughts can actually change the physical structure of the brain:

> Just thinking about playing a piano piece, over and over, can expand the region of motor cortex that controls those fingers; just thinking about depressive thoughts in new ways can dial down activity in one part of the brain that underlies depression and increase it in another, leading to clinical improvement.[27]

Professor Richard Davidson of the University of Wisconsin, Madison, and his colleagues, have found that practising metta meditation can lead to long-lasting changes to certain parts of the brain and make us more empathetic.[28]

In one study, Davidson and Lutz's research found that empathetic activity was significantly greater in monks with thousands of hours of meditation than the novices, even when those monks were not meditating. This was because the great number of hours of meditation had created enduring change in the region of the monks' brains that helped them show empathy and compassion towards others at all times. This finding essentially demonstrates that we can train our brains to become more compassionate towards others by following a systematic and rigorous program of meditation.[29]

Yet, we must remember that, in most cases, it takes time to begin to observe the physical, psychological or spiritual benefits of meditation. Therefore, when you commit to engage in regular meditation, watch for the slightest progress you make and give yourself credit every step of the way. Pay special attention to any positive changes in the way you think, feel or act that could have come from persistent meditation. If you see progress, celebrate by rewarding yourself, regardless of how small the progress is.

Today, the positive effects of meditation on human health are well established. Meditation is now widely recognized as one of the best ways to relax the mind; help gain control over thoughts, feelings and behaviour; improve general health; and even create lasting change in the structure and functionality of the brain.

Suggested meditation techniques

There are a wide variety of meditation techniques you can choose from. Among the more well-known approaches are:

- Single object meditation
- Breath awareness meditation
- Insight meditation
- Mindfulness of the present moment
- Mantra meditation
- Mantra writing
- Contemplation on the Word of God

- Metta meditation
- Mindfulness of God.

Effective meditation requires daily practice for 20 to 40 minutes, preferably at the same time every day. For a full discussion of the above techniques, you can refer to the book, *The Divine Art of Meditation.*[30]

Single object meditation

We can do this meditation with the use of a single object, such as a flower, a leaf, a candle, or a picture. Sitting in quiet, private space, we begin by focusing on the object of meditation with our eyes open. We need to see the object as if we have never seen it before. In other words, we need to look at it with curiosity as we explore its various parts with deep interest. During meditation, when our minds begin to wander, we can gently bring it back to the object of our meditation. The key in this and other forms of meditations is to be kind and gentle to ourselves and stay away from criticizing and judging our ability to meditate.

The practice of picture meditation and visualization

Today we know that visualization, like meditation, can also affect the brain in a positive way. In a study conducted at Yale University described by by Newberg and Waldman, scientists discovered that visualization can stimulate almost all the same areas of our brain that meditation techniques do.

The combined practice of picture meditation and visualization brings single-object meditation and visualization together, and creates a new technique for quieting the chatter of the mind and attaining inner peace and tranquillity.

To do this simple yet effective meditation/visualization practice, choose at least five pictures of beautiful places. You can use more pictures depending on the amount of time you are planning to spend on this activity. If you enjoy nature, you may want to choose pictures or paintings of beautiful scenery. That can include lakeside lodges, cozy cottages in beautiful flower gardens, log cabins in forests, and so on. This practice can be done by using paintings or actual photos you have found on the web. If you have a large number of such images, you may even want to put them in a PowerPoint or other digital slide deck to access on your electronic device at the time of your meditation.

To do the picture meditation/visualization technique, start by sitting quietly in your meditation place. Take a few deep breaths, then focus on the first picture. Treat it as if you have never seen it before. Pay close attention to everything you see in the picture. Do this with a fresh sense of curiosity and interest every time you do this meditation. When your mind begins to wander, gently bring it back to the picture. Having done the first part of your practice (picture meditation) for some time, now do the second part: visualization. To do this, imagine yourself in that picture doing all the things you would like to do, and try to do them with a smile on your face; this will help release endorphins, thus making you feel even happier and more peaceful. Feel free to bring loved ones into the picture with you. Add new images to your repertoire as you come across them.

Breath awareness and insight meditations

These two techniques, which supposedly go back to the time of the Buddha, continue to be among primary approaches to meditation for many Buddhist and non-Buddhist meditators. Through concentration on the *in* and *out* flow of breath, the breath awareness meditation calms the meditator's mind, whereas in insight meditation, the focus is on concentration on whatever arises during the meditation session.

Larry Rosenberg, the author of *Breath by Breath*, has an effective technique for dealing with distractions. He encourages the meditator to move from a 'doggy mind' to a 'lion mind':

> One time when I was visiting a friend, he kept playing with his dog, throwing a plastic bone for the dog to go fetch. It

not only wasn't a real bone, it wasn't even a convincing fake; pieces of meat were painted on the plastic. Yet no matter how many times he threw the bone, the dog ran after it, with great excitement. He kept chasing this plastic bone, which had no nourishment whatsoever, as if it could somehow satisfy him. Suddenly I realized: that's my mind, chasing after thoughts. The mind doesn't think it's chasing a plastic bone with pieces of meat painted on it, of course. It thinks it's pursuing something that will have a vital effect on its life. But if we look more closely at the objects that the mind chases, we notice a similar lack of nourishment. In contrast to that, think of a lion. Can you imagine how a lion – sitting in that majestic way they have – would react if you threw him a bone (especially a plastic one)? He wouldn't even notice. He'd just stare at you. Lions stay focused on the source. That's the attitude we need to have, sitting with that deep calm, that steadiness of purpose, not chasing after every bone that flies our way. We need to develop lion mind . . . our practice is to try to go from doggy mind to something more like lion mind, in which there is a deep steadiness.[31]

Mindfulness of the present moment

> Do not go after the past,
> Nor lose yourself in the future.
> For the past no longer exists,
> And the future is not yet here.
> By looking deeply at things just as they are,
> In this moment, here and now,
> The seeker lives calmly and freely.[32]

Our minds have a tendency to continuously put their attentions on the dead yesterdays or on the unborn tomorrows. Most of our thoughts seem to be about the regrets of the past or the worries of the future. In practising mindfulness, we try to overcome this tendency by focusing on the task at hand – whether it is eating, taking a shower, doing house chores, driving, working at the office, or simply talking to another person. When our minds wander to the regrets of the past, or the fears and worries of the future, we should not get angry with ourselves. We should just let such thoughts move on like clouds or birds in the sky of our minds, and gently bring the mind back to the present moment. Using a simple expression such as, 'Oh well', in such situations can be a good wakeup call in bringing our minds back to the task at hand.

Mindfulness is a great ally in disciplining the mind to stay in the present moment where our real life occurs, and where we can find true peace and tranquillity. In practising mindfulness, we give our complete attention to the task at hand with a sense of deep curiosity. For instance, in washing our hands and face, we try to feel the warm water on our hands and the soft touch of the towel on our face, and really savour the joy of the experience. In our daily practice of mindfulness, we come to view every task as a precious experience. This is due to the fact that all such experiences will provide us with opportunities to train our minds, and will lead us to a more peaceful life where we are in control of our thoughts and not a slave to them.

Our daily lives can provide us with many opportunities to practise mindfulness. Here are three examples:

Mindful eating

You can begin mindful eating by smiling to yourself and becoming aware of 'seeing' the food you are about to eat. Pay close attention to its shape, colour and scent. Note the anticipation in your mind of the food you are about to eat. The next step is to reach for the food mindfully. Raise your arm and lift the food into your mouth. As you put the food into your mouth, be mindful of the touch of the food on your tongue and how it tastes in your mouth as you are chewing it. Then, be mindful of the act of swallowing.

Eat slowly and mindfully, taking the time to enjoy every bite. Chew at least twenty times before you swallow. During mindful eating meditation, when other thoughts come to your mind, gently bring your mind back to the food. Throughout your practice, continue to be mindful of seeing, smelling, reaching, touching, tasting, chewing, swallowing, and enjoying.

Mindful shower

When you shower, *know* that you are taking a shower. Pay attention to the scent of the soap and every part of your body as you wash it. Be mindful of the warm water as it cascades over your skin. Now close your eyes and visualize yourself standing under a gentle waterfall on a beautiful tropical island. You are surrounded by fragrant flowering trees. The scent of the soap can be helpful in this visualization. Savour this experience with a smile

The litmus test for mindful bathing is this: by the time your bath is over, your mind should feel as peaceful and relaxed as your body.[33]

Mindfulness Jar practice

The practice of mindfulness provides us with a great opportunity to quiet the chatter of the mind, making it more focused, creative and peaceful. It also helps eliminate the attitude of rushing and being future-oriented. Furthermore, it enhances our appreciation of each moment, protects us from automatic responses and saves us vital energy. However, cultivating a mindful attitude towards life needs much time and effort.

One approach to cultivating such an attitude is through the practice of the Mindfulness Jar. To do this practice, you need to have an empty jar (which you can label the 'Mindfulness Jar') and some kind of container, perhaps a small bowl, which will hold loose change and be placed next to your Mindfulness Jar (see Fig. 8). Every time you are successful in your practice of mindfulness, you can reward yourself by taking a coin from the container and putting it in your Mindfulness Jar – for instance, whenever you eat your food mindfully, take a shower mindfully, do your house chores mindfully, and so on. As an alternative to loose change, you

Fig. 8
Mindfulness jars

can use beads or something similar and assign a monetary value – say, five or ten cents – to each bead. When your jar is filled, you can donate the money to the charity of your choice.

This practice will not only grant you a more peaceful, focused, and creative mind, but will also allow others to benefit from your generosity, making this a win-win situation.

To get ideas for your daily mindfulness practice, you can refer to *How to Train a Wild Elephant* by Jan Chozen Bays. In this book, the author provides her readers with 53 ways they can practise mindfulness in their daily lives.

Grateful awareness

Mindfulness is awareness. To practise grateful awareness, we bring two essential happiness-enhancing techniques of gratitude and awareness (mindfulness) together. To do so, we try to become aware of the task at hand throughout the day with a grateful heart and mind. This will not only help us stay in the present moment and live an awakened life, but will also help us see all the gifts for which we can be grateful at any given moment. For instance, when we bring grateful awareness into doing the dishes, we are not only absorbed in the task at hand, but we are also grateful for the ability to do the dishes, for the warm water, for the dishes to wash, and so forth. When we practise grateful awareness in driving our car, we are not only absorbed in the task of driving, we are also grateful for our car and the ability to drive it and to pay for the gas and for the places that we have to go to. With practise, little by little, both gratitude and awareness become a new way of life for us and help us live a happier and more peaceful life.

Mantra meditation (Japa meditation)

A mantra can be a sound like *OM* in Hinduism, a word like *Adonia* (Lord) in Judaism, or a group of words such as, '*Lord Jesus Christ, have mercy upon me*' in Christianity, which is believed to be capable of bringing about spiritual transformation. Mantra meditation is a popular method in many religious traditions, such as Tibetan Buddhism, Hinduism, Sufism (Islamic mysticism), and Orthodox Christianity. More recently, this approach has also been adopted by practitioners of Christian centring prayer, as well as those of transcendental meditation.

Since invoking the name of God can be equated to invoking His presence, mantra meditation can be viewed as an easy yet powerful approach for practising God's presence in our lives.

In practising mantra meditation, we need to be sure to choose a mantra that is meaningful to us. For example, if we are of the Hindu tradition, we may choose to meditate on the name of Rama or Krishna, who are among the Hindu deities. If we are of the Christian Faith, we may want to repeat the name of Christ, and so forth.

To practise the mantra meditation, we need to sit in our meditation space with our backs straight and our eyes closed. It would be helpful to use prayer beads to help us concentrate on our mantra. Then we can begin our practice by repeating the mantra of our choice out loud for a while, then follow with whispering, and then continue by reciting it in our mind. In the course of our manta meditation session, we can alternate (saying out loud, whispering, and reciting mentally) mainly when we encounter drowsiness. The recitation needs to be done gently, slowly and attentively. Additionally, a mantra can be repeated as a tool to quiet the mind in the course of the day. For instance, when we go for a walk, while we are stuck in traffic, when we are waiting for our turn at the doctor's office, are at the grocery store, or in traffic. It can be the first words we say in the morning as we open our eyes and the last when we close our eyes and fall sleep.

In addition to reciting the mantra, we could also write it in a notebook daily as an approach to meditation. This practice is called mantra writing or *Likhita japa*.[34]

Contemplation or reflection on the Word of God

> Do thou meditate on that which We have revealed unto thee, that thou mayest discover the purpose of God, thy Lord, and the Lord of all worlds. In these words the mysteries of Divine Wisdom have been treasured.[35]

Another form of meditation is contemplation and reflection on the deeper meanings enshrined in the sacred literature of the world's religions. Bahá'u'lláh supported this type of meditation and taught that it could help us discover the purpose of life.

However, it requires effort and a deep desire. The analogy he gives below reminds one of a treasure hunter who has to swim into the depths of the ocean before he can find treasure. It is symbolic of the amount of time and effort it will take for seekers of spiritual truths to discover the gems hidden in the sacred texts:

> Immerse yourselves in the ocean of My words, that ye may unravel its secrets, and discover all the pearls of wisdom that lie hid in its depths.[36]

For instance, if we contemplate on some of the passages in the Bahá'í writings about the station of humanity, we will discover that we are considered as God's noblest creation in potential; that we have been put on earth to know, love and praise our Creator; and that we are here to help carry forward an ever-advancing civilization. We are also here to grow our souls, since the seeds of divine virtues have been sown in the 'soil' of our souls. We can water those seeds daily by studying and contemplating the Word of God. Over time, this process leads to our spiritual transformation.

Many of us suffer from low self-esteem and lack of spiritual purpose in life, which can cause a great deal of psychological pain. However, when we engage in regular meditation and contemplation on the Sacred Word, we are gradually awakened to our true nature and nobility as God's creatures. This kind of enlightenment can be transformative.

The Bible also teaches us that contemplation on the Sacred Word and following the guidance offered by it, is a sure way to prosperity and success:

> This book of the law shall not depart out of your mouth, but you shall meditate on it day and night, that you may be careful to do according to all that is written in it; for then you shall make your way prosperous, and then you shall have good success. (Josh. 1:8)

Furthermore, contemplation on the Word of God can lead to changes in our character, wisdom, peace of mind, and spiritual elation.

When contemplating on the Word, we seek insights. This takes time and consistent effort. Therefore, developing the habit of reading at least a short passage in the morning will put us in the proper state of mind before leaving home and interacting with others at work or elsewhere, and reading another passage in the evening will conclude our day with contemplation on yet another spiritual theme. We are seeking insight, not cold hard facts. We are hoping for spiritual transformation rather than the mere acquisition of mundane information. Therefore, developing the habit of daily reading and contemplation on the Word is essential to seeking spiritual transformation and developing a closer relationship with our Creator.

Daily accountability

One of the most effective approaches to sparking a spiritual transformation – and, consequently, living a more peaceful, joyful and fulfilling life – is the practice of daily accountability. This practice can be done at the end of the day by reflecting on how our day went. The intention is to regularly assess our slow and gradual process towards spiritual transformation.

Since one of the primary goals of our existence is to acquire and manifest divine virtues, this practice can help us evaluate ourselves along this path. For instance, we can examine the interactions we had with others over the course of the day at work, at home and elsewhere, to decide if the decisions we made helped or hindered our spiritual progress. On any given day, we could look back and ask ourselves questions, such as, 'Today, based on my deeds, words or thoughts, did I become more or less patient, compassionate, polite, honest, fair-minded, truthful, loving or forgiving?'

The goal should be to learn from our mistakes, not to blame or beat ourselves up. We should simply want to grow in wisdom, and appreciate our efforts towards developing better habits and overcoming weaknesses:

Life's greatest achievement is the continual remaking of yourself, so that at last you know how to live.[37]

Bahá'u'lláh makes it clear that living a spiritual life is a requirement for progress in the afterlife and that we will be asked to give an account of our earthly deeds in the hereafter:

> O SON OF BEING! Bring thyself to account each day ere thou art summoned to a reckoning; for death, unheralded, shall come upon thee and thou shalt be called to give account for thy deeds.[38]

Mindfulness Matters

Mindfulness is a way of befriending ourselves
and our experience.
–Jon Kabat-Zinn

A story by Adam Avin

My great-grandfather inspired me to make a positive difference in the world. He was a very mindful person, and he taught me about positive thinking. He used to say things like 'Think well to be well,' and 'Every day, we have a new choice to make, so choose to be happy.'

When Grandpa Jack passed away, I wanted to honor him by teaching his messages of positivity, kindness, and happiness to other kids. I believe that the key to ending violence is teaching kids to be mindful when they're young. That's why I started the Wuf Shanti Children's Wellness Foundation, to teach kids to live a healthy and happy life, using his wisdom.

Wuf Shanti is a dog character that teaches mindfulness, social and emotional learning, kindness, and positivity to kids from three to ten years old. Wuf Shanti has produced seven books; a free mobile app with signature games; and 100 videos, which have run on local PBS stations, the Children's TV Network (the station in children's hospital across the nation), Adventure to Learning (health and fitness vid programming in 25,000 schools) and Kidoodle.TV (safe streaming network for kids).

In my Wuf Shanti dog costume, I traveled to schools and children hospitals to visit the kids and share our message with them. When I would walk into the hospitals and meet the kids, especially the ones who had cancer – many of them bald from treatment or hooked to tubes – they'd forget all that for a few minutes. They would smile and run up to Wuf to hug him, dance, or give a high-five.

Parents would cry with joy at seeing their kids smiling and happy. It had an impact on me. I felt sad seeing them like this, but happy about how my being there was helping their lives, even for a few minutes, made me realize how good my life is and how so many people need help to be happier.

One time, my little sister was crying, and I was able to share Grandpa Jack's message. I told her that she had a choice to make. She could choose to be upset about not getting what she wanted, or she could choose to be happy for what she did have. About five minutes later, I overheard her calming herself down by repeating 'think well, be well,' while tapping her fingers one at a time against her thumb, one of the exercises Wuf Shanti teaches. You don't realize how much of an impact you're making until you witness a five-year-old control her own temper tantrum and bring positivity back into her life.

I've used my grandpa's teaching often. For example, when I became a teenager, I got self-conscious when some of my friends teased me about being a dog character. So, I did what Grandpa taught me to do: I laughed. They stop teasing you if they see it doesn't bother you.

And I took action by expanding our curriculum for older kids, ages eleven to seventeen (minus the dog character). My mission is to provide kids and teens with coping tools so they grow up less depressed and anxious. I want them to become happy, peace-loving adults who solve their problems in productive ways. I consider these techniques to be life skills. My goal is to get these mindful social-and-emotional-learning programs into schools across the country as part of their core curriculums.

We live near Parkland, Florida and the tragic shooting that happened at Marjory Stoneman Douglas High School. That made me want to do even more, so I founded the Kids' Association for Mindfulness in Education for teens to collaborate and figure out ways to work together to make the world a better place. I also founded the international online Mindful Kids Peace Summit for middle schools and high schools. More than fifty subject-matter experts spoke about diversity, kindness, anti-bullying, communication, mindfulness, positivity, learning to interact with others, compassion, collaboration, positive psychology, and more.

Through working on all of this, I've learned that even when you feel like giving up (like when you see yet another shooting on the news), you have to work even harder. I've also learned that collaboration is key. We can't change the world alone. Even though I'm a mindful kid, I get sad or upset sometimes. Sometimes, I find it hard to put down my phone and look up, but I force myself to do it. I now tell people that if they can just practice mindfulness for five minutes every day it can help them.

Science has proven that mindfulness helps us relax, stay focused do better in school and sports, stay healthy, heal faster, get along better with others, and live a happier life. There will always be stress in life that we'll have to deal with, so we need to stop thinking negatively and start focusing on the positive. We need to connect with each other and smile. 'Think well to be well,' as my grandpa would say. It can change our lives and change the world. It's a lesson that I take to heart every day.'[39]

8

MARRIAGE AND FAMILY LIFE

> If love and agreement are manifest in a single family, that family will advance, become illumined and spiritual.[1]

Our family unit can be a source of joy and love, or a cause of unhappiness and great misery. More than any other single factor, unhappy people consider love – or its lack thereof – to be the main cause of their unhappiness. In his book, *Six Attitudes for Winners*, author Norman Vincent Peale offers his readers eight steps to a more peaceful family life.

1. Let it begin with you. Determine that you will begin to create within yourself the upbeat spirit that can rejuvenate family life.
2. Ask yourself this question: 'Am I personally contributing to family happiness or unhappiness?' Be sure you answer this question with absolute honesty.
3. Correct within yourself any mistrust or hostility, and practise treating everyone in the family not only with love, but with respect for their opinions. Give them genuine esteem.
4. Consider yourself a love 'cell' and act lovingly. Do not tell the family you have decided to be this new way. Just be it. They will pick up on it. The new spirit injected by you will have effect.
5. Encourage every other family member, young and old, to hold each other in esteem as persons. Everyone should accept each other and let everyone be himself or herself. Identity of personality must always be respected. Love within the family

will create a climate of goodwill and – what is equally important – real understanding.
6. Be realistic. Do not expect that everyone is going to change at once, or that change will necessarily come easily. There may be the resistance of long-held resentments, and even prejudice, that will be reduced only by a gradual process. The principal factor is that someone must start the change and let it pick up momentum from there.
7. Develop a profound faith and reliance upon God for guidance, within the home and in all the family connections. When the Bible says, 'Except the Lord build the house, they labour in vain that build it' (Ps. 127:1), it is a reminder of a time-tested truth that the family with religious faith tends to overcome problems and meet situations, while families without it often fail.
8. Begin a programme of definite, earnest prayer for each family member. One person doing this regular type of praying, though they may not mention it to the others, will, in time, unconsciously motivate others to a new, spiritually-oriented attitude. When prayer becomes a group activity in the family, the members will grow together in a deeper fellowship. It is quite true that the family that prays together stays together.[2]

The ideal home is one in which family members find love, joy, peace of mind, and comfort. However, it takes concerted effort by every member of the family to create such an environment. The first step in establishing a loving, peaceful atmosphere at home can be to develop a simple daily habit: make sure the first words you say to other members each morning are something positive and pleasant, and preferably said with a smile. It doesn't have to be anything elaborate or premeditated. It could be something as simple as, 'Good morning, honey.' This seemingly simple practice has the potential to set the mental and emotional tone for the rest of the day, at home and outside.

Communication among family members needs to be mature and rational, not juvenile and emotional. The fundamental principle underlying healthy communication is to be loving. When we are loving to each other, the accompanying feelings and attitudes – such as being sympathetic, unselfish, understanding, or cooperative – come to us much more easily.

Mealtimes are particularly important occasions for families. If spent properly, they can strengthen the bonds of love and fellowship. If not, they can lead to constant bickering or gripe sessions that may eventually undermine the very fabric of the family. Therefore, it is essential that we look at mealtimes as opportunities for coming together in love, unity and gratitude. We need to exert our very best effort to avoid all kinds of arguments, nagging, criticizing, and negative discussions, which can affect our digestion, among other things!

Most of us have heard the phrase, 'The family that prays together stays together.' In other words, for a family to thrive and experience true joy and tranquillity, it is essential that it comes together in prayer and contemplation. The value of prayer and virtues can be taught to children from an early age.

While it is true that, throughout history, many atrocities have been committed by humans in the name of God and religion, we should not forget that religion has also been integral to the lives and services of some of the greatest figures in our history, including Mahatma Gandhi, Mother Teresa, Martin Luther King, and Albert Schweitzer.

Therefore, even if we are not particularly religious or spiritual, we can perhaps keep an open mind about the value of prayer and cultivating virtues in our children. Virtues should be taught to children when they are young, so that they grow up to be spiritual beings whose main concern in life is to grow their own souls and dedicate their lives to the service of their fellow humans – the ultimate path to true and lasting peace and joy in life.

> The family, being a human unit must be educated according to the rules of sanctity. All the virtues must be taught the family. The integrity of the family bond must be constantly considered, and the rights of the individual members must not

be transgressed. The rights of the son, the father, the mother – none of them must be transgressed, none of them must be arbitrary. Just as the son has certain obligations to his father, the father, likewise, has certain obligations to his son. The mother, the sister and other members of the household have certain prerogatives. All these rights and prerogatives must be conserved, yet the unity of the family must be sustained. The injury of one shall be considered the injury of all; the comfort of each, the comfort of all; the honor of one, the honor of all.[3]

Marriage

> O Ye two believers in God! The Lord, peerless is He, hath made woman and man to abide with each other in the closest companionship, and to be even as a single soul. They are two helpmates, two intimate friends, who should be concerned about the welfare of each other.[4]

A great deal of one's happiness in life can depend on the quality of one's marriage. Picking the right partner can bring us a great deal of joy, peace and comfort. On the other hand, if we make the wrong choice, or are unwilling to make the necessary investment in making our marriage work, that union can literally ruin our lives. The quality of our marriage will go a long way in determining the quality of our lives and the degree of happiness we experience. We should remember that building a strong marriage is much like growing a beautiful garden. It doesn't happen overnight; it takes a great deal of time, effort, love, patience, and tender care. It also takes sweat and hard work. However, in the end, the harvest will also be very rich and rewarding for the people who are willing to make the necessary investments.

> Good marriages don't just happen, they have to be made to happen . . . it takes more brain and determination than some people are willing to invest . . . But when you do, the dividends are enormous.[5]

Again, a successful marriage can bring us a lifetime of joy, companionship and prosperity. By the same token, a poor marriage can change our lives into a living hell. Successful couples typically build their relationships on three types of mutual attraction: physical, spiritual and intellectual. As a first step, before matrimony, a couple should spend a great deal of quality time together to get to know each other's personality, as well as their strengths and weaknesses.

> Marriage is a good thing. Like any good thing, it exacts a price. To receive the reward of marriage, both wife and husband should pay their share of the costs. For marriage to deliver its happiness, we need to look beyond the obvious. Marriage is not simply a contract between two people to share a roof. More important are the spiritual considerations that make marriage what it should be. Bahá'í Scriptures call marriage 'a fortress for well-being and salvation' ordained by God. In this intimate context of dealing with another daily, we are challenged to acquire and practise virtues. Marriage is also the best arrangement for conceiving new human beings, training and educating them.[6]

Although physical attraction between the couple is important, intellectual and spiritual attractions are also critical. If the couple finds each other intellectually engaging, it makes holding conversations and discussions easier and richer for both sides. This goes a long way in enhancing the quality of the relationship and the hours of companionship they spend together. Yet, it is the spiritual dimension that can keep a marriage particularly strong and helps it grow over time.

> In every marriage that begins with the dizzying highs of romance, it is the deeper, quieter ways of love that ultimately sustain it. The Harvard Psychiatrist, George Vaillant, who has followed the lives of Harvard graduates for half a century, gives the example of a judge who met his wife in high school. At

age sixty-five, he reported that his love was 'much deeper than at the beginning'. At age seventy-seven, he said, 'As life gets shorter, I love Cecily even more.'[7]

Invest five hours a week and reap the rewards

One of the leading figures in the field of marriage is Dr John Gottman. He is a professor emeritus of psychology at the University of Washington, and the co-founder and co-director of the Seattle Marital and Family Institute. Gottman is believed to have revolutionized the study of marriage by using scientific methods to observe the habits of a large number of married couples in detail over many years. His now classic book, *The Seven Principles for Making Marriage Work*, offers many practical techniques to help couples establish harmonious, long-lasting relationships.

In the last chapter of the book, Gottman offers his readers what he refers to as a 'concentrated refresher course in the Seven Principles' or 'the Magic Five Hours'. He suggests to his readers to spend five hours weekly in the following manner to make their marriage more loving and successful.

1. Partings
Make sure that before you say goodbye in the morning, you've learned about one thing that is happening in your spouse's life that day – from lunch with the boss, to a doctor's appointment, to a scheduled phone call with an old friend.

Time: 2 minutes a day x 5 working days
Total: 10 minutes

2. Reunions
Be sure to engage in a stress-reducing conversation at the end of each workday.

Time: 20 minutes a day x 5 days
Total: 1 hour and 40 minutes

3. Admiration and appreciation
Find some way every day to communicate genuine affection and appreciation to your spouse.

Time: 5 minutes a day x 7 days
Total: 35 minutes

4. Affection
Kiss, hold and touch each other during the time you're together. Make sure to kiss each other before going to sleep. Think of that kiss as a way to let go of any minor irritations that have built up over the day. In other words, lace your kiss with forgiveness and tenderness for your partner.

Time: 5 minutes a day x 7 days
Total: 35 minutes

5. Weekly date
This can be a relaxing, low-pressure way to stay connected.

Time: 2 hours once a week
Total: 2 hours

Grand Total: Five hours![8]

Gottman believes it is important to establish routines or rituals if one wants to have a happy marriage. As an example, he gives this simple after-dinner routine practised by sociologist William Doherty:

> [Bill] and his wife, Leah, created the tradition of after-dinner coffee in which their children played or did homework while he and his wife had coffee and talked. They all cleaned up after dinner, then Bill made coffee and brought it out to Leah in the living room. It was a time of peace and connection.[9]

Own up to your mistakes

The protection of one's ego can be one of the most destructive impulses in any relationship, and particularly in marriage. No human being is perfect, so the sooner we accept this fact the sooner we can start building a strong relationship with our partner. That includes the practice of admitting mistakes when we make them. Most parents are not easily persuaded to do this, especially in front of children. Gottman explains why owning up to our mistakes is critical, particularly in front of children:

> One of the most meaningful gifts a parent can give a child is to admit his or her own mistake, to say, 'I was wrong here' or 'I'm sorry'. This is so powerful because it also gives the child permission to make a mistake, to admit having messed up and still be okay. It builds in the forgiveness of self. In the same way, saying 'I'm sorry' and meaning it to your spouse is a very significant event. The more you can imbue your relationship with the spirit of thanksgiving and the graceful presence of praise, the more meaningful and fulfilling your lives together will be.[10]

Take delight in your spouse's success and good fortune

> Love is the condition in which the happiness of another person is essential to your own.[11]

Responding to our spouse's good fortune with enthusiasm and happiness can play a critical role in strengthening the bond of marriage. When we appreciate and express genuine joy in our spouse's good news, they can not only see that we are sincerely happy for their achievement, but that we also truly respect their dreams and values – and those outward expressions of joy and respect will go a long way in strengthening bonds of love and affection.

> If your partner is excited to tell you something, pay close attention, ask lots of questions, and relive the experience with

him. If you're happy for him, express it, and, if appropriate, insist on celebrating and tell others about it.[12]

Give compliments and express genuine appreciation to your spouse

Appreciation is among the main elements of a successful marriage. Sometimes we forget the importance of giving compliments to our spouse when they do something well, or showing them appreciation for who they are or what they do.

In her book, *The Adventure of Being a Wife*, Ruth Peale, makes a few suggestions:

> Appreciation . . . can be a casual compliment: 'My, that's a pretty dress . . . or a good-looking tie!', 'Darling, I don't know what I'd do without you!' It can be a smile or simple, 'Well-done!' . . . It helps when someone asks, 'How did your day go? What happened at the office?'[13]

She goes on to present the following simple example from what the wife of a friend does when the husband goes on a trip:

> Whenever he goes on a trip, his wife writes him a little note and hides it in his suitcase or in one of his pockets, just a line or two, telling him that she loves him, that she will miss him, that she thinks he's wonderful, that she knows the trip will be a success.[14]

Showing genuine appreciation can start with a simple *thank you*, but it shouldn't end there. Displaying genuine appreciation takes more work. We should provide specific details about what in our spouse's deeds, words or achievements led us to express our appreciation. Providing those details will show the spouse that we were paying deep attention, and that is a telling sign of genuine care, love and respect.

On the other hand, if we take our spouse for granted and focus only on the negative or on things we believe should be improved in our spouse, the marital bond will gradually weaken:

> When someone becomes part of the furniture of our life, we forget to notice what they do and it doesn't occur to us to give them compliments. In fact, we may only comment on the negative, the things we see that we think need to be changed. Without our intending it, this can gradually impart a negative feeling tone to the entire relationship. The practice of actively noticing what a person does well and giving genuine compliments can add new warmth, intimacy, and responsiveness to a relationship.[15]

Overcome anger

Like any type of human relationship, marital relationships also go through ups and downs. No two humans are exactly alike. Therefore, disagreements and even the occasional argument may arise between the couple. The key is to ensure that the disagreements remain civil and manageable, and do not spiral into anger or resentment. When a disagreement arises, do your best to deal with it calmly and rationally. If the situation worsens and the disagreement turns into a heated discussion, tell your spouse that you need to have some quiet time, leave the room and go to a private place in your home to calm yourself down. If you value a particular type of meditation, such as breathing or the practice of the presence of God, then use that technique. If you pray, you can draw strength and patience by repeating a simple prayer, such as this one from the Báb:

> Is there any Remover of difficulties save God? Say: Praised be God! He is God! All are His servants, and all abide by His bidding![16]

When you are calm and collected, and you feel your emotions are once again under control, go back to your spouse and try to resolve the issue peacefully.

Keep a marriage journal

> No one can go back and change how it started, but a new future for any marriage can begin the moment one person begins to invest in it.[17]

We would all love to go back in time and change at least a few things in our past. Perhaps we did or said something to our significant other and have regretted it ever since. But the fact is that, regardless of how badly we want to undo the damage, we cannot touch the past – indeed, that's precisely why it is called the 'past'. The best we can do is to learn from our mistakes and use them as opportunities for growth. However, we need to ensure that learning takes place.

One of the best ways to make sure that we learn from our marital experiences is to start a marriage journal in which we record any positive experiences, as well as unpleasant incidents, that may happen in our daily lives, and reflect upon how both the positive and unpleasant experiences made us feel. Recording positive experiences and the joy and satisfaction they bring will reinforce those behaviours and increase the chance of their reoccurrence. Taking note of negative experiences and how bad they made us feel can act as catalysts for preventing them from happening in the future.

To keep a marriage journal, buy a notebook and, on the first page, write a positive and inspiring prayer or passage on the power of love that can keep a marriage together, such as this one:

> In the world of existence there is indeed no greater power than the power of love.[18]

Also, don't just limit yourself to negative experiences in the marriage journal; record the positive ones, too! Recall the beautiful memories you have made with your spouse. Travel back in time to when you fell in love – the great times you spent together dating, eating, watching a sunset, or seeing a great movie together. Think of the day of your proposal, the engagement period, the night of the wedding, the honeymoon, the birth of your first child, and so on. Relive those joyous moments and gain strength and patience from them to deal with the problem at hand.

Think especially of the times when your spouse expressed genuine love for you, in words or deeds, and write them down in as much detail as you can remember. Next, list all of their good qualities and make a note of the kind and thoughtful things they have done for other people. Keep writing in the journal when new good things happen in your relationship. Then, go back to the journal periodically and read over some of the content. When negative feelings arise between the two of you, or when you go through tough times together, return to the journal and draw joy and strength from it. The marriage journal can be a great tool for rekindling love and romance in your life, and can also be a resource for drawing strength for overcoming marital tests in life.

Have fun together

A key to maintaining happiness in a marriage is to ensure you and your spouse have fun together. That could be as simple as having family game-nights, watching funny movies together, sharing jokes, going on a picnic or out on a 'date' with your spouse, or just eating out together. If you both love nature, depending on where you live, you may be able to take a day trip to a small town, spend time together on a scenic drive, go bird watching or visit a vineyard. At home, you can do gardening or landscaping together. When you need to rest, do it together while listening to relaxing music or reminiscing by the fireplace on cold winter nights. Thanks to YouTube, you can now even subscribe to channels that provide all sorts of content, including meditative and relaxing videos. As an example, for several years now our family has been subscribed to Tatiana Blue's YouTube channel, which features a lot of relaxing music, and we get notified every time a new video is added to the channel. The key to cementing the marital bond is to spend quality time together and truly enjoy each other's company, even if that time is spent doing the most mundane tasks such as laundry, cooking or grocery shopping.

Demonstrate mutual love and respect

> Happy marriages begin when we marry the ones we love, and they blossom when we love the ones we marry.[19]

To turn the flower of mutual love into delectable fruit in marriage, the couple must demonstrate love and mutual respect to each other – not just in words but in actions. It is in action that the spouse finds assurance and confidence in the genuineness and sincerity of his or her partner's motives. There are myriad ways of showing love and respect through action. Here are a few suggestions:

- Buy flowers for no special reason.
- Offer to take care of the kids while your spouse takes off to do what they consider fun.
- Turn off the TV so you can do something you both enjoy.
- Encourage and support your spouse to finally pursue that special dream they have had for years, and let them know you think that the time has come to make that dream a reality.
- Plan a 'week of appreciation' by preparing yellow sticky notes with examples of how your partner has made a difference in the family life (or in the lives of others), and then hide them all over the house. Let your partner find the sticky notes throughout in a week long 'treasure-hunt'.
- If you have musical talent, write and record a love song for your spouse.
- Praise your spouse's talents and accomplishments and, again, cite specific examples of those talents and accomplishments that have made a positive contribution to your life, the life of your family or those of others around you.

Be your spouse's best friend

After marriage, if your spouse can continue to claim someone else is still their best friend, then you have work to do! A successful marriage – which is a key to your enduring happiness – is one in which you and your spouse are each other's best friends. The two of you complement each other and help one another to improve. How do you do this? There are lots of ways. Below are a few:

- Spend time with your spouse. Communicate. Then communicate some more. Communication is one of the most important aspects of a relationship. Talk about the important activities and events of the day. Laugh, share and express emotions and feelings towards each other.
- Listen to your spouse and show genuine interest in what they are saying – whether they are talking about problems, feelings, interests and hobbies, likes and dislikes, or goals and dreams – without side-tracking them or turning the conversation into something about you or someone else.
- Be worthy of your spouse's trust. Show loyalty and honesty in the relationship. Without trust and loyalty in a marriage, the relationship is built on a shaky foundation that can easily crumble into pieces with the first signs of serious trouble.
- Maintain a kind, loving tone in all communications with your spouse. Be nice and polite. Even when you are angry inside, try to maintain your composure and express your feelings in as calm a manner as you can. Never take out your anger on them.
- Be willing and ready to compromise. Adjust your schedule. Don't insist on watching that game live; record it and watch it at a different time.
- Treat your spouse as a genuine equal. Marriage is a partnership of equals. If you can't treat your spouse as your equal, then you can forget about being each other's best friends.

Pray for each other

If prayer plays an important part in your life, don't forget to include your spouse. After all, they are your 'significant other'. You may not always have the time to write long letters or emails, or get loving cards for your spouse; but if you pray regularly, including your spouse in those prayers does not require a great deal of additional investment in time. Praying daily for your spouse will deepen your love for them and strengthen the bond of your marriage. You can pray for your spouse's health, happiness, protection, and success in their personal and professional life, as well as in becoming a contributing member of society and rendering service to the community. When praying, you can also express gratitude for the gift of a good spouse and a loving relationship.

Use a positive approach to resolving conflicts and disagreements

While it is acceptable to express one's feelings and frustrations in a relationship, it is not okay to engage in overly critical methods of communication, because criticism is perhaps more toxic in a marital relationship than anything else. We marry someone so the two of us can be on the same 'team'. However, too many of us these days end up undermining our partner on the team by criticizing them in front of our friends and family – or worse yet, in front of our children. Mature couples soon realize that there is a difference between offering constructive criticism – which is high-minded and aims to help the recipients improve themselves – and spiteful criticism, which is destructive and is designed to hurt or humiliate others. Critique or constructive feedback is a positive trait, and criticism is negative and can be a destructive force in any relationship.

If marital disagreements or conflicts arise, it is imperative that we don't allow discussions to turn into bickering sessions. As soon as we begin finding faults in our partner, communication begins to break down and the real issues will remain unresolved.

For starters, the way we present a marital issue, big or small, can make all the difference in how it is received. Consider these two extremes in presenting the same issue and ask yourself to which of these two methods you would respond better:

1. You are a selfish, thoughtless idiot! I have asked you a hundred times to put your dirty dishes in the dishwasher. Do you ever listen to me? I always do all the work around here and you never do anything. You just sit there and watch TV. I'm sick of it!

2. Honey, I know you work hard, and I know you're tired at the end of the day. However, I feel pretty frustrated when I see that dishes are left on the table. As you know, a clean house is important to me. I'd really appreciate it if you would pay attention to this and make it a priority to put your dishes in the dishwasher after we eat.

Here, the first method will be perceived as an attack, and the natural reaction to an attack is often a counterattack. That's a survival mechanism, so there's no surprise in adopting that approach. Some of us may choose to run away or walk away from a tense situation. Others among us may begrudgingly cave in to a request, but we will secretly remain resentful, even angry, and that may beget passive-aggressive behaviour further down the road. The sum total of adopting any of these methods will be negative, for both sides.

However, if we adopt the kinder, gentler approach and use milder language, it will be received as a positive, loving and respectful request by someone who is dear to us. Therefore, we will be more inclined to comply with the request. We will take criticism a lot better when we feel it is coming from someone we admire, particularly if they have shown us love, affection and respect. In the words of the late Stephen Covey, every time we communicate with someone with love and affection, we are making a deposit in our 'emotional bank account' with them.[20] Therefore, over time, we can create a reservoir of goodwill with them, from which we can draw in times of conflict.

In addition, instead of dragging ancient history into the conversation and using superlatives such as 'you always' or 'you never' (which is often an exaggeration), try to come up with a concrete solution to the problem at hand. If you feel you have to offer criticism, first pause and reflect for a while. Don't be impulsive or emotional about it, because it may lead to a rush judgment. Then, use 'the sandwich approach': start and end with something positive about the person or the situation, and then offer the criticism in kind, loving language.

Avoid using the language of blame

Instead of, 'How could you have possibly forgotten to call me? Didn't I tell you to do that as soon as you got there?', simply explain the experience you went through when that phone call didn't take place. For example, 'I felt really worried and frustrated when you didn't call to say you'd be late. I thought you had gotten in a serious accident. I'd appreciate it if you pay more attention to this next time and call.'

If you and your spouse have frequent arguments, set aside a regular time to air grievances. Again, those times should not be turned into bickering or attack sessions, which can lead to defensiveness and counterattacks. Rather, they should be occasions for rationally presenting your case in a safe and loving environment.

Be realistic about your expectations

Evaluate your expectations to ensure they are not too high. Critical couples often have very high expectations of each other. If you find yourself constantly annoyed or disappointed by your spouse, your expectations of your partner may be too high. Pause and reflect on those expectations; you may have to adjust them. If you sent an email or a text to your spouse 30 minutes ago and have not yet received a response, is it reasonable for you to feel annoyed or disappointed when your spouse may be tied up in a meeting at work?

Be aware of the importance of trust

A key component of any relationship is the virtue of trust. Even in work environments, the value of trust has now been scientifically demonstrated: 'Compared with people at low-trust companies, people at high-trust companies report: 74% less stress, 106% more energy at work, 50% higher productivity, 13% fewer sick days, 76% more engagement, 29% more satisfaction with their lives, 40% less burnout.'[21] In family life, if there is trust in a relationship – and the couple knows that there is genuine love, affection and care on both sides – they can overcome virtually any issues or problems.

Focus on the behaviour, not the person

If you notice that your spouse consistently does something that bothers you, don't make the situation personal. Separate him or her from the negative behaviour that is causing the aggravation. Criticizing the person can backfire and result in a counterattack. In contrast, focusing on the behaviour itself and offering suggestions on how to rectify the negative behaviour can lead to a potential solution. Say your spouse consistently forgets to pay your monthly mortgage bill and this results in unnecessary late payment fees. You have two approaches at your disposal here: the negative approach and the positive one. Here's the negative approach:

> Why can't you pay our mortgage bill on time? This is the fourth time this year we have had to pay $25 in late payment fees. That's $100 down the drain, and it's all because you don't care or you are just a forgetful person!

And here's the more positive approach:

Honey, I noticed our bank's online services now offers automated payments for free. Since our home mortgage amount is fixed, and we know when our last payment is going to be, why don't you set up our monthly mortgage payments as an automated item? That way, we don't have to remember to make the payment every month and will also avoid any potential late fees.

Put yourself in their shoes

There is nothing more effective in understanding someone's point of view or perspective than putting ourselves in their shoes. That is why, in some cases – like large-scale conflicts – a popular method of resolution these days is to require each party to take on the role of the opposing side and realistically play that part so they can truly feel and experience what the other side goes through. In your marital relationship, when extremely difficult or controversial cases arise, you and your spouse may have to make use of this conflict resolution method and take on the role of your spouse, and present all the feelings and grievances of your spouse in a realistic and comprehensive way so you could truly appreciate 'their side of the story'.

Look for a mutually agreeable solution to your problem

The ultimate goal of any conflict resolution method for couples should be to arrive at a mutually agreeable solution that can be considered a win-win situation for both parties. A marriage without compromise is a recipe for divorce. Therefore, both spouses should accept that it is neither fair nor healthy that one person consistently gets everything they want in marital conflicts. Instead, both should be willing to 'give some to get some'. When both parties in a marriage adopt that as an approach and a philosophy, they can expect less headaches and heartaches.

A Story for Valentine's Day

Larry and Jo Ann were an ordinary couple. They lived in an ordinary house on an ordinary street. Like any other ordinary couple, they struggled to make ends meet and to do the right things for their children. They were ordinary in yet another way – they had their squabbles. Much of their conversation concerned what was wrong in their marriage and who was to blame. Until one day when a most extraordinary event took place.

'You know, Jo Ann, I've got a magic chest of drawers. Every time I open them, they're full of socks and underwear,' Larry said. 'I want to thank you for filling them all these years.'

Jo Ann stared at her husband over the top of her glasses. 'What do you want, Larry?'

'Nothing. I just want you to know I appreciate those magic drawers.'

This wasn't the first time Larry had done something odd, so Jo Ann pushed the incident out of her mind until a few days later.

'Jo Ann, thank you for recording so many correct check numbers in the ledger this month. You put down the right numbers 15 out of 16 times. That's a record.'

Disbelieving what she had heard, Jo Ann looked up from her mending. 'Larry, you're always complaining about my recording the wrong check numbers. Why stop now?'

'No reason. I just wanted you to know I appreciate the effort you're making.'

Jo Ann shook her head and went back to her mending. 'What's got into him? she mumbled to herself.

Nevertheless, the next day when Jo Ann wrote a check at the grocery store, she glanced at her check book to confirm that she had put down the right check number. 'Why do I suddenly care about those dumb check numbers?' she asked herself. She tried to disregard the incident, but Larry's strange behaviour intensified.

'Jo Ann, that was a great dinner,' he said one evening. 'I appreciate all your effort. Why, in the past 15 years I'll bet you've fixed over

14,000 meals for me and the kids.' Then, 'Gee, Jo Ann, the house looks spiffy. You've really worked hard to get it looking so good.' And even, 'Thanks, Jo Ann, for just being you. I really enjoy your company.'

JoAnn was growing worried. 'Where's the sarcasm, the criticism?' she wondered.

Her fears that something peculiar was happening to her husband were confirmed by 16-year-old Shelly, who complained, 'Dad's gone bonkers, Mom. He just told me I looked nice. With all this make-up and these sloppy clothes, he still said it. That's not Dad, Mom. What's wrong with him?'

Whatever was wrong, Larry didn't get over it. Day in and day out he continued focusing on the positive. Over the weeks, Jo Ann grew more accustomed to her mate's unusual behaviour and occasionally even gave him a grudging, 'Thank you'. She prided herself on taking it all in stride, until one day something so peculiar happened, she became completely discombobulated.

'I want you to take a break,' Larry said. 'I am going to do the dishes. So please take your hands off that frying pan and leave the kitchen.'

(Long, long pause.) 'Thank you, Larry. Thank you very much!'

Jo Ann's step was now a little lighter, her self-confidence higher and once in a while she hummed. She didn't seem to have as many blue moods anymore. 'I rather like Larry's new behaviour', she thought.

That would be the end of the story except one day another most extraordinary event took place. This time it was Jo Ann who spoke.

'Larry,' she said, 'I want to thank you for going to work and providing for us all these years. I don't think I've ever told you how much I appreciate it.'

Larry has never revealed the reason for his dramatic change of behaviour, no matter how hard Jo Ann has pushed for an answer, and so it will likely remain one of life's mysteries. But it's one I'm thankful to live with. You see, I am Jo Ann.[22]

9

POSITIVITY

> The greatest discovery of my generation is that a human being can alter his life by altering his attitudes of mind.[1]

A great deal of our happiness depends on our general attitude towards life and everything we encounter during our daily experiences. These experiences range from our relationships and conversations with family, friends and colleagues at work, to how we respond to economic, social or political news. If we look at our lives as a glass of water, for some of us the glass is always half full, for others it's half empty. Yet, it's the same glass of water. Therefore, it all goes back to our perspective – to what kind of lenses we are wearing when we look at the world and its people.

For instance, looking at what is good or positive about a person comes to some naturally, while others struggle to see anything positive in another. Ryan offers a powerful story on how simply focusing on what is right in other people, rather than what is wrong in them, can change our outlook on life in general, and how we look at people in particular:

> We are so incredibly well trained to notice what's wrong in any given relationship, work situation, or experience that it's easy to overlook what's right. But what if we have it backwards? . . . What if we spent as much energy in relationships noticing and appreciating the other person's gifts and talents and the strengths and beauty of the relationship itself as we do exposing and dealing with its flaws?
>
> An 'asset focus' – noticing and appreciating . . . is an

incredibly powerful tool for creating connection, fostering creative thinking, and overcoming obstacles. I saw this most powerfully at an office retreat in which we honoured the twelve people who worked at Conari Press. We went around the room, focusing on one person at a time. The rules were simple: Anyone who wished to could say what they appreciated about that person; no one had to speak . . . People laughed and cried. By the end, the sense of camaraderie, connection and team were the strongest I ever felt.[2]

Over the last 20 years or so, Barbara Fredrickson, author and professor of social psychology, has done a great deal of research on human emotions, particularly positive emotions and their benefits. According to Fredrickson, positivity can take various forms, 'ranging from joy, gratitude, serenity, and interest, to hope, pride, amusement, inspiration, awe, and – last, but not least – love. Each of these ten forms of positivity can change your life – and your future.'[3] Adopting a positive attitude in life has many benefits. Most of us are naturally more drawn to positive people – simply because they are more fun to be around – rather than negative people, who are constantly either complaining about their own lives or the lives of others. Therefore, it is easier to connect with positive individuals, which means they usually have wider and stronger networks of friends on whom they can fall back in times of trouble. In addition, positive people are more resilient by nature because they tend to bounce back from defeats and misfortunes more quickly and emerge stronger from them. They resist succumbing to feelings of despair and hopelessness. Thus, by adopting positivity as an attitude in life, we can take a significant step towards enhancing feelings of happiness.

In his book, *The Amazing Results of Positive Thinking*, Norman Vincent Peale – regarded by many as the father of positive thinking philosophy in America – defines a positive thinker as one who 'chooses to keep his mind fixed on the bright future that is always just around the corner, and in this way . . . helps make the dark moments more cheerful, productive and creative'.[4]

Physiological benefits of positivity

Fredrickson is among the social psychologists who have gathered research over the years that points to a strong connection between positivity and human health. Her research has led her to conclude that the daily practice of positivity has many physical benefits, including fewer instances of sore throat, less cases of acne and lower levels of stress hormones. Fredrickson believes these and other health benefits occur because positivity 'sends out more dopamine and opioids, enhances immune system functioning and diminishes inflammatory response to stress . . . People high on positivity also have lower disease risks. They are less likely to have hypertension, diabetes, or a stroke.'[5] Positive people also have lower blood pressure, experience less pain and fewer colds, and sleep better.[6]

Keeping an optimistic attitude has also been shown to affect life longevity. In a longitudinal study spanning over 30 years, Mayo Clinic physicians used the Minnesota Multiphasic Personality Inventory to identify patients as being optimistic, mixed and pessimistic. At the end of the study, the researchers found that for every ten-point increase in a patient's score on the optimism scale, their risk of early death decreased by 19 per cent.[7] That is a massive amount of improvement, especially when considering that the difference between sudden death risk factors for smokers and non-smokers is between 5 and 10 per cent.

Optimism among patients who deal with life-threatening diagnoses, such as cancer, has also been linked to a substantially better quality of life, compared to that of pessimistic individuals.[8,9] In another study, Matthews et al. showed that optimism can protect patients against the development of chronic diseases. A group of middle-aged women was tested for precursors to atherosclerosis at a baseline, and then again three years later. Those at the baseline assessment were significantly more likely to have thickening arteries, while optimistic women showed no such increase in thickness.[10]

Optimism has also been demonstrated to have a positive impact on HIV patients' immune system. For instance, Ironson and colleagues found that HIV patients with the highest levels of optimism had the best suppression of viral load and greater number of helper T cells, both of which were critical factors in the progression of HIV.[11] In a longitudinal study, Blomkvist et al. showed a positive relationship between optimism and lower mortality rates among HIV patients.[12]

Psychological benefits of positivity and optimism

Not surprisingly, studies have also shown that individuals with a positive attitude are generally more psychologically healthy, and this enables them to deal better with the tests and trials of life. For instance, in a 1992 study, Taylor and colleagues found that optimistic people dealt more effectively with the news of being diagnosed with HIV, and that their positive mental state had an effect on their immune system and their ability to fight the disease.[13] Pregnant women who are optimistic have also been shown to deliver healthier, heavier babies.[14]

Additionally, evidence suggests that positive people who maintain a more optimistic perspective on life are generally more satisfied with their lives and enjoy higher self-esteem.[15] A positive state of mind can also serve as a protector against depression and more serious medical issues, such as a coronary heart disease.[16] In contrast, a negative, pessimistic attitude has been linked to depression, stress and anxiety.[17]

In another study, Segerstrom and Sephton examined whether optimism predicted positive outcomes in life. Their hypothesis – that changes in positive versus negative outlooks in life would predict changes in the nature of the outcomes that people experienced – was proven to be true. In other words, the more optimistic the individual, the higher the chance of increased positive effect, and vice versa. This means that positive people, who are more optimistic about life generally, enjoy happier lives.[18]

Optimists generally recover from disappointments more quickly too, because they tend to focus on positive outcomes rather than negative ones. In a 1992 study, Litt and colleagues investigated optimism and pessimism in couples who underwent in-vitro fertilization (IVF) attempts. Forty-one couples were interviewed two weeks prior to an IVF attempt and then two weeks after a pregnancy test. Among the women who received a negative pregnancy test result, optimists coped with the failed fertilization attempt much better than the pessimists, looking for positive outcomes from the setback, such as, 'this experience has made our relationship stronger'. Pessimists, on the other hand, were more likely to blame themselves for the failed IVF attempt and display depressive symptoms.[19]

When facing difficult situations in life, optimists are also more likely to think rationally and engage in problem solving, which itself is a manifestation of increased psychological wellbeing. In one study, Taylor and colleagues investigated the link between optimism and stress in a group of 550 men who were HIV-positive and at risk for developing AIDS. Among these individuals, patients with a more positive attitude about their condition were more likely to plan their recoveries, seek further information on their condition and avoid self-blame.[20]

How can we cultivate positivity?

Positivity is a trait that can actually be developed and nurtured. A positive thinker looks for happiness, expects happiness and, in time, recognizes it when it comes his or her way. However, many of us appear to be negative by nature, and there's a reason for it:

> Recent breakthroughs in the ability to see the brain function – through MRIs – reveal that we all have two prefrontal lobes in our neocortex. When the left is activated, we think thoughts of peace, happiness, joy, contentment, optimism. When the right is activated, we think thoughts of gloom, doom, worry, pessimism. It turns out that each of us has what they call a tilt – a tendency for whatever happens to stimulate one side or the other. That's what creates the difference between optimists and pessimists. Whether we're born that way or develop it very young is not clear. But by the time we're adults, we have a

deeply grooved tendency to activate either the right (negative) or left (positive) no matter what's going on.[21]

If you consider yourself a negative or pessimist, take heart. Change is possible; but remember, it will take some effort and perseverance. There is a wide range of methods we can use to gradually overcome negativity and become more positive. Here are eleven different methods that can help:

1. **Count your blessings**
   A positive person starts with what they have, rather than what they don't have. We all have things to be thankful for. These can range from our health to family, friends and colleagues, to a good job, and to the gifts and inner talents that lay hidden within us and that we should try to bring out to the open, for our own benefit and the benefit of society.

2. **Stay away from negative people**
   Positive thinkers also consciously stay away from negative individuals, because negative people not only sap their energy but also model bad behaviours. Positive people even stop engaging in negative thoughts or using negative words, 'they drop every negative word that gets in the way of personal growth and development – words such as if, can't, and impossible . . . they chuck them out of their vocabulary and thinking'.[22]

3. **Replace 'if only' with 'next time'**
   When making a mistake, positive thinkers don't keep blaming themselves or living in the past. They don't think in terms of 'if only'; for instance, 'If only I had said or done that instead, I could have avoided that undesirable outcome.' Positive thinkers realize they can't touch the past, so they focus on the future instead. They replace negative, energy-sapping phrases like, 'if only', with hopeful, vitalizing phrases like, 'next time', because they are logical enough to know that they cannot change the past, but they are in control of their own future. The fruits

of 'next time' thinking are optimism, hope and a chance to apply what one has learned from the past. Adopting such a perspective motivates positive thinkers to move forward and do better next time. The fruit of 'if only' thinking, on the other hand, is nothing but helplessness, which only brings sadness and despair, and results in a waste of our precious lives.

A somewhat similar approach was promoted by Peale, who suggested that a negative person needed to become a *how thinker*, not an *if thinker*:

> The if thinker broods over a difficulty or a setback, saying bitterly to himself, 'If only I had done thus and so . . . If only this or that circumstance had been different . . . If others had not treated me so unfairly . . .' The world is full of defeated *if* thinkers.
>
> The how thinker, on the other hand, wastes no energy on post-mortems when trouble or even disaster hits him… He asks himself, 'How can I use this setback creatively? How can I work something good out of it?'[23]

4. **Trust in a higher power**
   Positive thinkers often also believe in a higher power. In times of trouble, they draw energy and hope from that source. When things get tough, they know they can reach out to that source for assistance and strength.

   > They shall run and not be weary. They shall walk and not faint. (Is. 40:31)

   This attitude gives them resilience, which enables them to bounce back from adversity and come out of tests and trials stronger. The same tests and difficulties could have devastating consequences for negative thinkers.

   Positive thinkers realize that what often seems to be an adversity in their lives could, in reality, be a chance for spiritual growth and development.

My calamity is My providence, outwardly it is fire and vengeance, but inwardly it is light and mercy.[24]

They have the assurance that they can go through the ups and downs of life with a Companion – a loving God who is always with them. Therefore, when adversity comes, they do their very best, but leave the rest in God's hands, believing that, 'Nothing save that which profiteth them can befall My loved ones.'[25]

5. **Be strong in faith, thought and character**
Peale believes that 'positive thinking is for strong people; strong in faith, strong in thought, strong in character. And if they are not so, when they embrace positive thinking, the struggle to become positive will make them strong.'[26]

Positive thinking can also help us overcome pain, or at least rise above it, so that it does not interfere with leading a productive life. Positive thinking 'keeps the negative in proper size and grows the positive big. Thus, it enables countless men and women to have serenity and power – despite continuing pain.'[27]

6. **Remember, you can change**
Unfortunately, for most of us, negative thinking seems to come more naturally than positive thinking. Perhaps because of the competitive or perfectionist environment at home, school and work, or in the general environment we grew up in, looking for the negative has become a learned characteristic. The good news is that all habits, including negative thinking, can be unlearned. Scientific research on the neuroplasticity (or malleability) of the brain has shown that, contrary to what we had previously thought, our brains are not hardwired for life by the time we are adults.

On the contrary, our brains are capable of change at any stage in our lives. They can form new connections or new wires that enable us to engage in new thoughts or behavioural patterns – and those new thoughts or behavioural patterns can run counter to the previous ones. This means we can unlearn undesirable characteristics, such as negative thinking, and form new brain connections that promote and strengthen its opposite – positive thinking. However, it takes persistence and perseverance to form those new connections in the brain.

Positive thinking starts with the thoughts, then the words that we choose to express those thoughts, and eventually those words will translate into deeds and attitudes that we adopt in life. The religiously-minded can seek assistance from God in the battle against negative thinking. They can take comfort in the fact that, 'With God all things are possible' (Matt. 19:26). Therefore, they don't have to fight negativity alone.

7. **Practise mindfulness**
The practice of mindfulness can also help cultivate positive thinking. As Frederickson explains, 'It alters the basic metabolism in brain circuits known to underlie emotional responding, reducing activity in circuits linked with negativity, and increase activity in circuits linked with positivity. This means that you can wilfully change the way your brain works – you can harness neuroplasticity to reinforce the move you make in your own mental riverbed.'[28]

8. **Practise positive affirmations**
In the next chapter, we will talk about the use of positive affirmations, which is a method of self-improvement for cultivating happiness. The same technique is also a great tool for developing positive thinking, which is essential for achieving happiness. You can come up with your own list of daily affirmations, or choose from among the ones below:

- I choose to be happy.
- I choose to be kind.
- I choose to be positive.
- I choose to be peaceful.

- I choose to be patient.
- I choose to be optimistic.
- I focus on thoughts and things that make me happy.
- I acknowledge my own self-worth; my confidence is soaring.
- I am full of zest for life.
- I can learn new things.
- I never give up.
- I accept with serenity what I cannot change in my life.
- I make the best of every situation.
- In every difficult situation, I do the best I can, but leave the rest to God.
- I look for humor and fun in life.
- I am grateful to God for this wonderful life.
- I enjoy my life to the fullest.
- I have control over my thoughts, feelings and attitudes.
- When something unexpected happens, I always turn to God for guidance.
- I choose to be happy at the start of each day.
- I live a life based on noble values and morals.
- I treat others with respect and dignity.
- I put my talents and knowledge to work for the benefit of all.
- I am determined to make a positive difference in the lives of others.
- Happiness is my natural way of being.
- In talking with others, I am always careful with my first reaction.
- Every day I become more energetic and healthier.
- My happiness increases all the time.
- For me, the future is always bright and happy.

9. **Change your media diet**

    We watch what we eat, but we don't always watch what we watch. We refuse to put trash in our mouth but don't hesitate to allow trash into our mind. Depending on the media diet that we choose, our world of television, movies, music, games, and social media can be positive, entertaining, informative, and thought-provoking, or negative, violent, depressing, and destructive. An unhealthy diet of greed, violence, fear, anxiety, and worry leads to the growth of the same negative qualities in our minds. Over time, those qualities become our character:

> Science shows that as you consume violent media, you increase the odds of becoming violent yourself . . . Your media diet is double-edged; it informs and entertains you, but often at a price of lowering your positivity ratio . . . the negativity spawned by the media is often far more subtle than violence. Consider . . . the implicit messages about thinness, sexuality, beauty . . . our media teaches us what's to be expected and what's 'normal'. It is not hard for viewers . . . to feel that they don't measure up.[29]

Therefore, our mental diet should be as important to us as our regular diet.

> Whatever is true, whatever is noble,
> whatever is right, whatever is pure,
> whatever is lovely, whatever is admirable
> if anything is excellent or praiseworthy
> think about such things. (Phil. 4:8)

10. **Notice and savour positive moments**
We can also train our minds to become mindful of positive moments in life, as they occur; moments in our daily lives for which we should be grateful. These could be things we would usually take for granted or consider very ordinary, such as feeling the cool breeze on our face or listening to the sound of a bird chirping as we go for a walk, becoming absorbed in the beauty of a flower blooming in our backyard, feeling the warm water on our body as we take a shower, enjoying the taste of our favourite food, the aroma of our tea or coffee, appreciating the hug we receive from a loved one, or a nice compliment we

get at work for the good job we did on a project, and so forth.

As you become aware of such positive moments, make a conscious effort to store them in your memory. Tell yourself, 'this is a positive moment', or 'this is a gratitude moment. Let me feel it for a second.' Then, take a snapshot of it in your mind so you can go back to it in the future and relive the moment during difficult times.

Articulate the moment in your mind, take in the visual and form a mental snapshot. Also, notice any sounds, smells or physiological reactions you have – smiling, relaxation of tensed muscles, and so forth. What you want to do is imprint this experience in your mind, using as many sensory modalities as possible, thereby strengthening positive neural pathways in your brain.[30]

With enough practice, we can train our minds to become aware of such moments in the course of the day as they occur. Consequently, little by little, we can condition our brains to focus on the positive, joyful moments of life as they happen, and de-emphasise the negative. If we are keeping a happiness journal, then such positive moments should be recorded in that journal.

> A brain that imprints positive emotions becomes more resilient – you bounce back quicker from negative experiences and disappointments. And, a focus on positive emotions dials down the release of stress hormones, which lessens the negative physiological effects of stress.[31]

11. **Stop comparing yourself to others**

A frequent cause of unhappiness among many of us is the tendency to compare ourselves to others, especially to those we consider better or more accomplished than ourselves. What we don't realize is that, often, we tend to underestimate our own gifts and talents and overestimate those of people we admire or envy.

If we cannot help comparing ourselves to others, it is better to engage in 'downward' rather than 'upward' comparison. Research shows that this kind of downward comparison – comparing oneself with someone who is worse off – is an effective strategy for combating feelings of pain and depression. It can also be an effective means for cultivating compassion.[32] In addition, while downward comparison can lead to gratitude and contentment, upward comparison can result in envy, jealousy or resentment.

Perhaps the best summary for the ideas presented in this chapter is Christian Larsen's 'The Optimist Creed', which includes the following ten principles:

Promise yourself:
1. To be so strong that nothing can disturb your peace of mind.
2. To talk health, happiness and prosperity to every person you meet.
3. To make all your friends feel that there is something in them.
4. To look at the sunny side of everything and make your optimism come true.
5. To think only of the best, to work only for the best and to expect only the best.
6. To be just as enthusiastic about the success of others as you are about your own.
7. To forget the mistakes of the past and press on to the greater achievements of the future.
8. To wear a cheerful countenance at all times and give every living creature you meet a smile.
9. To give so much time to the improvement of yourself that you have no time to criticize others.
10. To be too large for worry, too noble for anger, too strong for fear, and too happy to permit the presence of trouble.[33]

When life gives you lemons, make lemonade

This is the story of Thelma Thompson, as told by her to Dale Carnegie.

During the war, my husband was stationed at an army training camp near the Mojave Desert in California. I went to live there in order to be near him. I hated the place. I loathed it. I had never before been so miserable. My husband was ordered out on manoeuvres in the Mojave Desert and I was left in a tiny shack alone. The heat was unbearable – 125 degrees in the shade of a cactus. Not a soul to talk to. The wind blew incessantly, and all the food I ate and the very air I breathed were filled with sand, sand, sand!

I was so utterly sad, so sorry for myself that I wrote to my parents. I told them I was giving up and coming back home. I said I couldn't stand it one minute longer. I would rather be in jail! My father answered my letter with just two lines – two lines that will always sing in my memory – two lines that completely altered my life:

Two men looked out from prison bars.
One saw the mud, the other saw the stars.

I read those two lines over and over. I was ashamed of myself. I made up my mind I would find out what was good in my present situation; I would look for the stars.

I made friends with the local people, and their reaction amazed me. When I showed interest in their weaving and pottery, they gave me presents of their favourite pieces which they had refused to sell to tourists. I studied the fascinating forms of the cactus and the yuccas and the Joshua trees. I learned about prairie dogs, watched for the desert sunsets and hunted for seashells that had been left there millions of years ago when the sands of the desert had been an ocean floor.

What brought about this astonishing change in me? The Desert hadn't changed. But I had. I had changed my attitude of mind. And by doing so, I transformed a wretched experience into the most exciting adventure of my life. I was stimulated and excited by this new world that I had discovered. I was so excited I wrote a book about it – a novel that was published under the title *Bright Ramparts* . . . I had looked out of my self-created prison and found the stars.[34]

CHAPTER 10

HAPPINESS TECHNIQUES

> *Happiness is a perfume you cannot pour on others without getting some on yourself.*[1]

We doubt you have ever met a person in your life who doesn't want to be happy. Seeking happiness seems to be the ultimate goal of everyone on the planet. After all, if given a choice, why would anyone among us want to be miserable and unhappy? By nature, human beings are driven towards seeking pleasure and happiness. We want to be as far away as possible from the feelings of pain and misery. It is only natural. Yet, many of us don't achieve this goal. Why? Because we often fail to realize that, to a large extent, feeling happy or miserable lies in our own hands.

Of course, some of us tend to play the victim game and attempt to blame others or circumstances out of our control for our unhappiness. That's why, as Norman Vincent Peale explains:

> [We may] manufacture our unhappiness by thinking unhappy thoughts, by the attitudes which we habitually take, such as the negative feeling that everything is going to turn out badly. Our unhappiness is further distilled by saturating the consciousness with feelings of resentment, ill will and hate. The unhappiness-producing process always makes important use of the ingredients of fear and worry.[2]

Hence, at the end of the day, we can be as happy or as unhappy as we make up our mind to be.

What science says

There are now scientific studies that prove we are in control of a substantial portion of our own happiness. In one study, Martin Seligman, a psychologist and professor at the University of Pennsylvania, taught a simple happiness-enhancing technique to a group of people who were suffering from severe depression. These individuals were so depressed that they had a hard time even leaving their beds in the morning. Participants were asked to recall and write down three good things that happened in their daily lives. Within a period of only fifteen days, their depressive moods were improved from 'severely depressed' to 'mildly or moderately depressed'. The vast majority (94%) had found relief through this simple exercise.[3]

Studies by the University of California professor of psychology, Sonja Lyubomirsky, and her colleagues, Ken Sheldon and David Schkade, led them to the conclusion that three factors were the most important in determining human happiness.

Growing research with identical and fraternal twins led Lyubomirsky and her colleagues to the conclusion that about 50 per cent of the differences in the level of happiness among people can be attributed to their genetic disposition, which they call 'set points'. We inherit our set points from our mothers, fathers or both. Our set point is our baseline or potential for happiness, to which we typically return after every major setback or triumph. Another 10 per cent can be explained by differences in our life circumstances, such as the amount of wealth, health or beauty we have, our marital status, and so on.

Lyubomirsky provides several studies to back up her conclusions. One study that focused on the level of the happiness of the rich (those making at least US$10 million a year) demonstrated that their level of personal happiness was only marginally higher than that of the staff who worked for them. Another study covering married and single people from across 16 different countries showed that only 25 per cent of married people described themselves as very happy, versus 21 per cent of singles.[4] A meta-analysis of these and similar studies show that we cannot reasonably expect lasting happiness from 60 per cent of the variables in our life, because those variables are due to factors outside our control (50 per cent due to genetic predisposition and 10 per cent due to life conditions). However, the good news is that we are in control of the remaining 40 per cent (see Fig. 8). That is still a substantial amount of control over our happiness, which can be achieved by habitually monitoring and regulating our thoughts and behavioural patterns.

In studying the behaviour of happy people, Lyubomirsky observed that they were more sociable, optimistic, grateful, mindful of the present moment, cooperative, charitable, likeable, flexible, and productive. More specifically, they:

- Spent more time with family and friends, and nurtured those relationships.
- Were comfortable expressing a sense of gratitude for what they already had in life.
- Were often the first to offer helping others.
- Were more optimistic about the future.
- Savoured life's pleasures.
- Tried to live in the present, not the past or the future.
- Engaged in regular exercise.
- Were deeply committed to lifelong, meaningful goals and ambitions, such as teaching deeply held values to their children or fighting fraud.
- Had their own share of stresses and crises, and even tragedies. However, what set them apart was in how they responded to those circumstances – they did so with poise and strength.[5]

Many of us have conditioned ourselves to believe that we should wait for certain things to happen in the future before we are allowed to experience happiness, like having lot of money, a dream home, a beautiful car, or a great job. That is a myth. Countless studies have proven otherwise. Even winning the lottery not only won't guarantee happiness, it often leads to misery.[6,7,8]

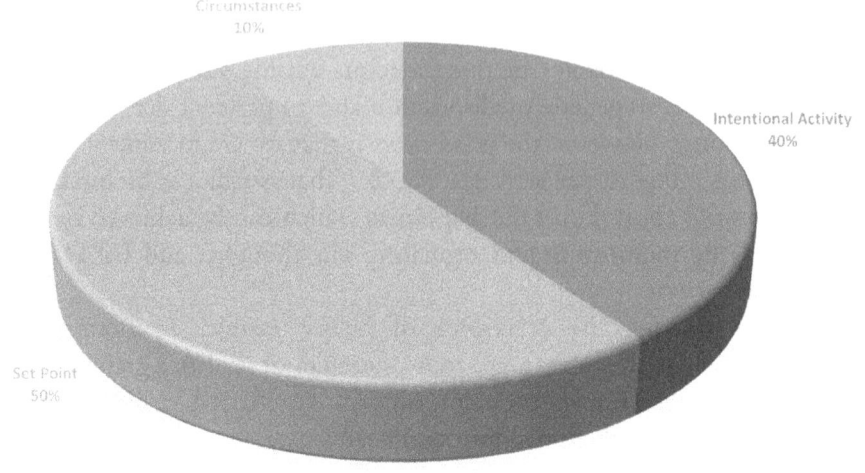

Fig. 9
What determines happiness
(image based on Sonja Lyubomirsky's *The How of Happiness: A New Approach to Getting the Life You Want*)

Thus, to secure a more lasting kind of happiness, Lyubomirsky suggests we observe the aforementioned behavioural patterns of truly happy people. There are intentional strategies we can choose from to regulate our behavioural and thought patterns to match those of happy individuals. For example, keeping a gratitude journal, cultivating optimism and hope, avoiding overthinking and social comparison, practising acts of kindness, savouring life's joys, practising religion and spirituality, and so on.

Like Lyubomirsky, Stephen Post also believes that:

> Our own behaviour, attitudes, activities, practices, and responses ultimately determine our happiness. One piece is biology. Just as some people are hardwired to be skinny and others seem to gain weight just by looking at food, some people are naturally happier than others . . . Yes, some babies are born smiling and

content, and others are born kicking and crying. But whatever hand we are dealt, we choose how to play the cards.[9]

Post offers four elements for happiness and believes all four have a spiritual foundation:

1. Love others and let their happiness be as significant to you as your own happiness.
2. Cultivate moral integrity. Live a life based on virtues.
3. Live a life of gratitude, simplicity and contentment.
4. Have high and noble goals, as well as a purpose in life that does not revolve around material things.[10]

So, to enjoy the highest quality of life and experience more lasting happiness, it seems essential to live a life filled with meaning and centred on moral values.

In their book, *Happiness: Unlocking the Mysteries of Psychological Wealth*, father and son professors of psychology, Ed and Robert Diener, describe a classroom experiment in which the participants were given two different activities. The first activity involved doing something fun such as dancing, enjoying a fancy dessert, driving a new car, etc. The next activity involved being engaged in a meaningful and rewarding experience, such as volunteering, cleaning up litter, helping a child with their homework, and so forth. A week later, the participants said that the first set of activities was undoubtedly fun, but the positive effect was short-lived. A large number of the participants also said that if they were to recommend one of the two kinds of activities to a friend, it had to be the meaningful one. As one of the participant explained, 'Even though the meaningful activities weren't always fun, they tended to feel good later because they resonated with deeply held personal values.'[11]

Arguably, the most significant study of the life course ever done – and the longest recorded longitudinal study – is the Harvard's Grant Study of Adult Development, which brims with wisdom. This revolutionary research, which began in 1938, has been following the lives of 268 male undergraduate subjects at

Harvard, and continues to this day (as some of the men are still alive, well into their 90s). The people behind the study felt the medical research of the time was putting too much emphasis on various diseases and how to fight them, and paid little attention to methods of coping with life – an approach that could prevent some of those diseases from being developed in the first place.

Nearly forty years after the research began, George E. Vaillant, the director of the study, published the results of his first measure of the Harvard Grant Study men in the now classic book, *Adaptation to Life*.[12] In that work, Vaillant poses fundamental questions about why different people confront life's stresses differently; in other words, why some of us cope with the most stressful situations wisely and calmly, while others among us get rattled by even the most insignificant issues in life and show little or no coping skills. Vaillant also asks if there are ways we can effectively change the behaviour patterns that make us unhappy, unhealthy or unwise. He uses these and other questions to come up with an adaptation measure that rates the subjects as mature, neurotic, immature, or psychotic, and illustrates each method of coping with specific case histories.

In 2012, Vaillant published his second report of the men in the sequel to *Adaptation to Life*, entitled *Triumphs of Experience: Men of the Harvard Grant Study*.[13] Taking a holistic approach, the sequel also reports on different aspects of these individuals' lives – from relationships, to the subjects' political and religious affiliations and opinions, to coping strategies, and even to their alcohol usage – with alcohol abuse being, by far, the greatest contributor to the men's ill-health and unhappiness. The second volume included some surprising findings, as well. For instance, the men who coped well with life's circumstances in old age did not necessarily do so well in midlife, and vice versa. Or, while it was possible for most men in the study to recover from a lousy childhood, memories of a happy childhood could become a source of strength for the rest of one's life. Married men experienced more contentment after age 70.

Of course, the Harvard Grant Study is not without its

limitations. The most obvious limitation is that it doesn't include any women. Yet, the study offers an incredibly deep look at the lives of a subset of humanity from one university, starting at a certain period in time and continuing for 77 years by collecting data on different aspects of their lives and reporting their findings at regular intervals. Among their conclusions that appear to be universally applicable are the following:

Love is the key ingredient

Above all else, the virtue of love matters the most. It is the key to happiness. You can have all the comfort and luxuries in the world but, without love, none of that will bring lasting happiness – not a six or seven-figure income; or a fat 401k; or the number of books, articles, or blog posts you wrote; or the number of friends or followers you had on social media; or how chiselled your body is; or the number of tech companies you worked for, the rank or position to which you were raised at those organizations, or how much power you wielded there. No, the biggest predictor of your happiness and fulfilment overall in life is, basically, love.

Meaningful relationships and connections matter a great deal

Our relationships with other people, especially those who are important to us, have a significant effect on our happiness. When we are young, we tend to show immaturity, even narcissism; but, as we grow older, most of us learn to move away from self-centredness and focus more on others and the quality of our relationships. Even if we had terrible childhoods, we can still find the right coping mechanisms and get over painful past experiences. Vaillant gives the example of Mother Teresa who, despite an awful childhood and painful inner spiritual life, found strength in serving others and led an exemplary life.

Don't abuse alcohol, period

There is a strong correlation between alcohol abuse and neurosis and depression. The abuse of alcohol was the leading cause of divorce among the 268 men. Combine alcohol abuse with cigarette smoking and you will raise your chances of an early death by a significant margin.

More money and power does not mean more happiness

Job satisfaction matters a lot more than how much money you make. If you don't feel connected to your work, it won't matter how much money you make. That doesn't mean money or traditional career success don't matter – they do. In the grand scheme of things, however, they will prove to be small parts of a much larger picture. Financial and career success may loom large for us in the moment. As we grow older, though, they will diminish in importance because we will begin to view them just as pieces of a puzzle in the context of a full life. Eventually, we will come to define achievement as being content at work and satisfied with our job.

Intelligence matters, but only up to a certain point

Above a certain level, having a higher IQ does not guarantee a higher level of emotional wellbeing. The men in the Harvard Grant Study with IQs between 110 and 115 were no more or less happy than men with IQs higher than 150.

It's never too late to find happiness in life, because people can change

Being born into a rich family does not guarantee happiness in later life. The opposite, too, is true. Just because you were once miserable doesn't mean you can't be happy in later life. In fact, one of the happiest people in the Harvard Grant Study was an individual who had attempted suicide before participating in the study. So, if we use appropriate coping mechanisms, we can turn hardships into positive learning experiences and find happiness.[14] The great German composer and pianist Ludwig van Beethoven's coping mechanism was to creatively express his agitation through his art and music. The outcome was one of the most beautiful pieces of music ever written: Symphony No. 9, which is usually associated with the well-known poem, *Ode to Joy*.

Happiness-enhancing activities

In our daily lives, there is actually a wide range of activities we can choose from to enhance our happiness. Among them are the following:

1. **Recalling past pleasant experiences**

A powerful way to cultivate happiness, especially during periods of inactivity, is to focus our attention on past pleasant experiences. Reviving and reliving such experiences helps stimulate the pleasure and weaken the displeasure systems in our brain. Famous Brooklyn Dodgers baseball pitcher, Carl Erskine – who once pitched a no-hitter and struck out fourteen New York Yankees in the 1953 World Series – had a formula for overcoming pressure:

> One sermon has helped me overcome pressure better than the advice of any coach. Its substance was that, like a squirrel hoarding chestnuts, we should store up our moments of happiness and triumph so that in a crisis we can draw upon these memories for help and inspiration. As a kid, I used to fish at the bend of a little country stream just outside of my hometown. I can vividly remember this spot in the middle of a big, green pasture surrounded by tall, cool trees. Whenever tension builds up both on or off the ball field now, I concentrate on this relaxing scene, and the knots inside me loosen up.[15]

In his book, *Spiritual Intelligence*, Khalil Khavari, professor emeritus of psychology at the University of Wisconsin-Milwaukee, shares a personal experience with regard to this practice:

> One day, as I was walking from my lab to a class, as is my habit, I was meditating and focusing on pleasant thoughts and, apparently, smiling. Suddenly, a graduate student I knew approached me, said hello and grinned from ear to ear. After a couple of ordinary exchanges, he finally got the courage to ask, 'Dr Khavari, what are you on?' For a moment I didn't understand. 'What do you mean?' I asked, puzzled. He said sheepishly, 'I mean I see you smiling to yourself walking in this freezing weather.' I was slow, but I finally got what he meant by 'on'. I said, 'I'm on a marvellous drug that we all carry inside our head, but seldom use. I am working the pleasure centres of the brain by meditating and recalling pleasant memories.' I'm not sure that he believed me or even wanted to believe me. He wanted the name of the chemical he thought I was using, so that he could also walk around smiling happily in the freezing snow. He grinned sceptically, shook his head and walked away.[16]

In a study by Lyubomirsky, subjects who recalled their past pleasant experiences for eight minutes daily for three consecutive days felt more intense positive emotions four weeks later.[17] Keeping a happiness journal can be a valuable tool in systematizing this practice. In our happiness journal, we can write about our joyful experiences as they occur. Then, as a part of our happiness-enhancing practice, we can recall a couple of those experiences daily and relive them in our mind, savouring their flavour with a smile. We can also relive our joyful experiences in moments of need.

2. **Keeping a happiness journal and a happiness jar**

Keeping a happiness journal is a simple yet powerful way to enhance our happiness daily and a great tool for overcoming sadness when we are faced with tests and trials in life. To start with this practice,

HAPPINESS TECHNIQUES

Fig. 10
A happiness jar

get yourself a notebook. On the first page, you may want to write some inspiring quotes on happiness and its significance. Then begin this practice by writing about positive and joyful experiences as they occur. Make sure you put the date at the top of each page as you write in detail about your joyful experience. As you continue with this practice, feel free to go back and read about your previous positive experiences. Relive them in your mind and savour their flavor with a smile. To enhance your happiness on a regular basis, you can make reading from your happiness journal a daily practice. You can also refer back to the journal in times of sadness when it is hard to remember the happy days you once enjoyed.

Keeping a happiness jar is another happiness-enhancing technique that can be practiced individually as well as with other family members. To do this practice, get a jar and put a notepad and pen next to it. When wonderful things happen in your life, write about your experience; fold the piece of paper and put it in the jar. When the jar is full, take out all the bits of paper, then read, relive, and savour the memories you wrote down with a smile. Doing this practice with other family members who live with us can make us even happier as we share our happy experiences with them and learn about theirs.

3. Reinforcing other people's good qualities

A great deal of our happiness depends on our relationships with family, friends, colleagues at work, and others who are indispensable parts of our daily lives. To a large extent, we can choose to have positive, peaceful relationships with these individuals, or negative, confrontational ones. Since no one likes to be criticized, if we choose to overlook the negative qualities of others and focus on their positive traits instead – and perhaps even reinforce and nurture such traits – we can count on solidifying our bonds with them.

> One must expose the praiseworthy qualities of the souls and not their evil attributes . . . must overlook their shortcomings and faults and speak only of their virtues and not their defects.[18]

In our daily conversations with our loved ones, 'the more often those qualities are expressed and approved, the more likely the relationship operates on a positive note. The individual learns to become a better human being and we stand to enjoy the benefits of his or her betterment.'[19]

Therefore, one approach to living a happy life is to love and respect the best in others. How we think about people, how we treat them and how we react to them are closely linked to our own happiness.

4. Practising sympathetic joy

> True peace and tranquility will only be realized when every soul will have become the well-wisher of all mankind.[20]

Simply stated, sympathetic joy means rejoicing in the good fortune of other people. It is always easy for us to show sympathy when others are faced with misfortune. However, is it just as easy to rejoice in their happiness? For instance, when someone we know gets a job promotion, welcomes a new child, gets married, graduates from college, or is enjoying a relaxing vacation, shouldn't we take a few minutes out of our lives to reach out to that person and express our happiness? That can be a five-minute phone call, a short e-mail, a social media message, or a card in the mail. To share in others' happiness is a sign of mental and spiritual health and maturity. It is also a great way of strengthening the bonds of friendship with others and bringing joy to their hearts, which will in turn lead to our own happiness.

In her research on the science of happiness, Lyubomirsky learned that 'the happiest people take pleasure in other people's successes and show concern in the face of others' failures.'[21]

The first step in practising sympathetic joy is to stop comparing ourselves to others and their achievements in life. We should be in competition only with our own innate talents. In other words, we should continuously work on improving ourselves and trying to realize our full potential in this life.

> Let each morn be better than its eve and each morrow richer than its yesterday.[22]

Since none of us is ever sure of exactly how far we can go in life, the journey towards self-improvement will be an endless one. Therefore, if we remain solely focused on our own development, we shouldn't even have time to worry about keeping up with the Joneses next door! Now, imagine being the recipient of a message that expresses your friend's sympathetic joy for your success. How would you feel when one of your friends takes the time to express his or her joy at your success or happiness? We can also celebrate others' joy and success by remembering them in our prayers and wishing that their happiness and success continue. Metta meditation can actually be a very effective tool for cultivating sympathetic joy. It can help us overcome the human tendency to feel that there is a limited supply of joy available to humanity and that someone else may be getting our share. Practising sympathetic joy can help us develop the capacity to truly love others and feel connected to them. This will not only draw us closer to the people who are important in our lives and diminish the chance of conflict with them, but it will also help us attain inner and outer peace.

5. **Using positive affirmations**

> Whatever is true, whatever is noble, whatever is right, whatever is pure, whatever is lovely, whatever is admirable – if anything is excellent or praiseworthy think about such things. (Phil. 4:8)

The use of positive affirmations is a method of self-improvement based on optimistic autosuggestion. It was first popularized by Émile Coué, the 19th century French psychologist and pharmacist. Positive affirmations are short, powerful statements which you repeat to yourself, describing the way you want to be. They are noble goals to which you aspire in the lifelong journey to becoming a better person. One of the first and best-known affirmations comes from Coué himself: 'Every day in every way, I'm getting better and better.'

The idea behind affirmations is that, when you repeat positive affirmations, or think them, or even hear them, they will gradually become your thoughts, and those thoughts will eventually become the driving force for positive action in your life, which will bring about the desired change. In short, positive affirmations will give you the confidence you need to overcome weaknesses and turn them into areas of strength. They will give control of your mind back to you and put you in the driver's seat.

Repeating affirmations and the images they conjure up affects our subconscious mind, leading to a change in our actions and reactions, habits and behaviours. The power of this self-improvement method lies in its ability to reshape our thinking. Over time, these positive statements will become a part of our internal dialogue, alter negative beliefs and ultimately rewire the brain.

Positive affirmations can basically help re-programme the mind into believing the stated concept, because the mind doesn't know the difference between what is real and what is fantasy. When you watch a movie and you start to laugh or cry, your mind is empathizing with the characters on the screen, even though it is only Hollywood magic. Negative affirmations are as powerful as positive ones. Their destructive force can ruin lives. Many of us have been the victims or witnesses of how negative affirmations have caused serious damage to the psyche, self-confidence and self-respect of individuals. We have seen how a child is berated by a teacher, a coach or a parent as lazy, good-for-nothing, fat, clumsy, and so on. Those unpleasant statements will subsequently become the internal dialogue of the child's mind, remain in their conscious or subconscious mind, and gradually become accepted as reality, thus causing damage to the child and hindering them from realizing their full potential in life.

Today, sports figures, entertainers, public speakers, and a wide range of other groups use positive affirmations – in combination with visualization – to achieve their goals. To start this practice, you can follow the steps below:

- Choose an area of your life that needs improvement.
- Write positive statements affirming the fact that you can achieve that goal.
- Write the goal in the form of a statement in the present tense.
- Say and repeat the words as you sit in front of a mirror. Alternatively, you can close your eyes and visualize yourself living your life based on the statement.
- You can write the statement on an index card or a sticky note and leave reminders in various places around the house, such as the kitchen table, computer monitor, bathroom mirror, etc. Each time you see the reminder, read, ponder and visualize the statement.
- If you don't have time to say your affirmation daily, make a recording on your smartphone and listen to the affirmation

during your free time, or as a way to relax. You can write as many as 15 to 18 affirmations. Repeat each of the statements three times until you have completed your list. Finish your recording by saying them one more time, but this time change the 'I' to 'you'. For example, 'I am a good public speaker' becomes, 'You are a good public speaker'. You do this because 'it recognizes our need to have external validation – someone else telling us we are doing a good job'.[23] You can also add some soothing background music to the last 'you' portion of your recording, because adding music can create feelings and stimulate the imagination.

Sample affirmations

Here are some suggested affirmations:

- Life is wonderful, God is with me. Today is a day full of beautiful moments.
- I don't allow negative emotions to affect my perception of reality. I know that the circumstances of life at a given moment are not necessarily permanent; they only seem that way at that moment.
- I avoid being attached to my opinions and actions. I see God present in the things I say and do; thus, I try to do what I believe will lead to His good-pleasure.
- I always replace 'if only' thoughts with 'next time', and go on with my life peacefully.
- With God in charge of my life, I know that things will work out for the best. So, why should I worry?
- Being a positive and optimistic person, I only look at the bright side of things and know that things will always work out for the best.
- I always leave judgment to God and only focus on improving my own life and contributing to the wellbeing of my loved ones.
- To me, the best cure for worry is prayer.

- With God's help, I can handle any tough situation.
- I like who I am and I feel good about myself and what I am doing in my life to serve others.
- I always look for the best in myself and in everything around me – and the more I look, the more I find.
- I live an active and fulfilling life.
- The more I invest in my marriage, the more valuable it becomes.
- I choose to think positive and happy thoughts all day long.
- God loves me more than I can ever imagine. He is with me. He wants the best things for me. He guides and protects me.
- When someone gives me good news, I share in their excitement and practise sympathetic joy.
- I am a good listener, especially at home and with my family. I see their point of view by listening mindfully.
- I always voice my opinions in a calm and loving manner.
- I create harmony and happiness in my home.
- My life doesn't have to be perfect for me to enjoy it. I can always find happiness in any day and in any situation.
- I believe that marriage, like a garden, takes time to grow, but the harvest is rich for those of us who patiently and tenderly care for the ground.
- I live with God and talk to Him all day long. I don't do anything, however small, without talking to God and seeking His guidance and assistance.
- Today, life gives me many reasons to smile.

6. **Developing an optimistic outlook**

Optimism motivates us and leads us to take initiative. Optimists don't easily give up. This is likely one major reason that optimists are more successful across a wide variety of arenas – professional, academic, athletic, social, and even health.[24]

An optimistic attitude can add immensely to our personal happiness. Imagine you are in a gathering of friends. On one side, a discussion is taking place among those of your friends who are optimists. They see the bright side of things. They have great plans for the future, are ready to face the obstacles and are confident they will overcome them. On the other side, you have friends who are engaged in a pessimistic, depressive dialogue. They see the future as bleak, have no confidence in how their lives will unfold and worry that everything that could possibly go wrong *will* go wrong. Which conversation would you likely join? That depends on the kind of person you are. If you have a positive attitude about life in general, about yourself and your present or future, you will probably join the positive discussion. If not, you will be drawn to the other discussion, which will reinforce your own negative perception of yourself and life in general.

The fact is that our general attitude about life and about ourselves matters. It matters a lot, in fact, because it directly affects how happy or miserable we feel, day in and day out. An optimistic person always looks at the bright side of things. Their cup is always half full, while a pessimistic person cannot find the good in any situation. Their glass is always half empty. In *The Happiness Makeover*, author Ryan shares a short personal experience about mountain climbing in Utah that accentuates the contrast between an optimistic and a pessimistic outlook in a time of crisis:

> My friend and I were lost on a mountaintop in Utah. I began instantly worrying. How will we ever get down? What if we freeze to death up here? My friend was looking around saying things like, 'Look at this fabulous scenery! Isn't it breathtaking?'[25]

As noted above, optimists are generally more successful in various endeavours because they are typically more resilient and do not give up easily. They persevere despite challenges, and even defeats. This enables them to cope better with adversity. They also show more vigour and enthusiasm when facing challenges in life. Their positive attitude also helps them lead healthier physical and mental lives, have higher self-esteem and assume better control of circumstances in life.[26]

Little wonder, then, that numerous studies have shown that 'pessimism decreases immunity while optimism increases immunity.'[27] In his New York Times article, *Research Affirms Power of Positive Thinking*, Daniel Goleman, the internationally known author, psychologist and former Harvard professor, notes that:

> Optimism – at least reasonable optimism – can pay dividends as wide-ranging as health, longevity, job success and higher scores on achievement tests. Pessimism not only has the opposite effect but also seems to be at play in such psychological disorders as extreme shyness and depression.[28]

How to cultivate optimism

A highly effective, science-based strategy for developing optimism is 'The Best Possible Self Exercise'. This technique can enhance the practitioner's happiness level, optimism, hope, and coping skills.

- Sit in a quiet place.
- Calm down your mind through breathing exercises.
- Spend the next 20–30 minutes visualizing a future for yourself where things have turned out the way you have wanted.
- Imagine yourself working hard to achieve your goal over the next several months or years to reach your goal.
- Next, write down what you have imagined. The writing will help you document the process and create a logical structure for the future you planned. It will help you to 'move from the realm of foggy ideas and fragmented thoughts to concrete, real possibilities.'[29]

Here are a couple of examples:

- I can envision starting a family. We are spending quality time together vacationing and are going to activities together in the city.
- I see myself doing work that is meaningful and fills me with

a sense of purpose as I help people reach their dreams on a daily basis.

7. Using the act 'as if' principle

If you want a quality, act as if you already had it.[30]

If we are not happy and excited about life, we can act as if we are and, with practise, we can gradually get there. This idea was first suggested by the 19th century psychologist and philosopher, William James, who believed that doing things differently – rather than just talking about what we would like to do – can lead to real changes in our feelings. Therefore, if we want to be happy and excited about life, we can act as if we are excited and the feeling will follow.

The sacred literature of the world's great religions teach us that the seeds of many positive, desirable qualities – such as being loving, kind, compassionate, patient, truthful, honest, and so on – are already latent within our souls. Our success in manifesting these qualities in the outer world, however, is dependent upon receiving the proper education in a positive, nurturing family environment. Yet, when we decide to act *as if* we have those desirable qualities, the decision and the action itself will begin to bring out what is already within us. According to most sacred texts, seeking God's grace in doing such practices will always be of great importance, since nothing can be done without His assistance.

8. Grateful savouring

Grateful savouring is the ability to notice, appreciate and enhance the positive moments in our lives. In practising grateful savouring, we are not only aware of the positive experiences, but also choose to focus on them with a grateful heart and mind. Most of us have the tendency to rush through our pleasant life experiences. Learning to savour them with a grateful heart will lead to a sense of joy, peace and contentment, no matter how small the experience might be.

Savouring positive experiences and thoughts will 'teach' the brain to fall into a more naturally positive pattern. Look forward to a positive experience, relish it while it's happening, and later allow the positive feelings to re-emerge as you hold the experience in your memory.[31]

To practise grateful savouring, you can enjoy a bite of your favourite food, take a sip of your warm drink in a cold day, smell the aroma of a scented candle, feel the breeze on your face as you walk in nature, listen to the birds chirping in your backyard, become absorbed in the beauty of flowers and trees, listen to a piece of calming music, and enjoy a nice compliment or a hug with a grateful mind and heart. For instance, as you hug your child or a friend, you can not only enjoy the hug, but also think about how grateful you are for having them in your life. When you listen to the birds chirping, you can not only be absorbed in the sound, but be grateful that you can hear.

To cultivate grateful savouring as a daily habit, you can use the Notion app[32] to keep track of positive experiences as they occur throughout the day. To maximize the benefits of this practice, you can refer to your daily list each evening and relive those pleasant moments with a grateful heart.

9. Anticipating a happy day upon waking up

I am enough of an artist to draw freely upon my imagination. Imagination is more important than knowledge. Knowledge is limited. Imagination encircles the world.[33]

Human imagination is a powerful asset. Most innovations and discoveries have their roots in imagination. However, imagination can also be used as a tool for relaxation and for adding joy and happiness to life. Here is a simple exercise: When you wake up tomorrow morning, stay in bed for a few more minutes. Think of the day ahead – but think only good and positive thoughts for this practice. Imagine your day filled with positive and joyous moments. Even if you expect something negative to happen – like having a meeting with a difficult boss or co-worker – imagine the meeting will go well. End the exercise with a smile on your face. Depending on your attitude during this simple exercise, it could have a positive effect on your outlook and your attitude towards the upcoming day. Remember, you control about 40 per cent of your happiness. So, tomorrow morning, you can choose to expect either the worst or the best. Your choice will affect your thinking, your thinking will influence your behaviour, and your behaviour will produce its own unique results.

Our lives are made up of a series of days, which in turn are made up of hours and moments. If we create joy and happiness in our moments and hours, we will eventually learn to have happy and joyous days. Again, our attitude towards life matters. Indeed, it matters a lot, and it starts from the moment we wake up every morning.

Here's how your typical morning can potentially start:

Start your day by bringing a series of joyful, positive thoughts to mind: 'This is going to be a fine day. I had a great night's sleep. I am glad to be alive. First, I will enjoy a good breakfast. Then, I will enjoy the company of my loved ones before the day's work begins – and all day long, I shall have the satisfying experience of being with people, doing some good, and performing some worthwhile service.'[34]

In other words, learn to see and appreciate all the good that life has to offer, instead of all the negativity that may surround us. We all are much richer than we think. Richness has nothing to do with how much money we have in our bank accounts; it has everything to do with how much joy we experience in life's moments.

10. **Nurturing enthusiasm**

Nothing great was ever achieved without enthusiasm.[35]

Enthusiasm is a powerful human trait. It can help us accomplish great things in life. It can also help us experience life more fully and joyfully, and contributes to our lasting happiness. However, like many other human characteristics, enthusiasm should be nurtured and reinforced within us, because some of us fail to fully understand how much of a positive effect this trait can have on our success and happiness. Many of us may, at first, lack enthusiasm towards a certain goal or task in life. However, since enthusiasm is embedded within our nature, like other God-given qualities, we can cultivate it through prayer, contemplation, affirmation, and action.

If we understand the value of enthusiasm in human endeavours, we are more likely to develop or display that characteristic in our efforts. For instance, if we understand and appreciate the fact that enthusiastic people typically have more energy to accomplish goals, take calculated risks, demonstrate more creativity, show more faith, and feel driven to accomplish great goals in life, we will be able to appreciate the value of enthusiasm more fully, and try to practise it throughout our lives, not just during active years.

> Possessed of enthusiasm one is a citizen of the present regardless of how many years he has dwelt upon earth. Such a vitalized person cannot possibly become a *has-been*. He is perpetually the *is-now* type.[36]

Additionally, enthusiasm can become contagious; it can stimulate and inspire others, too. Another approach to cultivating enthusiasm is to set new goals for ourselves and then work toward achieving them.

11. Developing confidence

Unfortunately, many of us suffer from lack of confidence in life. There may be a host of reasons for this feeling. For instance, maybe our parents didn't do a particularly good job of raising us in a nurturing, healthy environment. Perhaps we have developed a tendency to compare ourselves to others and believe that we are not good enough or smart enough or pretty or handsome enough – or that we are too fat or too thin, or too tall or too short, and so on. Yet, regardless of whether there is any truth or logic to any of that, the fact remains that our self-perception should not depend on these superficial factors; rather, it should solely depend on who we really are, in our essence.

> O SON OF BEING! With the hands of power I made thee and with the fingers of strength I created thee; and within thee have I placed the essence of My light. Be thou content with it and seek naught else, for My work is perfect and My command is binding. Question it not, nor have a doubt thereof.[37]

Our self-worth as a human being should be derived from the virtue of solely being a noble creature of God in potential; someone who has been put on this planet to know our Creator, love Him and try to manifest the divine attributes that are concealed within His Reality – and live a life of service that helps carry forward an ever-advancing civilization. We can accomplish this by living a God-centred life.

> I keep the Lord always before me: because he is at my right hand, I shall not be moved. Therefore, my heart is glad, and my soul rejoices: my body also dwells secure. (Ps. 16:8–9)

Reading from the sacred texts of the world every morning and evening – and reflecting on the meaning of what we read – keeps us focused on what really matters in life, rather than trivial things. Again, we should not forget who we are in our essence, and aim high in life with lofty and noble goals.

> O SON OF SPIRIT! I created thee rich, why dost thou bring thyself down to poverty? Noble I made thee, wherewith dost thou abase thyself? Out of the essence of knowledge I gave thee being, why seekest thou enlightenment from anyone beside Me? Out of the clay of love I molded thee, how dost thou busy thyself with another? Turn thy sight unto thyself,

that thou mayest find Me standing within thee, mighty, powerful and self-subsisting.[38]

In his book, *In God We Trust*, Norman Vincent Peale suggests that we fill our minds with God during the first and last five minutes of the day:

> Psychologists have said that the first five minutes at the beginning of the day, as you wake up from sleep, and the last five minutes of the day, as you fall asleep, are extraordinarily important, because then the mind, the consciousness is in its most malleable state. The first five minutes of the day should be dedicated to God . . . Nothing bad can get in when it is packed full of God.[39]

One way to boost our confidence – which, in turn, helps with our sense of self-image – is to seek every opportunity to do what we are really good at:

> Nothing builds confidence – and with it a strong self-image – like the repetition of superior performance . . . If you have a skill – and everyone has something they do well – seize every opportunity to exercise that skill. If you bake good cookies, bake them every chance you get. If you don't need them, give them away: the thanks and praise you get will strengthen your self-image. After a somewhat shaky start many years ago, I have become a reasonably proficient public speaker. Now I draw strength and reassurance from reaching an audience, feeling people respond. It reinforces my image of myself as a person whose purpose is to help people over the rough spots in life. So practise what you do well – and draw strength and confidence from your successes.[40]

12. Enjoying the beauty of nature

Although music or an ordinary pleasing voice is of the physical realm, yet it has an effect upon the spirit. In the same manner, freshness and purity of the air, the atmosphere, the scenery and sweet fragrances impart joy, spirituality, and comfort to the heart. Even though these are physical phenomena they have a great spiritual influence.[41]

Spending time in nature and appreciating the beauty of what we see around us can also be a source of joy, gratitude and happiness. The practice can also help bring us out of ourselves and what preoccupies our minds. It can reduce negative emotions – such as fear, anger, worry, stress, and anxiety – and increase positive feelings. There is no shortage of scientific studies now that show how being surrounded by nature can 'boost the immune system, lower blood pressure, reduce stress, improve mood, increase ability to focus, accelerate recovery from illness, increase energy level, and improve sleep . . . simply looking at trees reduces the stress-related hormones cortisol and adrenaline.'[42]

Being in nature can also help us with concentration. Studies show that, 'spending time in nature, looking at plants, water, birds and other aspects of nature gives the cognitive portion of our brain a break, allowing us to focus better and renew our ability to be patient.'[43]

Nature can help pain sufferers cope better with pain, too. As we are absorbed by the beauty of nature, we tend to be distracted from our pain. This was demonstrated in a study of patients who underwent gallbladder surgery. Half had a view of trees and half had a view of a wall. According to the physician who conducted the study, Robert Ulrich, the patients with the view of trees tolerated pain better, appeared to nurses to have fewer negative effects, and spent less time in a hospital.'[44]

Taking nature breaks

One approach to spending time in nature is taking nature breaks. Regardless of what we do for a living, if we can, we should take periodic nature breaks throughout the day to rejuvenate and clear our minds. If you are not near a forest, a park or a greenbelt, use your backyard – if you have any trees, plants, shrubs, or flowers there. Alternatively, you can simply take a five-minute break to get out of the house or office to get a breath of fresh air. If you can't afford to take breaks in the middle of the morning or afternoon, at least do it in the middle of the day, during your lunch hour. Weather permitting, try to eat in nature when possible. As you go out, take a deep breath, stretch your body and look for the beauty in the nature that surrounds you, such as flowers, birds, the colour of the leaves, the branches swaying in the wind, the clouds moving across the sky, and be absorbed in their beauty.

13. Smiling and laughing

Smiling can be defined as a silent form of laughter. Regular smiling, even when we don't feel like it, is another approach to developing inner joy and peace. Smiling is an important way of bringing peace and joy not only to our own lives, but also to the lives of others. It shows that we are in control, regardless of what is happening around us.

Wearing a smile has a positive influence, even if we are feeling sad and have to pretend to generate a smile. It also affects our self-image, and all the attitudes and feelings that it entails. Furthermore, smiling fosters proper movement of blood and energy in the body for healing, and enables our brain and nervous system to better work with and regulate our internal organs.

Today, the medical field is becoming more aware of the therapeutic value of smiling, and that one's facial expression does influence one's mood:

> The mere act of smiling repetitively helps to interrupt mood disorders and strengthen the brain's neural ability to maintain a positive outlook on life.[45]

Smiling can also help alleviate both physical and psychological pain:

Dr David Bresler, a former director of the pain control unit at the University of California in Los Angeles, encourages his patients to move away from their pain by smiling. He even writes prescriptions for his patients that direct them to go to the mirror and smile twice an hour.[46]

Smiling can also help strengthen the thymus gland, 'an important contributor to a healthy immune system, because the zygomaticus major (those smile muscles) and the thymus gland are closely linked'.[47]

In the course of the day, reliving happy memories, anticipating future joyful events and practising gratitude can be great tools for triggering a smile. In addition to smiling, laughter can be a great tool for happiness.

> 100 laughs is the aerobic equivalent of 10 minutes spent rowing . . . Laughter elevates the secretion of our natural mood-enhancing catecholamine and endorphin and decreases levels of the stress hormone cortisol.[48]

According to Post:

> One reason laughter is exhilarating may be that it releases the feel-good chemical, dopamine. Researchers used brain imaging to study individuals while they looked at funny cartoons, and they found that a region of the brain with reward centres that involve dopamine was activated. The degree of humour 'intensity' was positively linked to bold signal intensity in that area of the brain.[49]

Dr Lee S. Berk, an immunologist at Loma Linda University's School of Allied Health and Medicine, and his colleagues have also studied the effects of laughter on the regulation of hormones. Their research showed that laughter can actually help the human brain regulate cortisol and epinephrine, which are known as the 'stress hormones'. They also found a connection between laughter and the production of antibodies and endorphins, which serve as natural painkillers in our bodies.[50]

Additional studies have shown that laughter can lower blood pressure, relax muscles, lead to better brain function, lower stress, dissolve anger, and enhance relationships, especially within the family. Laughter can also provide us with a healthier heart, connect us to other people, regenerate our energy, and make us feel good altogether.[51] There are many different ways we can generate laughter in our lives:

- Read jokes.
- Watch funny videos on TV or on the web.
- Take five- to ten-minute humour breaks. Look at funny memes, quotes and pictures.
- Surround ourselves with positive, funny people and avoid negative individuals as much as we possibly can.

Finally, if seeking happiness seems selfish to you, remember this quote from Ryan:

> So if happiness seems a selfish act, don't do it for yourself – do it for the effect you will have on everyone around you. By choosing to be happy day by day, we have the potential to drive emotions in the positive direction of all those around us – our children and mates, our co-workers and friends, even the people we casually stand next to on the subway. It turns out that happiness truly is contagious.[52]

14. Bringing sunshine to the lives of others

> *Those who bring sunshine to the lives of others cannot keep it from themselves.* —James Barrie

Psychologically, we can say that 'by nature we are hardwired to feel good when we do good'.[53]

When we practise kindness, we are not only improving our

own mental and even physical health, but we can also inspire others who come into contact with us to practise kindness themselves. In other words, our kindness can have a ripple effect.

So, if we are experiencing a sad day but want to overcome our negative state of mind and enjoy a better day, we can ask ourselves, 'What can I do today to make another person happy?' We can then spend some time thinking about the person we have chosen to make happy and the manner in which this can be done. We can even visualize our kind act with a smile, savouring this positive thought and its potential to bring sunshine to another person's day. Having done so, if we are keeping a Happiness Journal, we can write about our positive experience in it with a grateful heart. Here are some ideas for practising kindness if we are experiencing a sad mood:

- Call, text or e-mail a family member or a friend and say some kind and encouraging words to them.
- Call or text someone who we know is going through a hard time. Offer them words of hope and encouragement, and ask if there is anything we can do to help them.
- Visit someone we know who is in need of some comfort and care. Take them a small gift if we can.
- If we are shopping and receive great service from a sales clerk, we can express our gratitude by letting their supervisor know. This also applies to any situation where we receive a lot of care and attention from an employee, such as the doctor's office, the post office, and so on.

In the following story, the author learns that 'the way to feel better is to be someone else's blessing'.

HAPPINESS TECHNIQUES

Out of the Blue

My friend Patty once shared the story of how she got over a bad case of 'the blahs', and within her account was the best advice I have ever received. It was a simple bit of wisdom, casually conveyed, but has since become a precept I try to live by every day.

Her tale began on a gray afternoon in late February, when winter's drab skies, barren trees and numbing cold had left Patty feeling forlorn.

'I was down in the dumps and just couldn't perk up,' she recalled. 'I tried giving myself a manicure, watching a bunch of sappy rom-coms, making double-fudge brownies – nothing helped; I was stuck in the doldrums.'

Desperate to overcome the gloom, Patty decided to try 'retail therapy', but even an impromptu shopping trip left her hollow. Weary and defeated, she retreated into the comfort of her favourite coffee shop for a caffeine boost.

As Patty sat sipping a double cappuccino, she noticed an older woman walk into the cafe, struggling with a half-dozen overstuffed grocery bags. The lady looked to be about sixty, well dressed but slightly dishevelled, and something about her was vaguely familiar. Patty kept glancing over, trying to place her, and it seemed the woman was doing likewise. After a few minutes, the stranger came up to Patty's table.

'Excuse me,' she said timidly. 'I hate to bother you, but I think I've seen you at church . . .'

Of course, that was it! Patty recognized her as one of the ladies who sang in the Sunday choir. The woman introduced herself and they chatted briefly before she asked for a favour.

'My car is in the shop, but I really needed to get to the store today so I walked,' she explained, setting her bags down on the table. 'Now it looks like it's going to rain any minute. If it isn't too much trouble, would you mind giving me a ride home? It's not too far from here.'

Patty told her it wouldn't be a problem, and the two headed out to the van. Before they left the shopping centre, Patty asked if there was anywhere else she needed to go, and the woman admitted she had hoped to get a few more errands done that afternoon. In the end, their trip included a visit to the pharmacy and a stop at the dry cleaner's to pick up her husband's shirts.

And sure enough, just as they pulled into the woman's driveway, an icy sleet began drizzling down. If the woman had walked home, she would have been caught in the storm long before reaching her house. The two joked about the timing of the wicked weather, and then Patty helped carry the thankful woman's parcels inside.

'I had so much to do today. I was praying God would help me make it through,' she told Patty as the two were saying goodbye. 'You were the answer to that prayer.'

Patty smiled, hugged her and returned to the van, feeling better than she had in months. The blues were gone, replaced by a deep and dynamic jubilance. She turned on the radio and sang along with the music, her mood a complete contrast to the dismal day around her.

'I felt wonderful!' Patty exclaimed, relating the story to me. 'All the while, I had been trying to cheer myself up and nothing worked because I was going about it all wrong. That day, I realized that the way to feel better is to be someone else's blessing.'

Be someone else's blessing.

Over the years, that simple, straightforward concept has become a goal I try to meet every day. And whenever I've been fortunate enough to accomplish it, I find that helping others not only gives me a sense of purpose, but also reminds me of the many, many things I have to be thankful for in my life. There are always plenty of ways to be someone else's blessing. Some are big opportunities like volunteering at the local soup kitchen or leaving a huge tip for the server who looks exhausted and overwhelmed. Others are small gestures that can have a big impact, such as letting the frustrated driver cut into the lane, or offering kind words to the mom whose toddler is having a meltdown. Oftentimes, these actions begin a ripple effect, with one good deed setting off a chain reaction of kindness, until it's hard to tell exactly where the blessings began and knowing they may never end.[54]

Helen Steiner Rice writes:

The more you love, the more you'll find
That life is good and friends are kind
For only what we give away
Enriches us from day to day.[55]

Making others happy is conducive to our own happiness

In December, five years ago . . . I was engulfed in a feeling of sorrow and self-pity. After several years of happy married life, I had lost my husband. As the Christmas holidays approached, my sadness deepened. I had never spent a Christmas alone in all my life; and I dreaded to see this Christmas come. Friends had invited me to spend Christmas with them. But I did not feel up to any celebration. I knew I would be a wet blanket at any party. So, I refused their kind invitations. As Christmas Eve approached, I was more and more overwhelmed with self-pity. True, I should have been thankful for many things, as all of us have many things for which to be thankful.

The day before Christmas, I left my office at three o'clock in the afternoon and started walking aimlessly up Fifth Avenue, hoping that I might banish my self-pity and sadness. The avenue was jammed with happy crowds – scenes that brought back memories of happy years that were gone. I just couldn't bear the thought of going home to a lonely and empty apartment. I was bewildered. I didn't know what to do. I couldn't keep the tears back. After walking aimlessly for an hour or so, I found myself in front of a bus station. I remembered that my husband and I had often boarded an unknown bus for adventure, so I boarded the first bus I found at the station. After crossing the Hudson River and riding for some time, I heard the bus conductor say, 'Last stop, lady.' I got off. I didn't even know the name of the town. It was a quiet, peaceful little place.

While waiting for the next bus home, I started walking up a residential street. As I passed a church, I heard the beautiful song of 'Silent Night'. I went in. The church was empty except for the organist. I sat down unnoticed in one of the pews. The lights from the decorated Christmas tree made the decorations seem like myriads of stars dancing in the moonbeams. The sound of music – and the fact that I had forgotten to eat since morning – made me drowsy. I was weary, so I drifted off to sleep.

When I awoke, I didn't know where I was. I was terrified. I saw in front of me two small children who had apparently come in to see the Christmas tree. One, a little girl, was pointing at me and saying, 'I wonder if Santa Claus brought her.' These children were also frightened when I awoke. I told them that I wouldn't hurt them. They were poorly dressed. I asked them where their mother and daddy were. 'We ain't got no mother and daddy,' they said.

Here were two little orphans much worse off than I had ever been. They made me feel ashamed of my sorrow and self-pity. I showed them the Christmas tree and then took them to a drugstore and we had some refreshments, and I bought them some candy and a few presents. My loneliness vanished as if by magic. These two orphans gave me the only real happiness and self-forgetfulness that I had had in months. As I chatted with them, I realized how lucky I had been. I thanked God that all my Christmases as a child had been bright with parental love. Those two little orphans did far more for me than I did for them. That experience showed me again the necessity of making other people happy in order to be happy ourselves. I found that happiness is contagious. By giving, we receive. By helping someone and giving out love, I had conquered worry and sorrow and self-pity, and felt like a new person. And I was a new person – not only then, but in the years that followed.[56]

> The man who forgot himself in service to others, would find the joy of living . . . forget yourself by becoming interested in others. Every day do a good deed that will put a smile of joy on someone's face.[57]

HAPPINESS TECHNIQUES

God Give Me Joy

God give me joy in the common things:
In the dawn that lures, the eve that sings.
In the new grass sparkling after rain,
In the late wind's wild and weird refrain;
In the springtime's spacious field of gold,
In the precious light by winter doled.
God give me joy in the love of friends,
In their dear home talk as summer ends;
In the songs of children, unrestrained;
In the sober wisdom age has gained.
God give me joy in the tasks that press,
In the memories that burn and bless;
In the thought that life has love to spend,
In the faith that God's at journey's end.
God give me hope for each day that springs,
God give me joy in the common things! [58]

11

GRATITUDE

> Be thou happy and well pleased and arise to offer thanks to God, in order that thanksgiving may conduce to the increase of bounty.[1]

The word gratitude comes from the Latin, *grātus*, meaning 'thankful'. It has the same ancestry as the word 'grace'. That is why many cultures still 'say grace' to express gratitude before meals. Therefore, offering gratitude can be defined as a voluntary expression of thanks for a blessing or bounty we feel we have received in our lives. Most of us actually have a tendency to take for granted the many things we should be thankful for, from general health, to family, friends, and a host of other things. Focusing on those gifts can be a great antidote to feeling sorrow, envy, regret, fear, anxiety, resentment, jealousy, and a range of other negative emotions that can undermine our health and happiness.

In his book, *Today We Are Rich*, author and motivational speaker, Tim Sanders, says:

> Gratefulness will push fear and anxiety out of your consciousness. It's a powerful cleansing agent for your psyche, dissolving any resentment, jealousy and envy that clog your attitudes with emotional sludge.[2]

As we focus on what is right in our life and all that we are grateful for, we will notice that our fears, anger and other negative states of mind will gradually melt away. Gratitude also helps us overcome worry. Worry always deals with a future scenario – one that may never happen. Gratitude, on the other hand, is about the present moment, where real life happens, and it reminds us of all the wonderful things that are working for us at this moment. If we change the focus of our thinking on what we have, rather than what is missing, we will realize how rich we already are, today. Over time, this will help us develop an attitude of gratitude, which will boost our health and happiness.

Once we realize how rich we are *today*, we will be more amenable to demonstrating generosity towards others:

> The more you feel grateful, the stronger is the impulse toward giving. And the more you give, the more you get-love, friendship, a sense of purpose, and accomplishment . . . When we live with a grateful heart, we will see endless opportunities to give; a flower from the garden to a co-worker, a kind word to our child, a visit to an old person. You will know what to do.[3]

If we allow an attitude of gratitude to permeate our life, it has the potential to reshape the way we look at everything around us. It opens new vistas before our eyes that we didn't even know existed:

> Gratitude is like a flashlight. If you go out in your yard at night and turn on a flashlight, you suddenly can see what's there. It was always there, but you couldn't see it in the dark . . . You're just standing in your yard, but suddenly you realize, Oh, there's the first flower of spring struggling to emerge from the snow; Oh, there's a deer emerging from the scrub brush; Oh, there's the measuring cup you've been looking for that your daughter was using to make mud pies. It's just your ordinary old backyard, but suddenly you are filled with happiness, thankfulness and joy.[4]

There are also times when a grateful outlook can help us see the bigger picture in life, and find things or moments – seemingly ordinary and not worthy of our attention – for which we can be grateful.

In her answer to the question of what gratitude is, Sonja Lyubomirsky writes:

> [Gratitude] is wonder; it is appreciation; it is looking at the bright side of a setback; it is fathoming abundance; it is thanking someone in your life; it is thanking God; it is counting your blessings; it is savouring; it is not taking things for granted; it is being present-oriented.[5]

Robert Emmons, another leading expert on the psychology of gratitude, characterizes gratitude in these terms:

> I believe that gratitude is the best approach to life. When life is going well, it allows us to celebrate and magnify the goodness. When life is going badly, it provides a perspective by which we can view life in its entirety and not be overwhelmed by temporary circumstances. And this is what grateful people do. They have learned to transform adversity into opportunity no matter what happens, to see existence itself as a gift. Seeing life in this way requires that gratefulness be a deep and abiding aspect of a person's character, developed patiently . . .[6]

If we are open to seeing the everyday things going on around us with a sense of novelty, even awe, we will perceive more potential gratitude moments. Emmons cites a few examples of people who often render a service in our lives whom we hardly notice as unique individuals – a postal worker, a UPS driver, or a pharmacist.[7] We often take the services of these hardworking people for granted, usually because we are too preoccupied with our own lives and concerns, or have simply grown so accustomed to these services that they don't even register in our minds as things we should be grateful for. Truly, if these people were not around to help us, our lives would be noticeably more difficult to live.

Perhaps this is a good litmus test for determining what is worthy of our gratitude: if the absence of a certain thing would affect us negatively, then we should cherish the presence of that thing and be grateful for it. To quote Charles Dickens, it would be better for us to 'reflect upon [our] present blessings – of which every man has many – not on [our] past misfortunes, of which all men have some'.[8]

'Abdu'l-Bahá offered numerous reasons we should all be grateful in life:

> Do you realize how much you should thank God for His blessings? . . . We were not in the world of existence, but as soon as we were born, we found everything prepared for our needs and comfort without question on our part. He has given us a kind father and compassionate mother, provided for us two springs of salubrious milk, pure atmosphere, refreshing water, gentle breezes and the sun shining above our heads. In brief, He has supplied all the necessities of life although we did not ask for any of these great gifts. With pure mercy and bounty, He has prepared this great table. It is a mercy which precedes asking. There is another kind of mercy, which is realized after questioning and supplication. He has bestowed both upon us – without asking and with supplication. He has created us in this radiant century, a century longed for and expected by all the sanctified souls in past periods. It is a blessed century; it is a blessed day. The philosophers of history have agreed that this century is equal to one hundred past centuries. This is true from every standpoint. This is the century of science, inventions, discoveries and universal laws.[9]

Real gratitude and lip service

'Abdu'l-Bahá once made an important distinction between thanks offered in the form of lip service and expressions of genuine gratitude. Concerning the former, he said:

> Thankfulness is of various kinds. There is a verbal thanksgiving which is confined to a mere utterance of gratitude. This is of no importance because perchance the tongue may give

thanks while the heart is unaware of it. Many who offer thanks to God are of this type, their spirits and hearts unconscious of thanksgiving. This is mere usage, just as when we meet, receive a gift and say thank you, speaking the words without significance. One may say thank you a thousand times while the heart remains thankless, ungrateful. Therefore, mere verbal thanksgiving is without effect.[10]

What, then, constitutes real, sincere gratitude? According to 'Abdu'l-Bahá, we demonstrate true thankfulness through actions:

> But real thankfulness is a cordial giving of thanks from the heart. When man in response to the favors of God manifests susceptibilities of conscience, the heart is happy, the spirit is exhilarated. These spiritual susceptibilities are ideal thanksgiving.
> There is a cordial thanksgiving, too, which expresses itself in the deeds and actions of man when his heart is filled with gratitude. For example, God has conferred upon man the gift of guidance, and in thankfulness for this great gift certain deeds must emanate from him. To express his gratitude for the favors of God man must show forth praiseworthy actions. In response to these bestowals he must render good deeds, be self-sacrificing, loving the servants of God, forfeiting even life for them, showing kindness to all the creatures.[11]

The effects of gratitude

In his seminal work, *Gratitude Works!*, Robert Emmons explains how gratitude allows us to develop positive feelings and character traits, and mitigate the corrosive influence of negative qualities:

> Gratitude has one of the strongest links to mental health and satisfaction with life of any personality trait – grateful people experience higher levels of positive emotions such as joy, enthusiasm, love, happiness, and optimism, and gratitude as

a discipline protects us from the destructive impulses of envy, resentment, greed, and bitterness.[12]

Emmons goes on to say that, 'Experiencing gratitude leads to increased feeling of connectedness, improved relationships, and even altruism. When people experience gratitude, they feel more loving, more forgiving, and closer to God.'[13] Emmons also provides the following list of benefits that gratitude can offer[14]:

- Increased feelings of energy, alertness, enthusiasm and vigour.
- Success in achieving personal goals.
- Improved ability to cope with stress.
- Increased feelings of self-worth and self-confidence.
- Solidified and secure social relationships.
- Generosity and helpfulness.
- Prolonging of the enjoyment produced by pleasurable experiences.
- Improved cardiac health through increases in vagal tone.
- Greater sense of purpose and resilience.

In *The How of Happiness*, Sonja Lyubomirsky has identified the following eight ways gratitude boosts happiness[15]:

1. Grateful thinking promotes the savouring of positive life experiences.
2. Expressing gratitude bolsters self-worth and self-esteem.
3. Gratitude helps people cope with stress and trauma.
4. The expression of gratitude encourages moral behaviour.
5. Gratitude can help build social bonds.
6. Expressing gratitude tends to inhibit invidious comparisons with others.
7. The practice of gratitude may diminish or deter feelings like anger, bitterness and greed.
8. Gratitude helps us thwart hedonic adaptation.

The benefits of expressing gratitude are not secrets that have only recently been unearthed. Some of the most eminent sages of past eras have also recognized the importance of this constructive practice. For instance, as far back as 6th century BCE, the character trait of gratitude is glorified, even in a wild animal such as a lion in the classic fable, *Androcles*:

> A slave named Androcles once escaped from his master and fled to the forest. As he was wandering about there he came upon a Lion lying down moaning and groaning. At first he turned to flee, but finding that the Lion did not pursue him, he turned back and went up to him. As he came near, the Lion put out his paw, which was all swollen and bleeding, and Androcles found that a huge thorn had got into it, and was causing all the pain. He pulled out the thorn and bound up the paw of the Lion, who was soon able to rise and lick the hand of Androcles like a dog. Then the Lion took Androcles to his cave, and every day used to bring him meat from which to live. But shortly afterwards both Androcles and the Lion were captured, and the slave was sentenced to be thrown to the Lion, after the latter had been kept without food for several days. The Emperor and all his Court came to see the spectacle, and Androcles was led out into the middle of the arena. Soon the Lion was let loose from his den, and rushed bounding and roaring towards his victim. But as soon as he came near to Androcles he recognized his friend, and fawned upon him, and licked his hands like a friendly dog. The Emperor, surprised at this, summoned Androcles to him, who told him the whole story. Whereupon the slave was pardoned and freed, and the Lion let loose to his native forest.[16]

According to Aesop, the author of *Androcles*, the moral of his fable is that gratitude is a sign of a noble soul. In the New Testament, we are instructed to give thanks in all circumstances. (1 Thess. 5:18)

The science behind gratitude

Science has just recently begun to corroborate the positive effects of sustained gratitude, as well as the best practices for 'exercising the gratitude muscle', so to speak. For instance, a 1995 study undertaken by Dr Rollin McCarthy, director of research for the Institute of Heart Math, in Boulder Creek, California, found that just five minutes of gratitude can shift the nervous system to a calm state. His study found that when we were in a state of appreciation and gratefulness, our body was in a more efficient energy state, whereas in stressful situations, emotions such as anger, frustration and anxiety would lead to erratic behaviour in our heart rhythms.[17]

If the practice of showing gratitude is longer than five minutes, the effects will increase proportionately. This was demonstrated in another study by McCarthy, in which a fifteen-minute focus on appreciation led to an immediate and considerable increase in levels of secretory IgA, an immune antibody. This antibody is one of the body's chief defences against invading microbes. When this fifteen-minute gratitude practice was maintained on a daily basis and extended to a full month, 30 of the participants showed a 100 per cent increase in dehydroepiandrosterone (DHEA) – a powerful and beneficial hormone – as well as a 30 per cent reduction in cortisol, the notorious stress hormone.[18]

One well-known undertaking, known as the 'Nun Study', yielded an interesting finding about the extent to which having a positive attitude has the potential to increase quality of life in one's later years. The lead researcher of this longitudinal study, David Snowdon, examined the autobiographies of several nuns who participated in the study, and found that those who described people, places and events using more positive words and emotions – including gratitude and contentment – generally lived longer than their more negative counterparts.[19] One corollary to this finding is the possibility that having a positive outlook on life can also play a role in the fight against dementia. The Nun Study is still ongoing, so time will tell whether this will prove to be yet

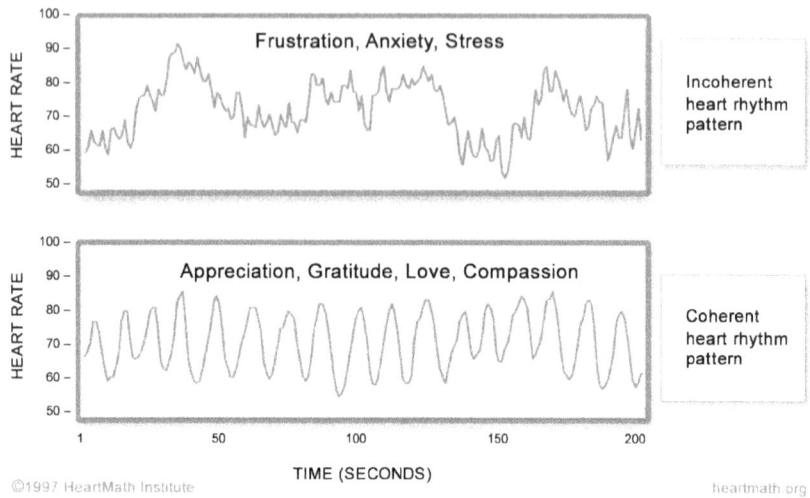

Fig. 11
The Heart Rhythm
(© HeartMath Institute)

another benefit – among the many others already borne out by science – of having an attitude of gratitude.

In his book, *Thanks!: How the New Science of Gratitude Can Make You Happier*, Robert Emmons explains the relationship between gratitude and happiness:

> Gratitude, we have found, maximizes the enjoyment of the good – our enjoyment of others, of God, of our lives. Happiness is facilitated when we enjoy what we have been given, when we 'want what we have'. Gratitude elevates, it energizes, it inspires, it transforms. People are moved, opened, and humbled through experiences and expressions of gratitude.[20]

Finally, according to Emmons, when we experience positive feelings such as gratitude, compassion and love, our heart 'produces coherent or smooth rhythms that enhance communication between the heart and brain' (see Fig. 11).[21]

Practising gratitude

> Both abundance and lack exist simultaneously in our lives, as parallel realities. It is always our conscious choice which secret garden we will tend . . . when we choose not to focus on what is missing from our lives but are grateful for the abundance that's present – love, health, family, friends, work, the joys of nature and personal pursuits that bring us pleasure – the wasteland of illusion falls away and we experience heaven on earth.[22]

As we begin to look for things in our lives to be thankful for and gradually cultivate an attitude of gratitude within ourselves, we will begin to appreciate simple pleasures and things we used to take for granted. Thus, we will not only notice the little 'gifts' that come our way daily, but we will also look for the good, even in undesirable situations. Here are some ways to cultivate the attitude of gratitude in our lives:

Keeping a gratitude journal

It will be a lot easier to know what deserves our appreciation if we can actually identify specific things or events we are grateful for. Keeping a gratitude journal can be a great help here. To keep a gratitude journal, at the end of the day, write a list of at least five things for which you are grateful. This list can include things that brought you joy over the course of the day, such as people, events, and the like.

As you list these items, associate them with the word 'gift'. For example, I am thankful to God for the gift of faith, the gift of my family, the gift of my friends, or the gift of the opportunity of service which brings happiness to my heart. As we write about each gift, we can savour it in our imagination. Those who keep a gratitude journal may find themselves jotting down mental notes of additional items to include in their list throughout the day.[23]

The Buddha once spoke of 'cultivating the mind'. By shifting your primary focus to positive events rather than negative ones, you can begin to cultivate a strong sense of gratitude and continue to develop it until it becomes second nature to you. Our thoughts are what we become, as the old adage goes. If we choose to preoccupy ourselves with negative thoughts, we will see the world through a jaded lens, but if we put a premium on the positive things in life, then we will start to recognize them more readily and treasure their priceless value.

Robert Emmons notes some additional benefits of sustained gratitude journaling:

> By writing each day, we magnify and expand on these sources of goodness. Setting aside time on a daily basis to recall moments of gratitude associated with even mundane or ordinary events, personal attributes one has, or valued people one encounters has the potential to weave together a sustainable life theme of gratefulness just as it nourishes a fundamentally affirming life stance.[24]

One study showed that counting blessings once a week resulted in significant emotional and health benefits, and helped participants feel happier by a full 25 per cent over other participants.[25] It is not difficult to imagine why this is the case. After all, gratitude journaling helps us savour positive life experiences and situations by recreating them in a concrete way that can be consulted again later – perhaps at a time when we feel that happiness and fortune have abandoned us. In so doing, a fundamental shift in our mindset takes place – one that moves away from what is lacking and orients itself towards what we already have.

In addition, research has shown that consistently writing in a gratitude journal can help people – even those who are chronically ill – sleep better, feel happier, more optimistic, and more connected to others.[26] Research has also demonstrated that gratitude is the kind of gift that keeps on giving. One act of gratitude encourages another and creates a circle of reciprocal love.[27]

Indeed, science is also beginning to unearth the neurological dynamic at play whenever we express gratitude:

> We know that dopamine and serotonin circulating in certain regions of the brain are related to happiness and other pleasurable feelings. A number of converging lines of evidence indicate that the neurotransmitter dopamine is required for the short-term perception and expression of gratitude . . . Dopamine juices the joy we experience when we celebrate goodness from reflecting on what is in our gratitude journals. Dopamine release does occur during periods of grateful feelings.[28]

In his book, Emmons relays the following:

> A nurse who attended a gratitude workshop that I led told me that the day after the workshop her husband was laid off at work. She said he usually gets severely depressed when events of this magnitude happen. Every morning they have devotionals or 'quiet time' together, and so she told him about the benefit of writing blessings.
>
> She wrote three and he wrote three and then they shared them with each other.
>
> After doing that for about three weeks, he began job hunting and his mood became much more optimistic. She couldn't believe the difference in him. Even their friends said to her, 'What's with your husband – why isn't he depressed?' Shortly thereafter, he secured a good position.
>
> In treating depression, we need to emphasise on building positive thoughts. By practising gratitude, attention is directed away from the self and more to others and what they are providing for us.[29]

Gratitude journaling clearly has a positive effect on those who are willing to engage in it with an open mind and serious resolve.

Emmons offers several tips for effective gratitude journaling:

- Seek gratitude density. Be specific. Go for depth over breadth. Give details for each entry. The journal is more than just a list of stuff.
- Try to include some surprise. What unexpected blessings did you benefit from today? What were you dreading that did not happen?
- Use the language of gifts. Think of the benefits you received today as gifts. Relish and savour the gifts you have been given.
- Think about the people to whom you are grateful and why. Who deserves your thanks? What have you received or are receiving from them?
- Think about and then write down those aspects of your life that you are prone to take for granted. Instead, take them as granted.
- Let your gratitude last a long time. It is OK to repeat a blessing day after day. But do elaborate on each blessing; give details.
- Don't only journal about people who helped you, but also about those who have helped people whom you love. We may overlook these sources of gratitude.
- Be grateful for the negative outcomes that you avoided, escaped, prevented, or redeemed into something positive.[30]

Expressing gratitude to another person

> To speak gratitude is courteous and pleasant, to enact gratitude is generous and noble, but to live gratitude is to touch Heaven.[31]

If someone has done something to brighten your life or enrich it in some way, you may want to show them how grateful you are for it. That expression of gratitude will make them feel appreciated. It will also make you feel good. Theodore Roosevelt had an interesting custom to this effect. Whenever he left his private train, he was in the habit of stopping to 'thank the engineer and fireman for a safe and comfortable trip. It took but a fraction of a minute of his time, but he had two more friends for the rest of his life.'[32]

There are a number of ways to express gratitude. One common way is to give the person a phone call. If you're feeling especially grateful to them, you could get them a small gift. But perhaps the most time-honoured method is writing a letter. And although it would usually be nice to let the person on the other end know how you feel, there are times when what you're feeling is so detailed or so intimate, that you're not sure how they will take it. In those cases, we can find solace in the results from one study, which indicate that the mere act of writing the gratitude letter – without actually sending it – can be enough to significantly increase the writer's level of happiness.[33]

When we express our appreciation to others for their help, not only will we feel good, but we will also reinforce the virtue of kindness in them.

> Two of the most joy-filled people I know are Joel and Michelle Levey. They seem literally to glow from the inside with the light of vitality and love. One of the greatest things about them is how exquisitely they give thanks for whatever is done for them. I've seen the letter they sent to their publicist after a recent book tour. They thanked her so eloquently and personally that she cried. When I asked them about the letter, they said they make it a habit to thank in writing people who treat them well. 'In our professional corporate work,' they write, 'we really value the help and support of reliable, qualified, capable people.' So they not only let the person know how grateful they are, but they tell the person's boss as well.
>
> As a consequence of such a practice, wherever they go, Joel and Michelle leave a trail of happiness, from the ticket agent at Alaska Airlines; to the waitress who served them with a smile; and the mechanic who fixed their car. Because they try not to

take anything for granted, their eyes are open to the gift in the most ordinary situations, and by thanking people for those gifts, they spread the gift around.[34]

Arrange weekly gratitude sessions

When possible, schedule a weekly gratitude session at home with other members of your family. This practice can help bring together all the members in a spirit of gratitude, unity and love. If you are religious or spiritual, you can start your weekly gratitude sessions with prayers, and perhaps even read and reflect on inspiring passages from the sacred literature of different religions of the world. Then, each member of the group can name or talk about the things that happened to them in the course of the past week for which they are grateful.

Keep a gratitude box

An alternative to talking about the things for which we are grateful is to keep a gratitude box (see Figs. 12 & 13). To do this, get a nice box and put it where the whole family can see. Put a notepad and a pen next to the box. In this daily practice, at the end of the day, each member of the family writes one thing that has happened to them in that particular day for which they are grateful. It can range anywhere from receiving good grades in school to a nice conversation with a friend, and so forth. Then, just like the weekly gratitude session, the whole family can come together at the end of the week, and – having said some prayers to get into the right frame of mind for gratefulness – the shuffled notes are distributed among the different family members, who take turns reading each note. A member of the family can then collect the notes and keep them in a bag. During the last session of the year, you can bring back the pile of the notes, and spend the first few minutes reading ten or more of the notes from the previous year. This will help you remember and reminisce about all the 'gifts' for which your entire family should be grateful during the year that is coming to a close.

GRATITUDE

Fig. 12
The authors' Gratitude Box

Fig. 13
Closeup of the authors' Gratitude Box

Both the weekly gratitude and gratitude box practices continue to be among our own family's most favourite approaches.

Gratitude mug

An easy yet powerful way to cultivate gratitude is the use of a gratitude mug as a reminder for the things we are grateful for daily. These days, thanks to a growing interest in the practice of gratitude for better mental, spiritual and physical health, we can find various items with positive messages of gratitude available for purchase.

A friend of ours told us about her practice with a gratitude mug with the words 'Filled with Gratitude' she received once on Mother's Day. To cultivate an attitude of gratitude in her family, she decided to put the mug above her kitchen sink so the whole family can see it frequently, as they cook or do the dishes. She says that sometimes she uses the mug as a vase and puts fresh flowers in it to brighten her kitchen. Each time they see the mug, family members can ask themselves: 'What am I grateful for now, at this moment'? She says it is always easy to find at least one thing she or her family members are grateful for at such moments. This practice continues to make her and her family more conscious of the many gifts and blessings in their lives.

Throw a gratitude party

Many of us arrange or participate in a wide range of parties, from birthday parties to anniversary parties to office parties. Yet, hardly anyone among us thinks of throwing a gratitude or appreciation party for someone who is dear to us. Think of your parents, siblings, friends, teachers, or anyone you want to honour. Then, surprise them with a gratitude party. It is a wonderful way to show your appreciation for all they have done for you. The celebration can include the guest of honour's favourite dinner, cards with heartfelt messages or poetry, small gifts, their favourite cake, even a banner welcoming them to their gratitude party. When our family arranged a gratitude party to honour someone who is very dear to all of us, it brought her much joy and left us all feeling wonderful for many days. The party included a humorous slide show of some of the more memorable events in her life, as well as pictures of her with children and grandchildren. After the party, she said that for those hours, she felt as if she was in heaven.

Have a 'Day of Gratitude' each week

We can set aside one day of the week and call it the Day of Gratitude. For our family, it is Sundays, since we have the whole family together. We start the day with gratitude prayers and contemplate on gratitude-related divine verses. Then, as we go through the day, we try to find things in everyone we meet and every situation to be grateful for. In other words, it is a day when we are more aware of every 'gift' that comes our way. Gradually, we will start to notice that the practice is becoming second nature to us and we will eventually begin to extend our one day of gratitude to multiple days during a week.

Take gratitude breaks

Taking frequent breaks at the office and home is becoming more typical. One way you can spend at least some of those short breaks is to make them gratitude breaks. As we said earlier, science has shown that spending just five minutes of gratitude can shift our nervous system toward a calm state.[35]

Therefore, next time you are taking your five-minute break at home or at work, bring to mind and relish one thing in your life for which you feel particularly grateful. Spend the rest of the five minutes listening to some soothing music or, if you choose to go for a short walk, practise *grateful awareness* and become fully absorbed in the nature around you. Enjoy the beauty of the trees or flowers you walk by, or the clouds as they move across the sky above you. Alternatively, you can spend the entire five minutes recalling and savouring the things for which you feel grateful at that particular time in your life, having a smile on your face all the while.

Practising gratitude as a tool to overcome low moods

Sometimes, going over all the blessings and gifts in our lives can help us overcome sadness. A friend once told us of her experience with this practice. She said that one day she took her father to a doctor's office for some tests. As she was sitting in the waiting area, she felt that little by little her mood was changing. It was as if a cloud of sorrow was gradually covering the sky of her mind. She didn't know what to do and was worried that when the doctor would want to talk with her she might burst into tears. Then, a positive thought came to her mind. What if she started counting her blessings, focusing on all the things that were right in her life and being grateful for them? So, she began reviewing those things, one after another. The more time she spent on that practice, the better she began to feel. By the time her father's tests were done, she was all smiles. She spoke with her father and his doctor with joy and peace beyond what she could have imagined 30 minutes earlier.

So, the next time you feel down, think about all the gifts and blessings in your life and see if the practice will help you feel better.

Gifts of the Year notebook

As we go through the journey of life, we are faced with many ups and downs. Life gives us both tests and trials, as well as beautiful moments that fill our hearts with a deep sense of gratitude. What if, at the end of each year, we look back at our lives and try to remember the blessings that came our way that year? After contemplating and savouring the gifts of that year, we can write about them in a small notebook and call it Gifts of the Year. This practice opens our eyes to many gifts that each year brings us, thus changing our focus from what we didn't receive to all that we did receive in the course of that particular year.

Send gratitude letters

Norman Vincent Peale includes a story about a gratitude letter in one of his books, *How to Be Your Best*. The story involves William L. Stidger, a professor of theology, who, in Peale's words, was 'in his time, one of the most distinctive and persuasive preachers in this country'.[36] At one time, Stidger had a nervous breakdown, which lasted for months. During that time, he would sit in abysmal gloom and mental darkness. He eventually became inspired to write to his high school literature teacher – who had made a profound impression on him and had kindled his interest in the poet, Alfred Lord Tennyson, to express his appreciation for everything she had done for him. He sent the letter and his teacher responded very positively. The reaction Stidger's letter elicited from his former teacher, and the delightful feeling brought on by the appreciation Stidger was expressing while writing that letter, moved him to make a whole list of people who had made a significant impression on him or an important contribution to his life and to devise a plan to send a similar letter every Thanksgiving Day in November. That changed Stidger's life forever. Below is the full story in Peale's own words.

Gratitude

I remember the description he [Stidger] gave me of this nervous breakdown. He said, 'I cared nothing about anything. Everything was hopeless, everything was dark, everything was black – utter despondency.' And how do you think he emerged from this? By the practice of thanksgiving. One day, a friend told him that, with God's help, he could bring himself out of his despondency by practising thanksgiving. And this friend suggested the manner in which he might go about it. 'Think', he said, 'of people who have greatly benefited you in your life, and ask yourself the question whether you have ever thanked them.'

'I can think of many right away, but I do not recall having ever thanked a one of them,' Stidger said. 'Well,' his friend suggested, 'why don't you select one of them and write that person an affectionate letter of thanks?'

Stidger gave it some thought, and he remembered an old school teacher. Let us call her Miss Smith. He hadn't communicated with her in years, but he began to think about her. And he remembered the gift she had of being able to inspire. It was she who had given him an appreciation of literature and made him love the great poets (I never knew a man who could recite quite as much poetry – deeply meaningful poetry). So he sat down and wrote her a letter, telling her that her influence had been a great blessing to him and that he had never forgotten her. He wrote that he wanted to thank her for what she had done for him.

He received, in reply, a letter written in the shaky handwriting of an aged lady. 'Dear Willy,' she wrote, addressing him by the nickname used in his boyhood. 'When I read your letter, I was blinded with tears, for I remember you as a boy and, as I think of you, now, I see you as a little fellow in my class. You have warmed my old heart.' And she continued: 'I taught school for fifty years. Yours is the first letter of thanks I have ever received from a student, and I shall cherish it until I die.'

This brought a ray of sunshine into Stidger's mind, and encouraged him to try another letter of appreciation, and another, and another, until he had written 500 such letters! In the years that followed, whenever depression began to seize him, he would take out his copies of the letters of thanks he had written to people, and the happiness he had experienced in doing it would well up in his heart once again.[37]

Gratitude Poem
by Ralph Waldo Emerson

FATHER IN HEAVEN, WE THANK THEE

For flowers that bloom about our feet,
For tender grass, so fresh and sweet,
For song of bird and hum of bee
For all things fair we hear or see –
Father in heaven, we thank Thee!

For blue of stream, for blue of sky,
For pleasant shade of branches high,
For fragrant air and cooling breeze,
For beauty of the blowing trees
Father in heaven, we thank Thee!

For mother-love, for father-care,
For brothers strong and sisters fair,
For love at home and school each day,
For guidance lest we go astray –
Father in heaven, we thank Thee!

For thy dear, everlasting arms;
That bear us o'er [over] all ills and harms,
For blessed words of long ago,
That help us now Thy will to know –
Father in heaven, we thank Thee![38]

12

DAILY PRACTICES FOR CULTIVATING A SPIRITUAL ATTITUDE

The practices in this section of the book provide a daily schedule throughout the week to cultivate a spiritual attitude that can lead to living a more peaceful and happier life. The reader is encouraged to focus on one key virtue each day of the week. This can be done by first contemplating on the importance of the virtue and then practising it throughout the day.

As the virtues of *gratitude* and *love* are fundamental to living a happier life, more than one day a week is devoted to practising and cultivating these two qualities.

DAILY PRACTICES FOR CULTIVATING A SPIRITUAL ATTITUDE

Sunday – The Day of Gratitude

Verse for contemplation

> Be thou happy and well pleased and arise to offer thanks to God, in order that thanksgiving may conduce to the increase of bounty.
> 'Abdu'l-Bahá, *Tablets of Abdul-Baha Abbas*, vol. II, p. 483

For additional verses, please visit the 'Gratitude' section of the Cyber Temple website, at:
https://www.cyber-temple.org/gratitude.html.

Practices for the day

- Start the day with contemplation on a sacred verse about gratitude (see the link above). Read the verse a few times. See what it means to you, and think about how you can practise gratitude today.

- Hold a gratitude session with your family (see Chapter 11 above).

- Give compliments and express genuine appreciation to others. Encourage their good deeds by acknowledging them.

- Look for gratitude moments. Say to yourself 'This is a **GRATITUDE MOMENT. Let me savour it.**'

- Practise enjoying the beauty of nature with a sense of gratitude (see Chapter 10 above, 'Happiness-enhancing activities', no. 12).

Monday – The Day of Love

Verse for contemplation

> O FRIEND! In the garden of thy heart plant naught but the rose of love.
>
> Bahá'u'lláh, *Hidden Words*, Persian no. 3

For additional verses, please visit the 'Love' section of the Cyber Temple website, at:
https://www.cyber-temple.org/love.html.

Practices for the day

- Start the day with contemplation on a sacred verse about love (see the link above). Read the verse a few times. See what it means to you, and think about how you can practise love and kindness today.

- All through the day, be kind to yourself and others in your thoughts, words, and actions.

- Throughout the day, send 'metta' periodically to the people around you. Do this during heavy traffic, meetings, waits and delays at the store, and doctor's appointments, or at the airport, subway, bus stations, or when someone cuts you off while driving. Your time will go by faster, and you will feel much better (for more information, see Chapter 7).

DAILY PRACTICES FOR CULTIVATING A SPIRITUAL ATTITUDE

Tuesday – The Day of Peace and Tranquillity

Verse for contemplation

Better than a thousand useless verses is a single verse that gives peace.
Dhammapada 8:100–101

For additional verses, please visit the 'Peacefulness' section of the Cyber Temple website, at:
https://www.cyber-temple.org/peacefulness.html.

Practices for the day

- Start the day with contemplation on a sacred verse about peacefulness (see the link above). Read the verse a few times. See what it means to you, and think about how you can practise peace and tranquillity today.

- Make this a **day of mindfulness.** Do everything mindfully, from washing your hands and face, to driving your car, doing house chores, eating your meals, communicating with others, and so on.

- Choose at least one of the following meditation techniques, and practise it even if it is only for five minutes (for more information, see Chapter 7):

    - Single-object meditation (candle or flower)
    - Breath awareness and Insight meditations
    - Mantra meditation or writing

Wednesday – The Day of Joy and Enthusiasm

Verse for contemplation

> Joy gives us wings! In times of joy our strength is more vital, our intellect keener ... But when sadness visits us, our strength leaves us.
>
> 'Abdu'l-Baha, *The Divine Art of Living*, p. 55

For additional verses, please visit the 'Joyfulness' section of the Cyber Temple website at :
https://www.cyber-temple.org/joyfulness.html.

Practices for the day

- Start the day with contemplation on a sacred verse about joyfulness (see the link above). Read the verse a few times. See what it means to you, and think about how you can practise joyfulness today.

- Anticipate a happy day upon waking up. Tell yourself, 'This is going to be a great day.'

- Practise smiling, whether you are alone or with others.

- All through the day, notice and savour positive moments. For instance, listen to the sound of a bird chirping as you go for a walk, become absorbed in the beauty of a flower blooming in your backyard, feel the warm water on your body as you take a shower, or enjoy the taste of your favorite food, the aroma of your tea or coffee, the hug you receive from a loved one, a nice compliment you get at work for a job well done, and so forth.

- Choose at least one of the following happiness-enhancing practices:

DAILY PRACTICES FOR CULTIVATING A SPIRITUAL ATTITUDE

- Recall past pleasant experiences (see see Chapter 10 above, 'Happiness-enhancing activities', no. 1)
- Watch funny videos
- Take a humour break to look at funny memes, quotes, and pictures

Thursday – The Day of Gratitude

Verse for contemplation

> What is to come is better for you than what has gone before; for your Lord will certainly give you, and you will be content . . . Keep recounting the favors of your Lord.
>
> *Qur'án* 93:1–11

For additional verses, please visit the 'Gratitude' section of the Cyber Temple website, at:

https://www.cyber-temple.org/gratitude.html.

Practices for the Day

- Start the day with contemplation on a sacred verse about gratitude (see the link above). Read the verse a few times. See what it means to you, and think about how you can practise gratitude today.

- Practise grateful awareness. Become aware of God's beauty in flowers, trees, birds, and other things in nature. Praise and thank Him for His gifts in nature and for the ability to enjoy them.

- Write in your gratitude journal (see Chapter 11).

- Take at least one gratitude break by asking yourself, 'What am I grateful for now, at this moment?'

Friday – The Day of Love

Verse for contemplation

> In the world of existence there is indeed no greater power than the power of love.
> 'Abdu'l-Bahá, *Paris Talks*, p. 179

For additional verses, please visit the 'Love' section of the Cyber Temple website, at:

https://www.cyber-temple.org/love.html.

Practices for the day

- Start the day with contemplation on a sacred verse about love (see the link above). Read the verse a few times. See what it means to you, and think about how you can practise love and kindness today.

- All through the day, be kind to yourself and others in your thoughts, words, and actions.

- Practise celebratory love meditation, even if it is only for five minutes (for more information, see Chapter 7).

Saturday – The Day of Positivity and Optimism

Verse for contemplation

> Whatever is true, whatever is noble, whatever is right, whatever is pure, whatever is lovely, whatever is admirable—if anything is excellent or praiseworthy, think about such things.
> Philippians 4:8

For additional verses, please visit the 'Faith' section of the Cyber Temple website, at:
https://www.cyber-temple.org/faith.html.

Practices for the day

- Start the day with contemplation on a sacred verse on faith (see the link above). Read the verse a few times. See what it means to you, and think about how you can practise faith today.

- Repeat the following affirmation a few times: 'Life is wonderful. God is with me. Today is a day full of beautiful moments.' Then, go on to create many beautiful moments.

- Fill your conversations with positive, happy, and optimistic words.

- Watch your media diet. Today, choose what is positive, entertaining, informative, and thought-provoking, and avoid the negative, violent, depressing, and destructive. An unhealthy diet of greed, violence, fear, anxiety, and worry leads to the growth of the same negative qualities in our minds (see Chapter 9).

- Read and reflect on the Optimist Creed (see Chapter 9).

BIBLIOGRAPHY

'Abdu'l-Bahá. *Compilation of Compilations (compiled by the Research Department of the Universal House of Justice)*, vol. II, Mona Vale: Bahá'í Publications Australia, 1991.
— *Foundations of World Unity,* Wilmette, IL: Bahá'í Publishing Trust, 1979.
— *Paris Talks*, Wilmette, IL: US Bahá'í Publishing Trust, 2006.
— *Selections from the Writings of 'Abdu'l-Bahá*, Haifa: Bahá'í World Centre, 1978.
— *Star of the West, 1913*. Vols. IV, no. 11. Oxford: George Ronald, 1978.
— *Tablets of 'Abdu'l-Bahá Abbas*, Wilmette, IL: US Bahá'í Publishing Trust, 1909.
— *The Promulgation of Universal Peace*, Wilmette, IL: US Bahá'í Publishing Trust, 1982.
— *The Secret of Divine Civilization*. Wilmette, IL: US Bahá'í Publishing Trust, 1990.
Adioma. *9 Types Of Intelligence – Infographic*. n.d. See: <https://blog.adioma.com/9-types-of-intelligence-infographic/>.
Allen, Kimberly Jordan. *Is Meditation the Key to Reducing Racial Bias?* n.d. See: <http://www.sonima.com/meditation/reducing-racial-bias/>.
Androcles. *Æsop. (Sixth century BC) Fables*, n.d. See: <https://www.bartleby.com/17/1/23.html>.
Anonymous. 'University of Minnesota: Taking Charge of Your Health & Wellbeing. How Does Nature Impact Our Wellbeing?' See: <https://www.takingcharge.csh.umn.edu/how-does-nature-impact-our-wellbeing>.
Astin, John A. et al. 'The Efficacy of "Distant Healing": A Systematic Review of Randomized Trials', in *Annals of Internal Medicine,* vol. 132.11, (June 6, 2000), pp. 903–10.
Bahá'u'lláh. *Áthár-i-Qalam-i-A'lá, vol. 6,* pp. 194–7. Vol. 6. Ṭihrán: Mu'assisiy-i-Millíy-i-Maṭbú'át-i-Amrí, 132 BE [1975]. (Translated by

Adib Masumian), <https://adibmasumian.com/translations/desire-of-the-world/>.
— *Gleanings from the Writings of Bahá'u'lláh*, Wilmette, IL: US Bahá'í Publishing Trust, 1976.
— *Iqtidarat va Chand Lawh-i-Digar ['Tokens of Power' and Some Other Tablets]*, Cairo, Egypt: Maṭbúʻát as-Saʻádah, 1924.
— *Prayers and Meditations*, Wilmette, Illinois: US Bahá'í Publishing Trust, 2013.
— *The Seven Valleys and the Four Valleys*, Wilmette, IL: US Bahá'í Publishing Trust, 1991.
— *Tabernacle of Unity*, Haifa: Bahá'í World Centre, 2006.
— *Tablets of Bahá'u'lláh Revealed After the Kitáb-i-Aqdas*, Haifa: Bahá'í World, Centre, 1978.
— *The Hidden Words*, Wilmette, IL: US Bahá'í Publishing Trust, 2003.
Bahá'u'lláh, the Báb and 'Abdu'l-Bahá. *Bahá'í Prayers: A Selection of Prayers Revealed by Bahá'u'lláh, the Báb, and 'Abdu'l-Bahá*, Wilmette, IL: US Bahá'í Publishing Trust, 2002.
Bahai.org. *What Bahá'ís Believe: The Life of the Spirit* (https://www.bahai.org/beliefs/life-spirit/), n.d.
Baker, Michael. *Harlow's Studies on Dependency in Monkeys*, (16 December 2010) See: <https://www.youtube.com/watch?v=OrNBEhzjg8I>.
Bancroft, Anne. *The Buddha Speaks: A book of guidance from Buddhist scriptures*, Boston MA: Shambala Publications, 2000.
Barbor, Cary. *The Science of Meditation*, (1 May 2001). See: <http://www.psychologytoday.com/articles/200105/the-science-meditation>.
Barness, Sarah. 'Harvard's 75-Year Study Reveals The Secret To Living A Happy Life. And Here It Is.' (10 February 2015). See: <http://aplus.com/a/75-year-harvard-grant-study-happiness?no_monetization=true>.
Bayes, Jan Chozen. *How to Train a Wild Elephant*, Boston, MA: Shambhala Publications, Inc., 2011.
Begley, Sharon. *The Lotus and the Synapse* (25 March 2008). See: <https://www.newsweek.com/lotus-and-synapse-221406 >.
Benson, Herbert. *The Relaxation Response*, New York: Harpertorch, 1975.
Benson H.; Dusek J.A.; Sherwood J.B. et al. 'Study of the Therapeutic Effects of Intercessory Prayer (STEP) in cardiac bypass patients: a multicenter randomized trial of uncertainty and certainty of receiving intercessory prayer', in *American Heart Journal American Heart Journal*, vol. 151.4 (2006), pp. 934–42.
Benson, Herbert & William Proctor. *Beyond the Relaxation Response: How to Harness the Healing Power of Your Personal Beliefs*, New York: Times Books, 1984.
Blomkvist, Vania et al. 'Psychosocial self-prognosis in relation to mortality

and morbidity in hemophiliacs with HIV infection.' *Psychotherapy and Psychosomatics,* vol. 62.3, (1994), pp. 185–92.

Blumenfeld, Larry. *The Big Book of Relaxation: Simple Techniques to Control the Excess Stress in Your Life*, Relaxation Co, 1994.

Breathnach, Sarah Ban. *The Simple Abundance Journal of Gratitude*, New York: Warner Books, 1996.

Brussat, Frederic & Mary Ann Brussat. *Spiritual Rx: Prescriptions for Living a Meaningful Life*, Lebanon, IN: Hachette Books, 2001.

Brussat, Fredric & Mary Ann Brussat. *Fredric and Mary Ann Brussat.* n.d. See: <http://www.spiritualityandpractice.com/practices/alphabet/view/10/faith>.

Canfield, Jack, et al. *A 6th Bowl of Chicken Soup for the Soul: 101 More Stories to Open the Heart And Rekindle The Spirit*, Deerfield Beach, FL: Health Communications, 1999.

Canfield, Jack et al. *Chicken Soup for the Soul 20th Anniversary Edition: All Your Favorite Original Stories Plus 20 Bonus Stories for the Next 20 Years*, Cos Cob, CT: Chicken Food for the Soul Publishing, LLC, 2013.

Carey, Benedict. 'Long-Awaited Medical Study Questions the Power of Prayer', (31 March 2006). See: <http://www.nytimes.com/2006/03/31/health/31pray.html>.

Carnegie, Dale. *How to Stop Worrying and Start Living: Time-tested Methods for Conquering Worry*, New York: Pocket Books, 1984.

Carrington, Patricia. *The Book of Meditation: The Complete Guide to Modern Meditation*, Shaftesbury, UK: Element Books, LTD, 1998.

Carver, Charles et al. 'How coping mediates the effect of optimism on distress: a study of women with early stage breast cancer,' in *Journal of Personality and Social Psychology,* vol. 65.2, (1993), pp. 375–90.

Chan, Melissa. 'Here's How Winning the Lottery Makes You Miserable', (12 January 2016). See: <http://time.com/4176128/powerball-jackpot-lottery-winners/>.

Chernin, Dennis. *How to Meditate Using Chakras, Mantras, and Breath*, Ann Arbor: Think Publishing LLC, 2002.

Cliffe, Albert E. *Let Go and Let God: Steps in Victorious Living*, New York: Prentice Hall Press, 1987.

Coldicott, Hilary et al. *Change Management Excellence Using The Four Intelligences For Successful Organizational Change*, London: Kogan Page Business Books, 2004.

Covey, Stephen. *The 8th Habit: From Effectiveness to Greatness*, New York: Free Press, 2004.

Dahl, Melissa. 'A Classic Psychology Study on Why Winning the Lottery Won't Make You Happier', (13 January 2016). See: <http://nymag.com/scienceofus/2016/01/classic-study-on-happiness-and-the-lottery.html>.

Davich, Victor N. *The Best Guide to Meditation*, New York: Renaissance Books, 1998.

Davidson, R. J. et al. *Regulation of the Neural Circuitry of Emotion by Compassion Meditation: Effects of Meditative Expertise*, (26 March 2008). See: <http://www.plosone.org/article/info:doi/10.1371/journal.pone.0001897>.

Department of Environmental Conservation. *Immerse Yourself in a Forest for Better Health*. n.d. See: <https://www.dec.ny.gov/lands/90720.html>.

Dickens, Charles. *Sketches by Boz (1836)*. See: <https://ebooks.adelaide.edu.au/d/dickens/charles/d54sb/chapter34.html>.

Diener, Ed & Robert Wiswas-Diener. *Happiness: Unlocking the Mysteries of Psychological Wealth*, Malden, MA: Blackwell Publishing, 2008.

Emerson, Ralph Waldo. *Emerson: Essays and Lectures*, New York: Literary Classics of The United States, Inc., 1983.

Emmons, R.A. 'Is Spirituality an intelligence?', in *The International Journal for the Psychology of Religion*, (2000), pp. 27–34.

Emmons, Robert. *Thanks! How the New Science of Gratitude Can Make You Happier*, New York: Houghton Mifflin Company, 2007.

Emmons, Robert. *Gratitude Works!: A 21 Day Program for Creating Emotional Prosperity*, San Francisco: Jossey Bass, 2013.

Frankl, Viktor E. *Man's Search for Meaning*, Boston: Beacon Press, 2014.

Fredrickson, Barbara. *Love 2.0: Finding Happiness and Health in Moments of Connection*, New York: Plume, 2013.

— *Positivity: Top-Notch Research Reveals the Upward Spiral That Will Change Your Life*, New York: Crown Publishers, 2009.

Gaertner, Johannes A. *Worldly Virtues: A Catalogue of Reflections*, Grand Rapids, MI: Phanes Press, 2002.

Gardner, Howard. *Frames of Mind: The Theory of Multiple Intelligences*, New York: Basic Books, 1983.

— *Intelligence reframed: multiple intelligences for the 21st century*, New York: Basic Books, 1999.

— *Multiple Intelligences: New Horizons in Theory and Practice*, New York: Basic Books, 2006.

Gardner, Howard. *Frames of Mind: The Theory of Multiple Intelligences*, New York: Basic Books, 2011.

Gallup Poll. *Most Americans Practice Charitable Giving, Volunteerism*, (13 December 2013). See: <https://news.gallup.com/poll/166250/americans-practice-charitable-giving-volunteerism.aspx>.

Gendry, Sebastian. *Laughter Therapy History: Who, What, When*, n.d. See: <https://www.laughteronlineuniversity.com/laughter-therapy-history/>.

Goleman, Daniel & Richard Davidson. *How Meditation Changes Your Brain – and Your Life*, (7 May 2018). See: <https://www.lionsroar.com/how-meditation-changes-your-brain-and-your-life/>.

BIBLIOGRAPHY

Goleman, Daniel. *Emotional Intelligence: Why It Can Matter More Than IQ*, New York: Bantam Books, 2005.

— *Research Affirms Power of Positive Thinking*, (2 March 1987). See: <http://www.nytimes.com/1987/02/03/science/research-affirms-power-of-positive-thinking.html?pagewanted=all>.

— *The Meditative Mind: The Varieties of Meditative Experience*, New York: TarcherPerigee, 1996.

Gottman, John M. & Nan Silver. *The Seven Principles for Making Marriage Work*, New York: Random House, 1999.

Grimm, Jr. Robert et al. *The Health Benefits of Volunteering: A Review of Recent Research*, 2007.

Hafez. *Ghazal 317*, (translated by Adib Masumian). See: <https://adibmasumian.com/translations/hafiz-passage-ghazal-317/>.

Hammarskjöld, Dag. *Markings,* New York: Knopf, 1964.

Heinlein, Robert. *Stranger in a Strange Land*, New York: Penguin Putnam, Penguin Putnam, 1991.

Hellaby, William & Madeline Hellaby. *Prayer: A Baha'i Approach*, Oxford: George Ronald, Publishers, 1985.

Helmstetter, Shad. *What to Say When You Talk to Yourself,* New York: Simon & Schuster, 1987.

Hodge, David R. *A Systematic Review of the Empirical Literature on Intercessory Prayer, Research on Social Work Practice*, vol. 17.2, (March 2007), pp. 174–87.

Ironson, Gail et al. 'Dispositional optimism and the mechanisms by which it predicts slower disease progression in HIV: proactive behavior, avoidant coping, and depression', in *International Journal of Behavioral Medicine*, vol. 12.2, (2005), pp. 86–97.

Ishráq-Khávarí, Abdu'l-Hamid. *Muḥáḍirát (vol. 3), A Tablet from Bahá'u'lláh to Jamál Effendi dated 9 Shawwál 1305 AH* [*June 19, 1888*], Hofheim: Bahá'í-Verlag, 2009.

Jacobs, Gregg. *Say Goodnight To Insomnia*, New York: Holt Paperbacks, 2009.

Jankowski, P. J., & Sandage, S. J. 'Meditative prayer, hope, adult attachment, and forgiveness: A proposed model', in *Psychology of Religion and Spirituality*, vol. 3.2, (2 March 2011), pp. 115–31.

Kamen, Leslie P. & E. P. Seligman, Martin. 'Explanatory style and health', in *Current Psychology: Research and Reviews*, vol. 6.3, (1987), pp. 207–18.

Khavari, Khalil. *Spiritual Intelligence: A Practical Guide to Personal Happiness*, Ontario: White Mountain Publications, 1999.

King, David et al. 'A Viable Model and Self-Report Measure of Spiritual Intelligence', in *Interpersonal Journal of Transpersonal Studies*, (2009), pp. 67–85.

King, David. 'The Spiritual Intelligence Self-Report Inventory', in *International Journal of Transpersonal Studies*, vol. 28.1, (2009).
Klein, Allen. *The Healing Power of Humor*, New York: Penguin Putnam, 1987.
Koenig, Harold G. *The Healing Power of Faith*, New York: Simon & Schuste, 1999.
Lam, Bourree. 'What Becomes of Lottery Winners?' in *The Atlantic.com*, (2016). See: <https://www.theatlantic.com/business/archive/2016/01/lottery-winners-research/423543/>.
Lambert, Nathaniel M. et al. 'Can Prayer Increase Gratitude?' in *Psychology of Religion and Spirituality*, (2009). See: <http://citeseerx.ist.psu.edu/viewdoc/download?doi=10.1.1.720.5306&rep=rep1&type=pdf>.
Larsen, Christian D. *The Optimist Creed and Other Inspirational Classics: Discover the Life-Changing Power of Gratitude and Optimism*, New York: TarcherPerigee, 2012.
Lawrence, Brother. *The Practice of the Presence of God with Spiritual Maxims*, Grand Rapids, MI: Spire Books, 1967.
Lawson, Karen MD. 'University of Minnesota – Taking Charge of Your Health & Wellbeing', n.d. See: <https://www.takingcharge.csh.umn.edu/enhance-your-wellbeing/health/thoughts-emotions/increase-positivity >.
Lemonick, Michael D. & Alice Park Mankato. 'The Nun Study: How one scientist and 678 sisters are helping unlock the secrets of Alzheimer's,' (14 May 2001). See: <http://content.time.com/time/world/article/0,8599,2047984,00.html>.
Litt, Mark D. et al. 'Coping and cognitive factors in adaptation to in vitro fertilization failure,' in *Journal of Behavioral Medicine*, vol. 15.2, (1992), pp. 171–87.
Lobel, Marci et al. 'The Impact of Prenatal Maternal Stress and Optimistic Disposition on Birth Outcomes in Medically High-Risk Women', in *Health Psychology*, vol. 19.6, (2000), pp. 544–53.
Long, Jeffry & Paul Perry. *The Groundbreaking New Evidence for God and Near-Death Experience*, San Francisco: HarperOne, 2016.
Lucas, Richard E. et al. 'Discriminant validity of well-being measures', in *Journal of Personality and Social Psychology*, vol. 71.3 (1996), pp. 616–28.
Luks, Allan & Peggy Payne. *The Healing Power of Doing Good*, New York: Fawcett Columbine, 1991.
Lyubomirsky, Sonja. *The How of Happiness: A New Approach to Getting the Life You Want*, New York: Penguin Press, 2008.
Markel, Dr. Howard. *Dr Albert Schweitzer, a renowned medical missionary with a complicated history*, (14 January 2019). See: <https://www.pbs.org/newshour/health/dr-albert-schweitzer-a-renowned-medical-missionary-with-a-complicated-history>.

Maruta, Toshihiko et al. 'Optimists vs pessimists: survival rate among medical patients over a 30-year period', in *Mayo Clinic Proceedings*, (2000), pp. 140–43.

Maslow, Abraham. *Religions, Values, and Peak-Experiences*, New York: Penguin Group, 2014.

Masumian, Farnaz. *The Divine Art of Meditation*, Oxford: George Ronald, 2014.

Masumian, Farnaz, Bijan Masumian, & Adib Masumian. *Faith*, (October 2014). See: <https://www.cyber-temple.org/faith.html>.

Matthews, Karen A. et al. 'Optimistic attitudes protect against progression of carotid atherosclerosis in healthy middle-aged women', in *Psychosomatic Medicine*, 66.5 (2004), pp. 640–4.

Miskiman, D.E. 'The Treatment of Insomnia by the Transcendental Meditation Program,' in Farrow, Orme-Johnson D. W. & J. T. [Eds.]. *Scientific Research on the Transcendental Meditation Program: Collected Papers*, Livingston Manor, NY: Maharishi European Research University Press, 1978.

Mitchell, Marilyn. *Dr. Herbert Benson's Relaxation Response*, (29 March 2013), <https://www.psychologytoday.com/blog/heart-and-soul-healing/201303/dr-herbert-benson-s-relaxation-response>.

Mitroff, Ian & Elizabeth Denton. *A Spiritual Audit of Corporate America: A Hard Look at Spirituality, Religion, and Values in the Workplace*, San Francisco: Jossey-Bass, 2012.

Moore, Thomas & Frederic Brussat. *Spiritual Literacy: Reading the Sacred in Everyday Life*, New York: Simon & Schuster, 1998.

Motlagh, Hushidar Hugh. *On Wings of Destiny*, Mt. Pleasant, MI: Global Perspective, 2003.

— *The Spiritual Design of Creation: Solving the puzzle of human life and destiny*, Mt. Pleasant, MI: Global Perspective, 2015.

Mu'ayyad, Habib. *Khatirat-i Habib*, Tehran: Mu'assisiy-i-Millíy-i-Maṭbúʻát-i-Amrí, 1961.

Mullen, Tom. *Marriage*, n.d. See: <http://www.livinglifefully.com/marriage.htm>.

Nabíl-i-Aʻẓam (Muhammad-i-Zarandí). The Dawn Breakers. Nabíl's Narrative of the early days of the Baháʼí Revelation, Wilmette IL: Baháʼí Publishing Trust, 1932.

Newberg, Andrew & Mark R. Waldman. *How God Changes Your Brain: Breakthrough Findings from a Leading Neuroscientist*, New York: Ballantine Books, 2009.

Newmark, Amy. *Best Mom Ever: 101 Stories of Gratitude, Love, and Wisdom*, Cos Cob, CT: Chicken Soup for the Soul Publishing, LLC., 2017.

Newmark, Amy & Deborah Norville. *Chicken Soup for the Soul: Think Positive, Live Happy-101 Stories About Creating Your Best Life*. CT: Chicken Soup for the Soul Publishing, LLC., 2019.

Niemiec, Ryan M., Psy.D. 'The Best Possible Self Exercise (Boosts Hope)', (September 2012). See: <http://blogs.psychcentral.com/character-strengths/2012/09/the-best-possible-self-exercise-boosts-hope/>.

Orme-Johnson, DW. *Medical Care Utilization and the Transcendental Meditation Program*. n.d. See: <https://pdfs.semanticscholar.org/a752/287e3 e7ef788725173baefa282957e6736cd.pdf>.

Pathath, Abdul Wahab. 'Psychological Well-Being of the Elderly through Meditation,' in *The International Journal of Indian Psychology*, vol. 4.1, (2016), pp. 114.

Peale, Norman Vincent (ed.). *Treasury of Joy and Enthusiasm*, New York: Fawcett Crest, 1981.

Peale, Norman Vincent. *A Treasury of Courage and Confidence*, Pawling, NY: Peale Center for Christian Living, 1996.

— *Enthusiasm Makes the Difference*, Pauling, NY: Prentice Hall, 1967.

— *Faith is the Answer*, Englewood Cliffs: Prentice-Hall, 1955.

— *Faith Made Them Champions*. Carmel, New York: Guideposts Associates, 1954.

— *How to Be Your Best: A Treasury of Practical Ideas*, New York: Foundation for Christian Living, 1990.

— *In God We Trust*, Pawling, New York: Centre for Christian Living, 1994.

— *Positive Imaging: The Powerful Way to Change*, New York: Ballantine Books, 1982.

— *Positive Living Day by Day*, Ideal Publications, 2003.

— *Six Attitudes for Winners*, Wheaton, Illinois: Tyndale House Publishes, Inc., 1989.

— *Stay Alive All Your Life*, New York: Prentic Hall, 1985.

— *The Amazing Results of Positive Thinking*, New York: Prentice Hall, 1959.

— *The New Art of Living*, New York: Hawthorn Books, 1971.

— *The Power of Positive Thinking*, Upper Saddle River, New Jersey: Prentice Hall, Inc., 1956.

— *Why Some Positive Thinkers Get Powerful Results*, New York: Fawcett World Library, 1986.

Peale, Ruth (Stafford). *The Adventure of Being a Wife*, Englewood, New Jersey: Prentice Hall, Inc., 1971.

Popva, Maria. 'The Science of Stress and How Our Emotions Affect Our Susceptibility to Burnout and Disease', (20 July 2015). See: <https://www.brainpickings.org/2015/07/20/esther-sternberg-balance-within-stress-emotion/>.

Post, Stephen. *The Hidden Gifts of Helping: How the Power of Giving, Compassion, and Hope Can Get Us Through Hard Times*, San Francisco: Jossey-Bass, 2011.

Post, Stephen & Jill Neimark. *Why Good Things Happen to Good People*, New York: Broadway Books, 2007.

Powell L.H, Shahabi L., Thoresen C.E. 'Religion and spirituality. Linkages to physical health', in *The American Psychologist,* vol. 58.1 (2003), pp. 36–52.

Queensland Brain Institute. *What are neurotransmitters?* n.d.. See: <http://www.neurogistics.com/the-science/what-are-neurotransmitters>.

Rainforth, M.V. et al. *Stress Reduction Programs in Patients with Elevated Blood Pressure: A Systematic Review and Meta-Analysis*, (December 2007). See: <https://www.ncbi.nlm.nih.gov/pubmed/18350109>.

Roche, Lorin. *Whole Body Meditation: Igniting Your Natural Instinct to Heal*, Emmaus, PA: Roadle Books, 2002.

Rogers, George L. (Ed.). *Benjamin Franklin's The Art of Virtue; His Formula for Successful Living,* Midvale, Utah: ChoiceSkills, 1996.

Rosenberg, Larry et al. *Breath by Breath: The liberating practice of insight meditation*, Boston, MA: Shambala, 1998.

Ryan, M. J. *Attitudes of Gratitude*, San Francisco: Conari Press, 2009.

— Ryan, M. J., et al. *The Giving Heart*, Berkeley, CA: Conari Press, 2000.

— Ryan, M. J. *The Happiness Makeover: How to Teach Yourself to Be Happy and Enjoy Every Day*, San Fancisco: Conari Press, 2014.

Salzberg, Sharon. *Loving Kindness: The Revolutionary Art of Happiness*, Boston: Shambhala Publications, 2002.

— *Sympathetic Joy by Sharon Salzberg*, (18 December 2011). See: <https://www.upaya.org/2011/12/sympathetic-joy-by-sharon-salzberg/>.

Sanders, Tim. *Today We are Rich: Harnessing the Power of Total Confidence*, Carol Stream, IL: Tyndale House Publishers, Inc., 2011.

Schou, Inger et al. 'The mediating role of appraisal and coping in the relationship between optimism-pessimism and quality of life', in *Psychooncology,* vol. 14.9, (2005), pp. 718–27.

Segerstrom, Suzanne and Sandra E. Sephton. 'Optimistic Expectancies and Cell-Mediated Immunity: The Role of Positive Affect', in *Psychological Science*, vol. 21.3, (2010), pp. 448–55.

Shapiro, Eddie & Debbie Shapiro. *The Meditation Book*, New York: Sterling Publishing Company, 2000.

Shapiro, Eddie. *Peace Within the Stillness: Meditation & Relaxation for True Happiness*, Berkeley, CA: Berkeley, CA: Crossing Press, 1998.

Stafne, Gigi. *The Immune System: Immune System Clinical Basics*, (2014). See: http://greenwisdom.weebly.com/uploads/4/3/9/0/4390688/immune_system_primer_stafne.pdf/.

Shoghi Effendi. *Directives from the Guardian*, Wimette, IL: Bahá'í Publishing Trust, 1973.

— *The Advent of Divine Justice,* Wilmette, IL: US Bahá'í Publishing Trust, 2006.

Smith, Mark K. *Howard Gardner, multiple intelligences and education,* 2002.

Taylor, Shelley E. et al. 'Optimism, coping, psychological distress, and high-risk sexual behaviour among men at risk for acquired immunodeficiency syndrome (AIDS)', in *Journal of Personality and Social Psychology,* vol. 63.3, (1992), pp. 460–73.

The Institute for Research on Unlimited Love. *Our Mission,* n.d. See: <http://unlimitedloveinstitute.org/about.php>.

Tindle, Hillary A. et al. 'Optimism, cynical hostility, and incident coronary heart disease and mortality in the Women's Health Initiative', in *Circulation,* (2009), pp. 656–62.

Upton, Charles (trans.). *Doorkeeper of the Heart: Versions of Rabi'a,* New York: Pir Press, 2004.

Vaillant, George E. *Adaptation to Life,* Boston: Little Brown, 1977.

— *Triumphs of Experience: Men of the Harvard Grant Study,* Cambridge, MA: Belknap Press, 2012.

Viereck, George Sylvester. 'What Life Means to Einstein: An Interview by George Sylvester Viereck', in *The Saturday Evening Post,* (26 October 1929).

Walsh, Roger. *Essential Spirituality,* New York: John Wiley & Sons, 1999.

Ware, Deann. *Positive Neuroplasticity,* n.d. See: <http://www.dailyshoring.com/positive-neuroplasticity/>.

Weaver, Fawn. *Positive Marriage Quotes,* n.d. See: <http://www.happywivesclub.com/marriage-quotes/>.

Whipple, Carol, MS. *The Connection between Laughter, Humor, and Good Health.* See: <http://www2.ca.uky.edu/hes/fcs/>.

Wigglesworth, Cindy. *SQ21: The Twenty-One Skills of Spiritual Intelligence,* New York: Select Books, 2008.

Zak, Paul J. *The Neuroscience of Trust,* (January-February 2017). See: <https://hbr.org/2017/01/the-neuroscience-of-trust>.

Zarqani, Mahmud. *Mahmud's Diary: The Diary of Mirza Mahmud-i-Zarqani Chronicling 'Abdu'l-Bahá's Journey to America,* Oxford: George Ronald, 1998.

NOTES AND REFERENCES

Preface
1. Notion (https://www.notion.so/) is a note-taking and collaboration application that can be used to keep track of tasks, projects, and more. It can be accessed via mobile devices and through PCs and laptops.

Chapter 1: The Purpose of Life
1. Ryan, *The Happiness Makeover,* pp. 3–4.
2. Gardner, *Frames of Mind.*
3. Gardner, *Multiple Intelligences.*
4. Gardner, *Frames of Mind.*
5. Smith, 'Howard Gardner, Multiple intelligences and education'.
6. Goleman, *Emotional Intelligence.*
7. Gardner, *Intelligence reframed.*
8. Gardner, *The Nine Types of Intelligences.*
9. Wigglesworth, *SQ21.*
10. King, 'A Viable Model and Self-Report Measure of Spiritual Intelligence'.
11. King, 'The Spiritual Intelligence Self-Report Inventory'.
12. Emmons, 'Is spirituality an intelligence?'
13. Khavari, *Spiritual Intelligence,* pp. 33, 49.
14. Covey, *The 8th Habit.*
15. Mitroff & Denton, *A Spiritual Audit of Corporate America.*
16. Coldicott et al., *Change Management Excellence Using The Four Intelligences For Successful Organizational Change.*
17. Frankl, *Man's Search for Meaning,* p. x.
18. The authors are aware that God, or any conception of the Creator, cannot be limited to a gender. However, due to the limitations of language, in this book, any references to God take the pronoun 'He'.
19. Shoghi Effendi, *Directives,* p. 87.
20. 'Abdu'l-Bahá, *Paris Talks,* p. 119–20.
21. The term 'man', here and in the quotations below, refers to both men and women.
22. 'Abdu'l-Bahá, *Promulgation of Universal Peace,* p. 294.

23 'Abdu'l-Bahá, *Secret of Divine Civilization*, p. 19.
24 'Abdu'l-Bahá, *Promulgation of Universal Peace*, pp. 177–8.
25 Bahá'u'lláh, *Gleanings*, p. 327.
26 'Abdu'l-Bahá, *Paris Talks*, pp. 63–4.
27 'Abdu'l-Bahá, *Selections*, p. 138.
28 See: https://www.bahai.org/beliefs/life-spirit.
29 Hafez, *Ghazal* no. 317.
30 Ishráq-Khávarí, *Muḥáḍirát* (vol. 3).
31 'Abdu'l-Bahá, *Paris Talks*, p. 80–1.
32 Bahá'u'lláh, *Gleanings*, p. 65.
33 'Abdu'l-Bahá, *Foundations of World Unity*, p. 64.
34 Bahá'u'lláh, *Gleanings*, p. 149.
35 'Abdu'l-Bahá, *Promulgation of Universal Peace*, p. 121.
36 Bahá'u'lláh, *Tablets*, p. 257.
37 Rogers, *Benjamin Franklin's The Art of Virtue*, p. 40.
38 ibid. pp. 42–3.
39 'Abdu'l-Bahá, *Secret of Divine Civilization*, p. 103.
40 Bahá'u'lláh, *Tablets*, p. 86.
41 Walsh, *Essential Spirituality*, p. 4.
42 Pathath, 'Psychological Well-Being of the Elderly through Meditation'.
43 Masumian, *The Divine Art of Meditation*, p. 22.
44 Roche, *Whole Body Meditation*, p. 5.
45 Pathath, 'Psychological Well-Being of the Elderly through Meditation'.
46 See: http://www.psychologytoday.com/articles/200105/the-science-meditation.
47 Walsh, *Essential Spirituality*, p. 4.
48 Pathath, 'Psychological Well-Being of the Elderly through Meditation'.
49 Walsh, *Essential Spirituality*, p. 5.
50 Long & Perry, *God and the Afterlife*, pp. 76–8.

Chapter 2: The Practice of the Presence of God

1 Bahá'u'lláh, *Hidden Words*.
2 Mu'ayyad, *Khatirat-i Habib*, pp. 422–3.
3 Peale, *Faith is the Answer*, p. 158.
4 Peale, *Positive Living Day by Day*, p. 153.
5 For examples of verses from the sacred literature of different world religions, see: https://www.cyber-temple.org/faith.html.
6 'Abdu'l-Bahá, *Selections*, p. 187.
7 Peale, *A Treasury of Courage and Confidence*, pp. 261–2.
8 *Bahá'í Prayers*, p. 129.
9 Lawrence, *The Practice of the Presence of God with Spiritual Maxims*, p. 25.
10 ibid. p. 27.
11 ibid. p. 58.
12 ibid. p. 24.

13 ibid. p. 26.
14 ibid. p. 28.
15 ibid. p. 29.
16 ibid. pp. 31–3.
17 ibid. p. 47.
18 ibid. pp. 36–45.
19 ibid. p. 46.
20 ibid. pp. 52–9.
21 ibid. pp. 79–81.
22 ibid. pp. 82–3.
23 Upton, *Doorkeeper of the Heart,* p. 42.
24 ibid. p. 44.
25 ibid. p. 46.
26 Cliffe, *Let Go and Let God,* pp. 3–4, 59.
27 John Oxenham is a pseudonym for the prolific English journalist, novelist and poet, William Arthur Dunkerley (1852–1941).
28 Peale, *Treasury of Joy and Enthusiasm,* p. 27.

Chapter 3: Love

1 Bahá'u'lláh, *Tablets,* p. 155.
2 Bahá'u'lláh, *Hidden Words.*
3 ibid.
4 ibid.
5 Motlagh, *On Wings of Destiny,* pp. 130–1.
6 Bahá'u'lláh, *Bahá'í Prayers,* p. 19.
7 Motlagh, *On Wings of Destiny,* p. 181.
8 Bahá'u'lláh, *Hidden Words.*
9 Bahá'u'lláh, Tablets p. 167.
10 Post & Neimark, *Why Good Things Happen to Good People,* p. 4.
11 ibid.
12 ibid. p. 7.
13 Peale, *The Amazing Results of Positive Thinking,* pp. 81–2.
14 Bahá'u'lláh, *Hidden Words.*
15 ibid.
16 ibid.
17 The sacred language of some religious texts of Hinduism, and all texts of Theravāda Buddhism.
18 Masumian, *The Divine Art of Meditation,* p. 65.
19 Allen, *Is Meditation the Key to Reducing Racial Bias?*
20 Salzberg, *Loving Kindness,* p. 23.
21 Shapiro & Shapiro, *The Meditation Book,* p. 40.
22 Shapiro & Shapiro, *Peace within Stillness,* p. 165.
23 Shapiro & Shapiro, *The Meditation Book,* p. 40.
24 ibid. p. 41.
25 Davich, *The Best Guide to Meditation,* pp. 273–91.
26 Newberg & Waldman. *How God Changes Your Brain,* pp. 208–9.

27 Salzberg, *Loving Kindness*, pp. 36–7.
28 'Abdu'l-Bahá, *Promulgation of Universal Peace*, p. 9.
29 Fredrickson, *Love 2.0*, pp. 156–7.
30 See: https://www.upaya.org/2011/12/sympathetic-joy-by-sharon-salzberg/.
31 Fredrickson, *Positivity*, p. 94.
32 Lyubomirsky, *The How of Happiness*, pp. 148–9.
33 Post, *The Hidden Gifts of Helping*, p. 28.
34 'Abdu'l-Bahá, *Selections*, p. 73–4.
35 See: http://www.pursuit-of-happiness.org/history-of-happiness/barb-fredrickson.
36 Fredrickson, *Love 2.0*.
37 ibid. pp. 84–6.
38 ibid. p. 86.
39 Post & Neimark, *Why Good Things Happen to Good People*, p. 4.
40 See: http://unlimitedloveinstitute.org/about.php.
41 See: https://www.youtube.com/watch?v=OrNBEhzjg8I.
42 Fred Rogers (1928–2003) was a popular American television personality and the host of a long-running preschool television series titled, *Mister Rogers' Neighborhood*.
43 Post & Neimark, *Why Good Things Happen to Good People*, p. 5.
44 Newmark, *Best Mom Ever*, pp. 214–15.
45 Peale (ed.), *Treasury of Joy and Enthusiasm*, p. 187.

Chapter 4: Faith

1 Cliffe, *Let Go and Let God*, p x.
2 Brussat & Brussat, *Spiritual Rx*, p. 81–2.
3 Bahá'u'lláh, *Gleanings*, p. 233.
4 *The Dhammapada*, 10:144.
5 The *Báb*, quoted in *The Dawn-Breakers*, p. 94.
6 Bahá'u'lláh, *Gleanings*, pp. 106–7.
7 Bahá'u'lláh, *Tablets*, p. 138.
8 'Abdu'l-Bahá, *Selections*, p. 187.
9 Bahá'u'lláh, *Áthár-i-Qalam-i-A'lá*, vol. 6, pp. 194–7.
10 Peale, *The New Art of Living*, p. 73.
11 Cyber-Temple.org is a non-profit website with selections from the scriptures of different world religions on various spiritual themes and subjects, including faith. See: https://www.cyber-temple.org/faith.html.
12 Motlagh, *The Spiritual Design of Creation*, p. 244.
13 ibid. p. 245.
14 Bahá'u'lláh, *Hidden Words*.
15 Motlagh. *The Spiritual Design of Creation*, pp. 251–2.
16 Benson & Proctor, *Beyond the Relaxation Response*, pp. 6–8.
17 Canfield, *A 6th Bowl of Chicken Soup for the Soul*, pp. 358–9.

Chapter 5: Service

1. Bahá'u'lláh, *Gleanings*, p. 250.
2. Bhagavad Gita 3:10.
3. 'Abdu'l-Bahá, *Promulgation of Universal Peace*, p. 8.
4. ibid. p. 132.
5. Markel, *Dr. Albert Schweitzer, a renowned medical missionary with a complicated history*.
6. Moore & Brussat, *Spiritual Literacy*.
7. Post & Neimark, *Why Good Things Happen to Good People*, p. 35.
8. Post, *The Hidden Gifts of Helping*, pp. 35–6.
9. Luks & Payne, *The Healing Power of Doing Good*, p. 42.
10. ibid. p. 6.
11. ibid. pp. 9–11 and 47–51.
12. ibid. pp. 48–9.
13. Peale, *Stay Alive All Your Life*, p. 105.
14. Quoted in Post, *Why Good Things Happen to Good People*, p. 53.
15. Luks & Payne, *The Healing Power of Doing Good*, pp. 8 and 64–7.
16. ibid. p. 7.
17. ibid. pp. 64–5.
18. ibid. p. 68.
19. ibid. pp. 83–96.
20. Ryan, *The Giving Heart*, p. 17.
21. Luks & Payne, *The Healing Power of Doing Good*, p. 231.
22. ibid.
23. Vaillant, *Adaptation to Life*, p. 40.
24. Post & Neimark, *Why Good Things Happen to Good People*, p. 59.
25. ibid.
26. See: https://www.goodreads.com/quotes/29365-it-is-one-of-the-beautiful-compensations-of-life-that.
27. Luks & Payne, *The Healing Power of Doing Good*, pp. 119–24.
28. Post & Neimark, *Why Good Things Happen to Good People*, p. 5.
29. Frankl, *Man's Search for Meaning*, pp. 103–4.
30. Post & Neimark, *Why Good Things Happen to Good People*, pp. 6–7.
31. ibid. p. 7.
32. Walsh, *Essential Spirituality*, p. 254.
33. Maslow, *Religions, Values, and Peak-Experiences*, p. xii.
34. See, for example: volunteermatch.org, dosomething.org or onlinevolunteering.org.
35. Walsh, *Essentials of Spirituality*, p. 273.
36. Post, *The Hidden Gifts of Helping*, pp. 30–1.
37. ibid.
38. ibid. p. 31.
39. ibid. 91–2.

40   See: http://www.gallup.com/poll/166250/americans-practice-charitable-giving-volunteerism.aspx.
41   Post, *The Hidden Gifts of Helping*, pp. 30–1.
42   Post & Neimark, *Why Good Things Happen to Good People*, pp. 8–10; pp. 48–80.
43   See: https://www.nationalservice.gov/pdf/07_0506_hbr.pdf.
44   'Abdu'l-Baha, *Secret of Divine Civilization*, p. 103.
45   'Abdu'l-Bahá, *Paris Talks*, p. 223.
46   Peale, *The New Art of Living*, pp. 60–1.

Chapter 6: Prayer
1   Bahá'u'lláh, *Hidden Words*.
2   See: https://www.quotes.wiki/the-sovereign-cure-for-worry-is-prayer/.
3   'Abdu'l-Bahá, *Tablets* pp. 683–4.
4   The Qu'ran (50:17)
5   Bahá'u'lláh, *Hidden Words*.
6   Emmons, *Thanks! How the New Science of Gratitude Can Make You Happier*, p. 194.
7   Hellaby & Hellaby, *Prayer: A Bahá'í Approach*, p. 52.
8   ibid.
9   ibid.
10   Peale, *The Power of Positive Thinking* pp. 55–6.
11   'Abdu'l-Bahá, *Compilation of Compilations*, p. 23.
12   'Abdu'l-Bahá, *Promulgation of Universal Peace*, p. 247.
13   Bahá'u'lláh, quoted in Shoghi Effendi, *The Advent of Divine Justice*, p. 124.
14   *Bahá'í Prayers*, p. 158.
15   Bahá'u'lláh, *Tablets*, p. 189.
16   Buddha's Four Noble Truths are: 1. Suffering is universal; 2. Suffering arises from attachment to desires; 3. Suffering ceases when attachment to desire ceases; 4. Freedom from suffering is possible by practising Buddha's Noble Eightfold Path.
17   'Abdu'l-Bahá, *Tablets*, p. 483.
18   Emmons, *Thanks!*, pp. 194–5.
19   Khavari, *Spiritual Intelligence*. p. 115.
20   'Abdu'l-Bahá, *Selections*, p. 78.
21   *Bahá'í Prayers*, pp. 40.
22   Bahá'u'lláh, *Hidden Words*.
23   Bahá'u'lláh, *Iqtidarat va Chand Lawh-i-Digar*, p. 224.
24   Bahá'u'lláh, *Hidden Words*.
25   Carey, 'Long-Awaited Medical Study Questions the Power of Prayer'.
26   Koenig, *The Healing Power of Faith*, p. 223.
27   Benson et al., 'Study of the Therapeutic Effects of Intercessory Prayer (STEP) in cardiac bypass patients . . .'

28 ibid.
29 Astin et al., 'The Efficacy of "Distant Healing" . . .'
30 Powell, Shahabi & Thoresen, 'Religion and spirituality. Linkages to physical health'.
31 Hodge, 'A Systematic Review of the Empirical Literature on Intercessory Prayer'.
32 Jankowski, & Sandage, 'Meditative prayer, hope, adult attachment, and forgiveness: A proposed model'.
33 Lambert et al., 'Can Prayer Increase Gratitude?'
34 ibid.
35 ibid.
36 Peale, *Stay Alive All Your Life*, pp. 60–62.

Chapter 7: Meditation

1 'Abdu'l-Bahá, *Promulgation of Universal Peace*, p. 244.
2 ibid. pp. 147–8.
3 Bahá'u'lláh, *Gleanings*, pp. 65–6.
4 Bahá'u'lláh, *Seven Valleys*, p. 35.
5 Benson, *The Relaxation Response*.
6 Mitchell, *Dr. Herbert Benson's Relaxation Response*.
7 ibid.
8 See: https://www.ncbi.nlm.nih.gov/pmc/articles/PMC3694268.
9 Goleman, *The Meditative Mind*, p. 168.
10 Newberg & Waldman, *How God Changes your Brain*, p. 191.
11 Roche, *Whole Body Meditations*, p. 5.
12 Orme-Johnson. *Psychosomatic Medicine*, pp. 493–507.
13 Jacobs, *Say Goodnight To Insomnia*, p. 8.
14 Miskiman, 'The Treatment of Insomnia by the Transcendental Meditation Program', pp. 296–300.
15 Carrington, *The Book of Meditation*, pp. 198–9.
16 Barbor, *The Science of Meditation*.
17 Newberg & Waldman, *How God Changes Your Brain*, p. 191.
18 ibid.
19 Tim Sanders coined this term as it occurs in this context. One of the authors (Bijan Masumian) first heard Sanders mention the concept in a keynote speech he made at an e-learning conference in Austin, Texas in 2010.
20 Popva, *The Science of Stress and How Our Emotions Affect Our Susceptibility to Burnout and Disease*.
21 Queensland Brain Institute, *What are neurotransmitters?*
22 Newberg & Waldman, *How God Changes Your Brain*, p. 56.
23 Dennis, *How to Meditate Using Chakras, Mantras, and Breath*, pp. 47–8.
24 Masumian, *The Divine Art of Meditation*, p. 26.
25 Newberg & Waldman, *How God Changes Your Brain*, pp. 54–5.

26 ibid. pp. 19–20.
27 Begley, *The Lotus and the Synapse.*
28 Davidson et.al. *Regulation of the Neural Circuitry of Emotion by Compassion Meditation.*
29 Begley, *The Lotus and the Synapse.*
30 Masumian, *The Divine Art of Meditation.*
31 Rosenberg, et al., *Breath by Breath*, p. 22.
32 Bancroft, *The Buddha Speaks*, p. 111.
33 Masumian, *The Divine Art of Meditation*, pp. 51–2.
34 For details, see Masumian, *The Divine Art of Meditation*, pp. 91–2.
35 Bahá'u'lláh, *Gleanings*, p. 153.
36 ibid. p. 136.
37 Anonymous.
38 Bahá'u'lláh, *Hidden Words.*
39 Newmark & Norville, *Chicken Soup for the Soul: Think Positive, Live Happy*, pp. 301–3.

Chapter 8: Marriage and Family Life

1 'Abdu'l-Bahá, *Promulgation of Universal Peace,* pp. 144–5.
2 Peale, *Six Attitudes for Winners*, pp. 51–5.
3 'Abdu'l-Bahá, *Promulgation of Universal Peace,* p. 168.
4 'Abdu'l-Bahá, *Selections,* p. 129.
5 Peale, *The Adventure of Being a Wife,* p. 4.
6 Khavari, *Spiritual Intelligence,* p. 94.
7 Post & Neimark, *Why Good Things Happen to Good People,* pp. 3–4.
8 Gottman & Silver, *The Seven Principles for Making Marriage Work,* pp. 260–1.
9 ibid. p. 252.
10 ibid. p. 266.
11 Heinlein, *Stranger in a Strange Land*, p. 363.
12 Lyubomirsky, *The How of Happiness*, p. 145.
13 Peale, *The Adventure of Being a Wife*, p. 111.
14 ibid. p. 109.
15 Bayes, *How to Train a Wild Elephant*, p. 37.
16 *Bahá'í Prayers*, p. 221.
17 Weaver, *Positive Marriage Quotes.*
18 'Abdu'l-Bahá, *Paris Talks,* p. 229.
19 Mullen, *Marriage.*
20 Covey, *The 7 Habits of Highly Effective People*, p. 12.
21 Zak, *The Neuroscience of Trust.*
22 Canfield et al., *Chicken Soup for the Soul 20th Anniversary Edition*, pp. 66–8.

Chapter 9: Positivity

1 Author unknown.

NOTES AND REFERENCES

2. Ryan, *Attitudes of Gratitude*, pp. 145–6.
3. Fredrickson, *Positivity*, p. 9.
4. Peale, *The Amazing Results of Positive Thinking*, p. 16.
5. Fredrickson, *Positivity*, pp. 93–4.
6. ibid.
7. Maruta et al., 'Optimists vs pessimists: survival rate among medical patients over a 30-year period'.
8. Carver et al., 'How coping mediates the effect of optimism on distress: a study of women with early stage breast cancer'.
9. Schou et al., 'The mediating role of appraisal and coping in the relationship between optimism-pessimism and quality of life'.
10. Matthews et al., 'Optimistic attitudes protect against progression of carotid atherosclerosis in healthy middle-aged women'.
11. Ironson et al., 'Dispositional optimism and the mechanisms by which it predicts slower disease progression in HIV: proactive behavior, avoidant coping, and depression'.
12. Blomkvist et al., 'Psychosocial self-prognosis in relation to mortality and morbidity in hemophiliacs with HIV infection'.
13. Taylor et al., 'Optimism, coping, psychological distress, and high-risk sexual behavior among men at risk for acquired immunodeficiency syndrome (AIDS)'.
14. Lobel et al., 'The Impact of Prenatal Maternal Stress and Optimistic Disposition on Birth Outcomes in Medically High-Risk Women'.
15. Lucas et al., 'Discriminant validity of well-being measures'.
16. Tindle et al., 'Optimism, cynical hostility, and incident coronary heart disease and mortality in the Women's Health Initiative'.
17. Kamen & Seligman, 'Explanatory style and health'.
18. Segerstrom & Sephton, 'Optimistic Expectancies and Cell-Mediated Immunity . . .'
19. Litt et al., 'Coping and cognitive factors in adaptation to in vitro fertilization failure'.
20. Taylor et al., 'Optimism, coping, psychological distress, and high-risk sexual behavior among men at risk for acquired immunodeficiency syndrome (AIDS)'.
21. Ryan, *The Happiness Makeover*, p. 12.
22. Peale, *Why Some Positive Thinkers Get Powerful Results*, p. 131.
23. Peale, *Six Attitudes for Winners*, pp. 8–9.
24. Bahá'u'lláh, *Hidden Words*.
25. Bahá'u'lláh, quoted in Shoghi Effendi, *Advent of Divine Justice*, p. 82.
26. Peale, *Why Some Positive Thinkers Get Powerful Results*, pp. 183–4.
27. Peale, *In God We Trust*, p. 17.
28. Fredrickson, *Positivity*, pp. 167–8.
29. ibid. p. 173.
30. Ware, *Positive Neuroplasticity*.

31 ibid.
32 Walsh, *Essential Spirituality*, p. 270.
33 Larsen. *The Optimist Creed and Other Inspirational Classics*, p. 208.
34 Carnegie, *How to Stop Worrying and Start Living*, pp. 162–3.

Chapter 10: Happiness Techniques
1 Anonymous.
2 Peal, *The Power of Positive Thinking*, p. 60.
3 Lyubomirsky, *The How of Happiness*, p. 15.
4 ibid. p. 21.
5 ibid. p. 22–3.
6 Lam, 'What Becomes of Lottery Winners?'
7 Dahl, 'A Classic Psychology Study on Why Winning the Lottery Won't Make You Happier'.
8 Chan, 'Here's How Winning the Lottery Makes You Miserable'.
9 Post, *The Hidden Gifts of Helping*, p. 112.
10 ibid. pp. 94–5.
11 Diener & Wiswas-Diener, *Happiness*, p. 225.
12 Vaillant, *Adaptation to Life*.
13 Vaillant, *Triumphs of Experience: Men of the Harvard Grant Study*.
14 Barnes, 'Harvard's 75-Year Study Reveals The Secret To Living A Happy Life. And Here It Is'.
15 Peale, *Faith Made Them Champions*, p. 79.
16 Khavari, *Spiritual Intelligence*, p. 82.
17 Lyubomirsky, *The How of Happiness,* p. 197.
18 'Abdu'l-Bahá, *Star of the West*, vol. IV, no. 11, p. 192.
19 Khavari. *Spiritual Intelligence*, p. 86.
20 Bahá'u'lláh, *Tabernacle of Unity*, p. 41.
21 Lyubomirski. *The How of Happiness*, p. 117.
22 Bahá'u'lláh, *Tablets*, p. 138.
23 Helmstetter, *What to Say When You Talk to Yourself*, p. 219.
24 Lyubomirsky, *The How of Happiness*, p. 107.
25 Ryan, *The Happiness Makeover*, p. 12.
26 Lyubomirsky, *The How of Happiness*, p. 107.
27 See: http://greenwisdom.weebly.com/uploads/4/3/9/0/4390688/immune_system_primer_stafne.pdf.
28 Goleman, *Research Affirms Power of Positive Thinking.*
29 Niemiec, 'The Best Possible Self Exercise (Boosts Hope)'.
30 James, quoted in Peale, *Enthusiasm Makes the Difference*, p. 13.
31 Lawson, 'University of Minnesota – Taking Charge of Your Health & Wellbeing'.
32 32 Notion (https://www.notion.so/) is a note-taking and collaboration application that can be used to keep track of tasks, projects, and more. It can be used on both smartphones and computers.

NOTES AND REFERENCES

33 Einstein, quoted in Viereck, 'What Life Means to Einstein'.
34 Peale, *Stay Alive All Your Life*, p. 177.
35 Emerson, *Emerson: Essays and Lectures*, p. 404.
36 Peale, *Enthusiasm Makes the Difference*, p. 33.
37 Bahá'u'lláh, *Hidden Words*.
38 Bahá'u'lláh, *Hidden Words*.
39 Peale, *In God We Trust*, p. 181.
40 Peale, *Positive Imaging: The Powerful Way to Change*, pp. 183–4.
41 Zarqani, *Mahmud's Diary*, p. 204.
42 See: https://www.dec.ny.gov/lands/90720.html.
43 ibid.
44 Anonymous. 'University of Minnesota: Taking Charge of Your Health & Wellbeing'.
45 Newberg & Waldman, *How God Changes Your Brain*, p. 151.
46 Klein, *The Healing Power of Humor*, p. 96.
47 ibid. p. 97.
48 Post & Neimark, *Why Good Things Happen to Good People*, p. 130.
49 ibid.
50 Gendry, *Laughter Therapy History*.
51 See: http://www2.ca.uky.edu/hes/fcs/factshts/hsw-caw-807.pdf.
52 Ryan, *The Happiness Makeover*, p. 100.
53 Post and Neimark, *Why Good Things Happen to Good People*, p. 59.
54 Newmark, *Chicken Soup for the Soul: Your 10 Keys to Happiness*, pp. 87–9.
55 Peale, *Treasury of Joy and Enthusiasm*, p. 146.
56 Carnegie, *How to Stop Worrying and Start Living*, pp. 176–8.
57 ibid. pp. 184–5.
58 Peale, *Treasury of Joy and Enthusiasm*, p. 49.

Chapter 11: Gratitude

1 'Abdu'l-Bahá, *Tablets* vol. II, p. 483.
2 Sanders, *Today We are Rich*, pp. 131–2.
3 Ryan, *Attitude of Gratitude*, pp. 62–3.
4 ibid. p. 82–3.
5 Lyubomirsky, *The How of Happiness*, pp. 89–92.
6 Emmons, *Gratitude Works*, pp. 132, 134–5.
7 ibid. pp. 49–56.
8 Dickens, *Sketches by Boz*.
9 'Abdu'l-Bahá, *Promulgation*, pp. 187–8.
10 ibid. p. 236.
11 ibid.
12 Emmons, *Gratitude Works!*, pp. 9–10.
13 ibid.
14 ibid.
15 Lyubomirsky, *The How of Happiness*, pp. 92–5.

16　See: http://www.bartleby.com/17/1/23.html.
17　Post & Neimark, *Why Good Things Happen to Good People*, p. 31.
18　ibid.
19　Lemonick & Mankato, 'The Nun Study How one scientist and 678 sisters are helping unlock the secrets of Alzheimer's'.
20　Emmons, *Thanks!*, p. 12.
21　ibid. pp. 71–2.
22　Breathnach, *The Simple Abundance Journal of Gratitude*, p. 83.
23　For more information on this practice, see: *How to Train a Wild Elephant*, pp. 158–61.
24　Emmons, *Gratitude Works!*, p. 22.
25　ibid. p. 24.
26　Post, *Why Good Things Happen to Good People*, p. 28.
27　ibid.
28　Emmons, *Gratitude Works!*, p. 44.
29　Emmons, *Thanks!*, pp. 39, 41.
30　Emmons, *Gratitude Works!*, pp. 47–8.
31　Gaertner, *Worldly Virtues*, p. 19.
32　Peale, *A Treasury of Courage and Confidence*, p. 199.
33　Lyubomirsky, *The How of Happiness*, p. 99.
34　Ryan, *Attitude of Gratitude*, pp. 171–2.
35　Post & Neimark, *Why Good Things Happen to Good People*, p. 31.
36　Peale, *How to Be Your Best*, p. 48.
37　ibid. pp. 48–50.
38　Peale, *A Treasury of Courage and Confidence*, p. 204.

ABOUT THE AUTHORS

As a family, we have tried to apply as many of the practices that have come out of our research as possible, such as holding weekly gratitude sessions, writing in our gratitude journals, and practising grateful savouring with the Notion app.

* * *

Farnaz has an MA in Middle Eastern Studies (1985), and a BA in Oriental and African Languages with a specialization in the Arabic language (1983), both from the University of Texas at Austin. She taught world religions at institutions of higher education for 23 years, including the University of Texas at Austin, where she offered classroom and online courses for ten years. Farnaz's primary research interests have been in the areas of life after death, near-death experiences (NDEs), meditation, and positive psychology. Among her publications are several books, including *Life after Death: A Study of the Afterlife in World Religions* (Oneworld Publications, 1995, reprinted in 2002 by Kalimat Press), *Divine Educators* (George Ronald, 2005), which she co-authored with Bijan, and *The Divine Art of Meditation: Meditation and Visualization Techniques for a Healthy Mind, Body and Soul* (George Ronald, 2014).

In 2017, Farnaz retired from academic teaching to devote more time to research, writing, service-oriented projects, and offering workshops for various organizations, such as the Osher Lifelong Learning Institute (OLLI) program at the University of Texas at Austin. For more information about Farnaz, see her personal website: https://www.farnazmasumian.com/

Bijan obtained a PhD in Instructional Systems Design and Technology from the University of Texas at Austin (1986), an MA in Education and Human Development from George Washington University (1981), and a BA in English Language from the College of Translation in Tehran (1978). He served as Manager of Global Learning Technologies at AMD (Advanced Micro Devices) for 26 years before he retired in 2022.

His research interests are in the areas of Bábí and Bahá'í studies, world religions, human rights, and technology-based learning. He has co-authored *Divine Educators* (Oxford: George Ronald, 2005) with his wife, Farnaz, and several Bábí and Bahá'í Studies articles, independently and with his son Adib. Bijan's human rights efforts include publications in both English and Persian. He has also been published in the field of Learning Technologies. More information about him and his publications can be found on his personal website: https://www.bijanmasumian.com.

Adib has an MA in Learning Technologies (2015) and a BS in Corporate Communication (2012), both from the University of Texas at Austin. Adib enjoys researching Bábí and Bahá'í Studies and undertaking various translation projects. He is the author of *Debunking the Myths: Conspiracy Theories on the Genesis and Mission of the Bahá'í Faith* (Lulu Publishing, 2009). He has also published several articles, both independently and with other authors, in the peer-reviewed *Bahá'í Studies Review* journal. He is currently Manager of Global Learning Technologies at AMD.

For more information about Adib, his publications and translations, see his personal website: https://www.adibmasumian.com.

www.ingramcontent.com/pod-product-compliance
Lightning Source LLC
Chambersburg PA
CBHW060228190426
43200CB00040B/1680